INTERMEDIATE CANT

CW00554186

The second edition of *Intermediate Cantonese* is designed for learners who have achieved basic proficiency and wish to progress to more complex language. Each of the 25 units combines clear, concise grammar explanations with communicatively oriented exercises to help build confidence and fluency.
Features include:

- many authentic examples from contemporary media, including films, advertising, songs and soap operas
- clear differentiation between colloquial and more formal speech registers
- up-to-date analysis of contemporary Cantonese as spoken in Hong Kong.

Suitable for independent learners and students on taught courses, *Intermediate Cantonese*, together with its sister volume, *Basic Cantonese*, forms a structured course of the essentials of Cantonese grammar.

Virginia Yip is Professor at the Department of Linguistics and Modern Languages, The Chinese University of Hong Kong. She is Co-Director of the University of Cambridge-CUHK Joint Laboratory for Bilingualism and Director of the CUHK-Peking University-University System of Taiwan Joint Research Centre for Language and Human Complexity.

Stephen Matthews is Professor at the Department of Linguistics at the University of Hong Kong. They are the authors of *Basic Cantonese: A Grammar and Workbook* (2000), *Cantonese: A Comprehensive Grammar* (1994, 2nd edition 2011), *The Bilingual Child: Early Development and Language Contact* (Cambridge University Press, 2007), and co-directors of the Childhood Bilingualism Research Centre.

Titles of related interest published by Routledge

Basic Cantonese
A Grammar and Workbook
By Virginia Yip and Stephen Matthews

Cantonese
A Comprehensive Grammar
By Stephen Matthews and Virginia Yip

Colloquial Cantonese
A Complete Language Course
By Keith S. T. Tong and Gregory James

Basic Chinese
A Grammar and Workbook
By Yip Po-Ching and Don Rimmington

Intermediate Chinese
A Grammar and Workbook
By Yip Po-Ching and Don Rimmington

Chinese
An Essential Grammar
By Yip Po-Ching and Don Rimmington

Colloquial Chinese
A Complete Language Course
By Kan Qian

Colloquial Chinese
CD-ROM By Kan Qian

Colloquial Chinese (Reprint of the first edition)
By Ping-Cheng T'ung and David E. Pollard

INTERMEDIATE CANTONESE: A GRAMMAR AND WORKBOOK

Second Edition

Virginia Yip and Stephen Matthews

Routledge
Taylor & Francis Group

LONDON AND NEW YORK

Second edition published 2017
by Routledge
2 Park Square, Milton Park, Abingdon, Oxon OX14 4RN

and by Routledge
711 Third Avenue, New York, NY 10017

Routledge is an imprint of the Taylor & Francis Group, an informa business

First edition published by Routledge 2001

British Library Cataloguing-in-Publication Data
A catalogue record for this book is available from the British Library

Library of Congress Cataloging-in-Publication Data
Names: Yip, Virginia, 1962– author. | Matthews, Stephen, 1963– author.
Title: Intermediate Cantonese : a grammar and workbook / Virginia Yip
    and Stephen Matthews.
Description: Milton Park, Abingdon, Oxon ; New York, NY : Routledge, [2017] |
    Series: Grammar workbooks | Includes bibliographical references and index.
Identifiers: LCCN 2016038441 | ISBN 9780415815604 (hardback) |
    ISBN 9780415815611 (pbk.) | ISBN 9781315265223 (ebook)
Subjects: LCSH: Cantonese dialects—Grammar.
Classification: LCC PL1733 .Y565 2017 | DDC 495.17/95127—dc23
LC record available at https://lccn.loc.gov/2016038441

ISBN: 978-0-415-81560-4 (hbk)
ISBN: 978-0-415-81561-1 (pbk)
ISBN: 978-131-526-522-3 (ebk)

Typeset in Times Ten
by Apex CoVantage, LLC

For Alicia Tīn Wihng
in celebration of a new millennium –
Chīn Hēi Lìhn 千禧年

CONTENTS

ACKNOWLEDGEMENTS

Since the publication of *Basic Cantonese* and *Intermediate Cantonese*, we have been pleased to hear from readers from around the world. We thank them for their heart-warming feedback and appreciation. Foremost among their suggestions has been the inclusion of Chinese characters, which we are happy to supply in this revised edition. We hope that our books on Cantonese grammar and its acquisition by bilingual children will contribute to wider efforts in promoting the language and its culture and providing tools for learners and teachers of Cantonese.

Thanks are also due to our dear friends and colleagues who have supported us over the years, and to numerous Cantonese speakers who, whether under duress or inadvertently, have supplied us with lively and colourful examples. Special mention must be made of our captive informants in the Yip family: Peggy, Patrick and Linda, Dan and Kennis. Pride of place goes to our three children, Timothy, Sophie and Alicia, whose Cantonese advanced from 'basic' level to beyond the modest level of this book during the writing of the first edition.

For valuable input to the first edition of this book as well as to *Basic Cantonese*, we thank Umberto Ansaldo, whose suggestions as a linguist and learner of Cantonese led to numerous improvements. The discussion of tongue twisters and Japanese loanwords with Cream Lee and Shin Kataoka was also a timely gift. For work on the second edition, we thank our assistants Szeto Pui Yiu and Cindy Cheung Shu Ting for their careful editing and constructive suggestions. We thank the reviewers and the Routledge editorial team who have seen the project through. We naturally take responsibility for any errors which remain.

Finally, we take the opportunity to pay tribute to the many scholars who have contributed to uncovering the richness of Cantonese grammar. Among these, we feel particularly indebted to Thomas O'Melia, Y.R. Chao, Samuel Cheung Hung-Nin and Anne Yue.

INTRODUCTION

Designed as a companion volume to *Basic Cantonese*, *Intermediate Cantonese* covers further topics not introduced there and revisits others in more detail. Following on where *Basic Cantonese* left off, the grammatical topics become more intricate and the examples more complex. The approach taken is similar: we aim to describe the structure of the language as used by Cantonese speakers, rather than prescribing how it should be spoken. Together, the two workbooks should also make our *Cantonese: A Comprehensive Grammar* accessible to learners as a reference book.

At a more general level, this book should suit any learners of Cantonese who have achieved elementary proficiency and are looking to progress to more complex language, which will allow them to converse on more demanding topics: to express themselves and communicate in a more effective and sophisticated manner thoughts and feelings as well as mere information and to phrase questions politely, acknowledge compliments appropriately, complain and even make the occasional joke. Such uses of language call for the right choice of words and structures, to name just the bare essentials.

Cantonese in the twenty-first century

Since the transfer of sovereignty over Hong Kong in 1997 and Macau in 1999 to the People's Republic of China, Putonghua has become more widely used in these cities as well as in Guangdong province. Cantonese nevertheless remains vibrant and popular, spoken as a vernacular and written in various forms. Under the policy of 'one country – two systems' **(yāt gwok léuhng jai** 一國兩制**)** and the promise of 'no change for fifty years' **(ńgh-sahp lìhn bāt bin** 五十年不變**)**, which guarantee a distinctive cultural profile for Hong Kong, we expect that Cantonese will continue to thrive. Indeed, the continued and uninhibited use of Cantonese may be taken as one litmus test of these pledges.

From the outset of the Hong Kong Special Administrative Region, official policy has been for its citizens to be trilingual (in Cantonese, Mandarin and English) and biliterate (in written Chinese and English). This ideal is embodied in the slogan **léuhng màhn sāam yúh** 兩文三語 'two written languages **(màhn** 文**)** and three spoken languages **(yúh** 語**)**'. No doubt, such a trilingual policy and its success are vital to the future of Hong Kong as a commercial, cultural and technological hub of southern China and the international gateway to the rest of the world. Cantonese served as the main medium of instruction in most schools following the mother-tongue education policy **(móuh-yúh gaau-hohk** 母語教學**)** introduced in 1998. By 2016, a majority of schools had replaced Cantonese with Putonghua as the medium of instruction for Chinese. This shift, together with growing use of simplified characters and of Putonghua in other domains, has triggered concern over the decline of Cantonese and loss of the tradition of literacy in the language. Policy apart, most speakers have an attachment to their language as a marker of identity and as a vehicle for Cantonese culture, from traditional operas and nursery rhymes to soap operas, films and songs.

Cantonese is increasingly learnt and used in bilingual and multilingual contexts. A growing population is that of heritage learners who have grown up in Chinese families overseas. Often these learners acquired some Cantonese as children before shifting to English or another dominant language. Heritage speakers wishing to re-learn the language make up a substantial proportion of learners in Cantonese language classes around the world.

Speech registers

In any language, chat among friends is relatively informal and colloquial, whereas reports and presentations are more formal. Just as an apology to a close friend or family member couched in a formal way will seem absurd (or comical), addressing a meeting in overly colloquial language will be badly out of place. The book therefore concludes with a series of units focusing on the differences between formal and informal speech, especially as they affect grammar.

In order to do justice to the lively and colourful character of the language, we use authentic examples wherever possible. The examples aim to illustrate how speakers use the language in real-life situations as well as how the grammatical structures work. Hoping to convey a true picture of how Cantonese is used in the streets of Hong Kong, we have included examples from television advertisements, news reports, radio programmes, soap operas and films. The sources of such examples are indicated where they are of special interest.

Spoken Cantonese and written Chinese

Spoken Cantonese has a complicated relationship to Chinese writing. At the extremes, it is useful to distinguish 'High' and 'Low' Cantonese. 'High Cantonese' is the kind of language used in legal, academic and other professional contexts. It is close to standard written Chinese in grammar and vocabulary. Television news broadcasts, based on a written script but read with some spoken Cantonese features, epitomize this register. 'Low' Cantonese as used in domestic and other informal contexts diverges further from standard written Chinese, especially in terms of grammar and vocabulary: for example, comparisons are made colloquially with **gwo** 過 rather than **béi** 比 (see Unit 13).

Cantonese has developed its own written form, allowing the language to be written as it is spoken. Nearly all the words and phrases in this book can be written with characters, many of which do not exist in standard Chinese. Written Cantonese has never been standardized, however, and for some colloquial words (such as the adjective **lé-he** 'messy'), the necessary characters are lacking, or usage varies between alternative characters. Writers also resort to strategies such as using English letters ('D' to represent the comparative **dī** 啲) and quasi-phonetic spelling ('mit' for **mīt** 搣 'to tear'). Any such texts will fall foul of language purists who frown on such deviations from standard Chinese writing. Nevertheless, written Cantonese can be found in magazines, cartoons and internet forums. Stories which originate in online media have given rise to full-fledged Cantonese novels, as in the case of **làahmyán m̀h hóyíh kùhng** 男人唔可以窮 ('A man can't afford to be poor') by Sit Ho-Ching 薛可正.

Using this book

This grammar and workbook aims to achieve the following for the learner of Cantonese:

(a) provide exposure to a slightly more advanced level of input and grammatical patterns,
(b) raise the learner's metalinguistic awareness of many aspects of Cantonese grammar, and
(c) help those who approach the learning of language in an analytic manner by means of explicit explanation and highlighting of difficult points.

Note on exercises

The dagger † indicates more demanding exercises. Words given in parentheses can be left out. Many exercises permit more than one answer, and those given in the key are far from definitive. Language is inherently creative; once learners master the major rules and patterns, they will naturally use the language in a productive and creative way to come up with novel phrases of their own. We encourage active experimenting with the language and actual use of language whenever possible, hence the open-ended nature of some of the exercises. Learners who are able to consult a native speaker can check their responses and elicit alternatives. All should bear in mind that there is nothing wrong with making mistakes: indeed, Cantonese speakers are impressed when foreigners attempt their language, and they will be amused rather than offended by errors.

Finally, we hope that just as our own appreciation of Cantonese has increased by leaps and bounds as a result of much musing on its various intriguing properties and structures, so will any native or second language speaker's appreciation of the language. The grammar of Cantonese will no doubt continue to surprise and fascinate us, and hopefully our readers too.

Virginia Yip and Stephen Matthews
28 July 2016, Vancouver

UNIT 1
Consonants and vowels

In this unit, we assume familiarity with the basic sounds of consonants and vowels as described in *Basic Cantonese*. Building on this base, we review some of the main difficulties and delve further into variation among these sounds. To represent sounds accurately, symbols from the International Phonetic Alphabet (IPA) are given in square brackets: [ʃ], for example, represents the consonant in 'shoe'.

Difficulties for English speakers

Certain Cantonese sounds pose particular difficulties for native speakers of English and, in some cases, other European languages. These include:

- Front rounded vowels: **yu** [y] as in **syū** 書 'book'
  eu [œ:] as in **séung** 想 'want'
  [ɵ] as in **geuk** 腳 'foot'
- Affricates: **j** [ts] as in **jā** 揸 'drive'
  ch [tsʰ] as in **chóh** 坐 'sit'

Rounded vowels

Rounded vowels are produced with the lips 'rounded' or pursed. In English, only the back vowels **o** (as in 'hope') and **u** (as in 'who') are rounded. In Cantonese, the front vowels **yu** and **eu** are also rounded: **yu** is produced like **i**, and **eu** like **e**, with the addition of lip rounding. These vowels do not have precise equivalents in English, **yú** 魚 (fish) should not sound like English **you** nor should **jeuk** 著 (wear) sound like **jerk**: in each case, the lips must be rounded outwards to produce the right vowel sound (pouting may help here).

eu is especially difficult since its quality varies according to the following consonant sound:

Longer, lower [æ:]	Shorter, higher [ə]
chéung 搶 rob	**chéun** 蠢 stupid
chēung 窗 window	**chēut** 出 go out
leuhng 量 capacity	**leuht** 率 rate
jēung 張 a surname	**jēun** 樽 bottle
sèuh 嘘 slide	**sèuhn** 純 pure

Long and short diphthongs

While the short vowel **a** and the long **aa** are easily distinguished, the corresponding diphthongs can be more difficult:

Short			Long		
ai	**máih** 米	rice (uncooked)	**aai**	**máaih** 買	buy
	tāi 梯	ladder		**tāai** 呔	tyre
au	**gáu** 狗/九	dog; nine	**aau**	**gáau** 搞	manage; meddle
	làuh 留	leave behind		**làauh** 撈	scoop up

In addition to the difference in length, the short diphthong **ai** is noticeably different in quality from long **aai**, much as **a** differs from **aa**. It begins with a less open vowel and can sound almost like **ei**.

Alternative pronunciations

Alternative pronunciations of sounds (technically known as allophones) occur in certain positions. Learners should be able to recognize these and may try to produce them in appropriate places.

Like **eu**, the vowels **i** and **u** have a different quality before the velar sounds **k** and **ng**, where they are more open than usual. Consequently, they can sound like a different vowel altogether:

sihk 食 (eat) tends to sound like **sehk** 石 (stone)
duhk 讀 (study) tends to sound like **dohk** 度 (to measure)
dihng 定 (steady) tends to sound like **dehng** 訂 (to order, reserve)
sung 送 (give) tends to sound like **song** 喪 (to lose, as in **song-sāt** 喪失**)**

In fact, there is an uncertainty inherent in the language here, since in some cases both vowels are used for the same meaning: **sìhng** and **sèhng** 成 'whole', for example, are both used **(sihng** is the more formal pronunciation, mandatory in reading a text aloud and in certain words such as **sìhnggūng** 成功 'succeed', while **sèhng** is colloquial, as in **sèhng jīu** 成朝 'all morning').

Palatalization

The fricative **s** tends to change when followed by the rounded vowels **yu** and **eu**:

syū 書 book   [çy] – towards [ʃ] as in 'shoe'
séung 想 want   [çœŋ] – towards [ʃ] as in 'sherbet'

Just as in English 'issue' and 'tissue' may be pronounced carefully with [s] or more casually with [ʃ], so the Cantonese **s** tends towards [ʃ] when the following vowel is **yu** or **eu**. This effect, termed palatalization, also affects the affricates **j** and **ch** before the same vowels:

jyuh 住 to live   [tçy:] – towards [tʃ] as in 'Jew' (but still
                         unvoiced)
jeui 最 most   [tçøʏ] – towards [tʃ] as in 'Joe'
chyùhn 全 whole   [tçʰyn] – towards [tʃʰ] as in 'choose'
chéui 娶 marry (take a wife)   [tçʰøʏ] – towards [tʃʰ] as in 'church'

Consequently, the **ch** sound in these words resembles rather closely the English **ch** in 'choose'. Contrast this with the usual sound of **ch**, [tsʰ] as in **chóh** 坐 'sit' [tsʰɔ], which should not sound like English 'chore'.

Sound changes

A further source of variation involves ongoing sound changes, whereby particular sounds are being lost or are changing.

(a) Initial consonants:

n- becomes **l-**   **néui → léui** 女   daughter
ng- disappears   **ngóh → óh** 我   I
gw- becomes **g-**   **gwok → gok** 國   country
kw- becomes **k-**   **kwòhng → kòhng** 狂   crazy

Though purists may insist on **néih** over **léih** 你 'you', this pronunciation is becoming rarer and rarer as the sound change takes its course. This means that the words merge with existing words with **l-**, so that **nàahm** 南 'south' sounds the same as **làahm** 藍 'blue'. The form **nī** 呢 'this' shows some resistance to the change (apparently because there are no existing syllables of the form **lī** in Cantonese) so that one hears either **nīdouh** or **līdouh** 呢度 'here'. Since most dictionaries list these words as beginning with **n-**, many words pronounced with **l-** will be found under **n-**.

There is a tendency for **ng** to be lost at the beginning of a word, but many words vary:

> **aap** or **ngaap** 鴨 duck, **ōnchyùhn** or **ngōnchyùhn** 安全 safe
> **ūk** or **ngūk** 屋 house, **ok** or **ngok** 惡 fierce (of animals), strict (of teachers)

A traditional rule of thumb which remains useful is that **ng** appears in syllables with low tones:

High and mid tones	Low tones
aai 嗌 shout	**ngàaih** 捱 suffer
aau 拗 argue	**ngàuh** 牛 cow
Daaih Ou 大澳 Tai O	**gīu-ngouh** 驕傲 proud
tóuh ō 肚痾 diarrhoea	**tóuh-ngoh** 肚餓 hungry

Syllables beginning with **gw** tend to become **g** especially in casual speech:

> **Gwóngjāu → Góngjāu** 廣州 Guangzhou (Canton)
> **gwok-gā → gok-gā** 國家 nation

This change depends on the following vowel and does not generally affect syllables with the vowel **a**, as in **gwa** 掛 'hang' or **gwai** 貴 'expensive'.

(b) Syllabic consonants:

As initial **ng-** disappears, the few words consisting of the consonant **ng** alone change to **m**:

ng becomes **m**	**ńgh mān → ḿh mān** 五蚊	five dollars
	ngh-gáai → mh-gáai 誤解	misunderstanding
	Ǹgh síujé → Ǹh síujé 吳小姐	Miss Ng

This change affecting the surname **Ǹgh** 吳 leads to jokes whereby, for example, the well-intended girl's name **Ǹgh Sī-Màhn** 吳斯文 'Grace Ng' sounds like **ḿh sīmàhn** 'not graceful'.

(c) Final consonants:

-ng tends to become **-n**, especially after the long vowel **aa-**:

> **hohksāang → hohksāan** 學生 student

Again, this merger leads to more words sounding the same. For example, the word **sāang-duhng** 生動 'lively' sounds the same as **sāan-duhng** 山洞 meaning 'cave' (note that the change does not apply to **duhng** 洞 because of the different vowel). Similarly, **-t** and **-k** tend to merge so that **sāk-chē** 塞車 'congested' (traffic) sounds like **sāt-chē** 失車 'missing car', while **bākbihn** 北便 'north side' sounds like **bātbihn** 不便 'inconvenient'.

Exercise 1.1

Pronounce the following pairs with particular attention to the vowels.

1 **luhk** 六/綠 six; green   **lohk** 落 down
2 **muhk** 木 wood   **mohk** 幕 curtain
3 **tùhng** 同 go with   **tòhng** 糖 sugar
4 **gīng** 經 pass by   **gēng** 驚 be afraid
5 **sihk** 食 eat   **sehk** 石 stone
6 **waih** 胃 stomach   **waaih** 壞 broken
7 **bai** 閉 close   **baai** 拜 worship
8 **māu** 踎 crouch   **māau** 貓 cat
9 **sīng** 升 rise   **sēng** 聲 sound
10 **juhk** 俗 colloquial   **johk** 鑿 dig

Exercise 1.2

Pronounce the following pairs paying attention to the initial and final consonants and vowels:

1 **Bāt bin ge deihfōng**   **Bākbihn ge deihfōng**
   不變嘅地方   北便嘅地方
   Unchanged places   Northern places
2 **Kéuih jungyi choisām**   **Kéuih jūngyi chèuih sāam**
   佢鍾意菜心   佢鍾意除衫
   She likes vegetables.   She likes to take off her clothes.
3 **Kéuih fóngmahn-gwo yāt bun yàhn**   **Kéuih fóngmahn-gwo Yahtbún yàhn**
   佢訪問過一半人   佢訪問過日本人
   She has interviewed half of the people.   She has interviewed the Japanese.
4 **Jeui gīng haih léih**   **Jeui gēng haih léih**
   最勁係你   最驚係你
   You're the best.   You're the most afraid.
5 **Kéuih jeui léuihyán**   **Kéuih jēui léuihyán**
   佢最女人   佢追女人
   S/he's most like a woman.   S/he chases after women.

Exercise 1.3

Pronounce the following 'tongue twisters' widely circulated among Cantonese speakers, paying attention to the initial and final consonants. Begin slowly before gradually increasing speed.

1 **Jā sihdīk daap dīksí heui sihdō sihk dōsí** 揸士的搭的士去士多食多士
 Hold a stick take a taxi to go to the store to eat toast.
2 **Yahp sahtyihmsāt gam gán-gap-jai** 入實驗室撳緊急掣
 Go into the laboratory and press the emergency button.
3 **Mahkdōnghùhng daai Mahkdōng-nàh heui Mahkdōnglòuh sihk maht-tòhng lōu dōnggwāi** 麥當紅帶麥當娜去麥當勞食蜜糖撈當歸.
 Mak Dong Hung takes Madonna to McDonalds to eat honey mixed with **donggui** (Chinese medicine) (from the film **Gāmjī yuhkyihp** 金枝玉葉 'He's a woman, she's a man')
4 **Gwaht gām gwaht gāt gwaht gāi gwāt** 掘金掘桔掘雞骨
 Dig gold, dig orange, dig chicken bone.
5 **Chèuhng gok-lōk-táu bahng gān gām gwan** 牆角落頭繃根金棍
 A gold rod leans against the wall in the corner.
6 **A-Chēung heui gāaisíh máaih yùh-chéung, gin dóu yìh-jéung, gūkgūng yìh-jéung, dit-jó yùh-chéung, yìh-jéung bōng a-Chēung jāp fāan fu yùh-chéung**
 阿張去街市買魚腸, 見到姨丈, 鞠躬姨丈, 跌咗魚腸, 姨丈幫阿張執返副魚腸
 A-Tseung goes to market to buy fish intestine, sees uncle, bows to uncle, the fish intestine falls down, uncle helps A-Tseung to pick up the fish intestine.
7 **Yāt mān máaih gān gāi, yāt mān máaih gān gwāi, gāai tàuh máaih gān gāi,**
 一蚊買斤雞, 一蚊買斤龜, 街頭買斤雞,
 gāai méih máaih gān gwāi, gaugíng gāi gwai dihng gwāi gwai?
 街尾買斤龜, 究竟雞貴定龜貴?
 Buy a catty of chicken for one dollar, buy a catty of turtle for one dollar, buy a catty of chicken at the beginning of the street, buy a catty of turtle at the end of the street. Which is more expensive, chicken or turtle?

Exercise 1.4

Pronounce the words/phrases and names first as written and then with the relevant sound changes.

1 **nàahm-sih** 男士 gentleman
2 **gwo hói** 過海 cross the sea/harbour
3 **yùh-sāang** 魚生 sashimi
4 **ǹgh gwok wuih-yíh** 五國會議 meeting of five nations
5 **Ngóh nāu gwo néih** 我嬲過你 I'm more angry than you.
6 **Gwūn Tòhng** 觀塘 Kwun Tong (a place in East Kowloon)
7 **Gwóngsāi** 廣西 Guangxi (a province in SW China)
8 **Ǹgh Méih-laih** 吳美麗 Ng Mei-lai ('pretty')
9 **Gwok Fu-sìhng** 郭富城 Aaron Kwok Fu-Shing (a singer and film star)
10 **Nàahm-gīng** 南京 Nanjing (a city in south central China)

UNIT 2
Tone contours

Tones remain a locus of difficulty for any learners of Chinese, especially for those whose own native languages do not use them. Recognizing, remembering and producing the tones correctly – or at least well enough to get by with only occasional misunderstandings – should be a priority. In this unit, we look in depth at tone contours, the actual pitch levels involved in pronouncing a given tone.

Entering tones

The so-called entering tones (known as **rusheng** in Mandarin or **yahp-sīng** 入聲 in Cantonese) are those which occur in 'checked' syllables ending in an unreleased stop (**-p**, **-t** or **-k**). When Cantonese is described as having nine tones, these three are included in addition to the familiar six. In this book, as in *Basic Cantonese*, the entering tones are simply treated as instances of the high, mid and low level tones:

	Entering tones	*Corresponding level tones*
High	**sāp** 濕 wet	**sā** 沙 sand
Mid	**gwok** 國 country	**gwo** 過 cross
Low	**siht** 蝕 lose	**sih** 事 matter

Note that only the three level tones generally occur in these 'checked' syllables. However, a rising tone can occur as a result of tone change (see Unit 3):

yuhk → **yúk** 玉 jade   **waht** → **wát** 核 seed, core
sehk → **sék** 石 stone   **dihp** → **díp** 碟 dish

Tone contours

The diacritics used in the Yale romanization system indicate the tones clearly as level, falling or rising, with the silent **h** indicating the three low register tones.

While this makes the tones relatively easy to remember, learners should be aware that these tone markings tend to simplify the actual contours involved, as do the conventional names of the tones. Hence we revisit them here in greater detail.

It can be useful to describe tone contours on a scale of 1 (low) to 5 (high), so that 55 represents a high level tone (starting and ending at level 5) and 25 represents a tone rising from low (2) to high (5):

High level:	55 or 53, as in **sān** or **sàn** 新 'new'
High rising:	25, as in **yám** 飲 'drink'
Mid level:	33, as in **fan** 瞓 'sleep'
Low rising:	23, as in **lóuh** 老 'old'
Low level:	22, as in **douh** 路 'road'
Low falling:	21 or 11, as in **wàahn** 還 'return (give back)'

Some learners also find it useful to draw lines above or beside the word to represent the tone contour as they hear it.

High level or high falling?

The first tone, shown in this book as high level (a), is sometimes pronounced with a high falling contour (shown in the Yale system as à). There is considerable variation here: in Hong Kong, the high level contour is increasingly dominant, while in Guangzhou a high fall (52) is common. Given that the two contours are largely interchangeable, learners should not worry unduly about the fact that they are distinguished in some dictionaries and course materials. There are, however, two particles which regularly have a high falling contour when they come at the end of a sentence: **sìn** 先 'first' and **tìm** 添 'in addition'.

High rising vs. low rising

The names of these tones might suggest that they go from mid to high and low to mid, respectively. In fact, these tones begin at the same lowish pitch (2 on the 1 to 5 scale). Moreover, both begin with a slight dip before the rise begins. The difference between them lies in how steeply the tone rises: as high as the high level tone in the case of the high rise (25), but only as far as the mid level tone in the case of low rising (23).

Examples:	**láu** 樓 25 flat, apartment vs. **láuh** 柳 23 willow
	mán 文 25 article, paper vs. **máhn** 吻 23 kiss

Low rising vs. low falling

Again, these two tones might appear to be the reverse of each other, but there is a marked asymmetry. The low rising tone (23) rises to mid level, as described above. The low falling tone begins near the level of the low rising and low level tones, but descends even further (21) – often as far as the speaker's voice range allows. Examples:

wáih 偉 23 great vs. **wàih** 圍 21 surround
síh 市 23 market vs. **sìh** 時 21 time

Low level vs. low falling

The difference between these two tones poses particular difficulty for many learners. The contours 22 and 21 are similar, and the difficulty is compounded by the fact that low falling (21) can sound level (11) at times (especially after another 21 tone). It can often be distinguished by the 'creaky' voice quality which results as the speaker's voice descends to the bottom of its range. Examples:

yuhng 用 22 use vs. **yùhng** 融 21 melt
yihm 驗 22 examine vs. **yìhm** 鹽 21 salt

Mid level vs. low rising

The difference in contour between mid level (33) and low rising (23) is rather small. Most speakers do make a distinction between 'minimal pairs' such as the following:

si 試 try	**síh** 市 market (as in **gú-síh** 股市 stock market, **gāai-síh** 街市 street market)
sin 線 string, line	**síhn** 鱔 eel
yau 幼 thin, slender	**yáuh** 有 have

In certain forms of Cantonese, however, including some varieties spoken in Malaysia, the two have merged so that 33 and 23 are merely alternative pronunciations of the same phonological tone, much like the high level 55 and high falling 53 tones as described above. In Hong Kong Cantonese, a similar tendency is apparent, with many younger speakers treating the mid level and low rising tones as interchangeable and even unable to perceive the distinction.

Other speakers treat the two rising tones as interchangeable. The result is that such speakers use a system of five tones rather than the traditional six.

Exercise 2.1

Pronounce the following pairs so that the difference is clear and give the tone numbers to represent the tone contours of each word.

1	**ngáahn** 眼 eye	**ngaan** 晏 late	
2	**tóuh** 肚 belly	**tóu** 土 earth	
3	**lùhng** 籠 cage	**lūng** 窿 cave, hole	
4	**máaih** 買 buy	**maaih** 賣 sell	
5	**ngāang** 罌 container	**ngaahng** 硬 hard	
6	**yeuk** 約 contract	**yeuhk** 藥 medicine	
7	**dāng** 燈 lamp	**dáng** 等 wait	
8	**séung** 想 want	**séuhng** 上 come up	

Exercise 2.2

Pronounce the following phrases noting where the crucial differences lie.

1a	**Waahk yāt tìuh sin** 畫一條線	Draw a line.
b	**Waahk yāt tìuh síhn** 畫一條鱔	Draw an eel.
2a	**Kéuih daai ngáahn-géng** 佢戴眼鏡	He wears glasses. (spectacles)
b	**Kéuih taai ngaahng-géng** 佢太硬頸	He's too stubborn. (*lit.* stiff-necked)
3a	**Yī hóu ngáahn-jīng** 醫好眼睛	Cure eyes.
b	**Yī hóu ngàahm-jing** 醫好癌症	Cure cancer.
4a	**Ngóh yiu cheung chín** 我要暢錢	I need to change some money.
b	**Ngóh yiu chéung chín** 我要搶錢	I want to rob (someone of) money.
5a	**Sung go jáu-gwaih làih** 送個酒櫃嚟	Deliver a drinks cabinet.
b	**Sung go jáu-gwái làih** 送個酒鬼嚟	Deliver an alcoholic. (*lit.* wine-devil)
6a	**Léih mohng mātyéh a?** 你望乜嘢呀?	What are you staring at?
b	**Léih mòhng mātyéh a?** 你忙乜嘢呀?	What are you busy with?
7a	**Ngóhdeih heui máaih dāng** 我哋去買燈	We're going to buy lights.
b	**Ngóhdeih heui maaih dang** 我哋去賣凳	We're going to sell chairs.
8a	**Ngóh jeui suhk haih Āu jāu sí** 我最熟係歐洲史	I'm most familiar with European history.
b	**Ngóh jeui suhk haih Āu jāu síh** 我最熟係歐洲市	I'm most familiar with the European markets.

Exercise 2.3

Pronounce the following triplets with distinct tone contours.

1 **láahn** 懶 lazy   **laahn** 爛 broken   **làahn** 難 difficult

2 **móhng** 網 net   **mohng** 望 stare at   **mòhng** 忙 busy

3 **chēui** 吹 blow   **cheui** 脆 crispy   **chèuih** 除 take off (clothes)

4 **chéung** 搶 rob   **cheung** 唱 sing   **chèuhng** 長 long

5 **máahn** 晚 evening   **maahn** 慢 slow   **(yéh** 野**) màahn** 蠻 barbaric

6 **tīu** 挑 carry   **tiu** 跳 jump   **tìuh** 條 a classifier for long, slender things

7 **būn** 搬 move   **bun** 半 half   **buhn** 伴 companion

8 **gōi** 該 should   **gói** 改 change   **goi** 蓋 cover

9 **syūn** 酸 sour   **syun** 算 calculate   **syùhn** 船 boat

10 **sīu** 燒 burn   **síu** 小 little   **siu** 笑 laugh

UNIT 3
Changed tones

Changed tones are cases where the expected ('citation') tone is replaced by a different ('changed') tone. The citation tone is the one which is used when a word is cited on its own, as when it is read from a written character. For example, **tìuh** 條 as a classifier is cited with the low falling tone and normally so pronounced, as in **tìuh fu** 條褲 referring to a pair of trousers. However, in words such as **syut-tíu** 雪條 (ice lolly) and **gām-tíu** 金條 (gold bar), it appears with the high rising changed tone. This results in alternations between a (usually low) tone and a high rising (occasionally high level) one. Such alternations are sufficiently frequent and systematic for learners to need to take note of the main patterns. The ability to produce changed tones serves as a kind of 'shibboleth' identifying the native Cantonese speaker.

The high rising changed tone

This 'tone change' is a process whereby a tone becomes a high rising tone. This happens in a wide range of circumstances, typically applying to the last syllable of a compound expression:

- In compounds with a specialized meaning:

  sin 線 string → **gong-sín** 鋼線 steel wire
  wàahn 環 ring, circle → **yíh-wáan** 耳環 earring
  yaht 日 day → **yàhn-yát** 人日 everyone's birthday (the seventh day of the Chinese New Year)
  jaahk-yaht 擇日 pick a day → **jaahk-yát** 擇日 pick a good day (for a wedding, moving house, Caesarean etc.)

- In names with the personal prefix **a-** or epithets such as **lóuh** 老 (old), typically referring to men familiar to the speaker:

Làih 黎 → **A-Lái** 阿黎	(Mr) Lai
Wòhng 黃 → **A-Wóng** 阿黃	(Mr) Wong
Chàhn 陳 → **Lóuh-Chán** 老陳	(Old) Mr Chan
Wùh 胡 → **Wú-jái** 胡仔	(Young) Wu

- In reduplicated names:

Lìhng-Líng 玲玲	Ling	
Mìhng-Míng 明明	Ming	
Sìhng-Síng 城城	(Nickname for the celebrity Aaron Kwok Fu Sing)	
Fèih-Féi 肥肥	Fatty (nickname for a portly character)	

- In reduplicated adjectives and adverbs, where the second syllable changes tone:

hàahm 鹹 salty → **hàahm-háam-déi** 鹹鹹哋	rather salty
wàhn 暈 dizzy → **wàhn-wán-déi** 暈暈哋	a bit dizzy
jeui 醉 drunk → **jeui-jéui-déi** 醉醉哋	a bit drunk, tipsy

As the examples suggest, this change applies largely to words with low tones, occasionally to those with mid level tones and not at all to those with high tones. Note also that most of these patterns involve the last syllable of a compound expression. When it is not the last syllable, the change does not apply:

sih-tàuh 事頭 → **sih-táu** boss but **sih-tàuh-pòh** 事頭婆 woman boss
mùih-yàhn 媒人→ **mùih-yán** matchmaker but **mùih-yàhn-pòh** 媒人婆 woman matchmaker

Some cases of tone change are more or less obligatory, while others are optional. The following forms involve obligatory tone change:

yàhn 人 person:	**léuih-yán** 女人 woman
	làahm-yán 男人 man
yáuh 友 friend:	**tō-yáu** 拖友 boy/girlfriend (*lit.* dating pal)
	faatsīu-yáu 發燒友 fanatic, aficionado
lìhn 年 year:	**seuhng-lín** 上年 last year
	chìhn-lín 前年 the year before last
	chēut-lín 出年 next year
	hauh-lín 後年 the year after next
hòhng 行 profession, company:	**leuhtsī-hóng** 律師行 solicitors' firm
	gīnggéi-hóng 經紀行 brokers' firm
	Taaijí-hóng 太子行 Prince Building in Central
	yèuhng hóng 洋行 foreign companies e.g.
	Taaigú yèuhng hóng 太古洋行 The Swire Company

daai 帶 as a verb 'to bring' is in the mid level tone:

Go mìhngsīng daai-jó go léui gin geijé 個明星帶咗個女見記者
The film star brought her daughter to see the reporters.

but when it functions as a noun for 'belt' or 'strap', the tone is always high rising.

bīu dáai 標帶 watch strap	**bung dáai** 繃帶 bandage

Similarly, **doih** 袋 as a verb 'to pocket' and classifier 'a bag of' (see below) but **dói** 袋 is a noun for 'pocket' or 'bag':

> **Kéuih doih-jó yāt baak mān lohk dói** 佢袋咗一百蚊落袋
> (*lit.* he pocketed one hundred dollars down pocket)
> He pocketed a hundred dollars.

Changed tone is also found in some idiomatic expressions:

> **tàuh → táu** 頭 as in **hám *táu* màaih chèuhng** 抌頭埋牆 bump one's head
>   against the wall
> **Kéuih gīk dou chā-dī hám táu màaih chèuhng** 佢激到差啲抌頭埋牆
> He's so angry that he almost banged his head against the wall.

In a number of combinations, the tone change is optional:

> **ngàhn-hòhng** or **ngàhn-hóng** 銀行 bank
> **gām lìhn** or **gām-lín** 今年 this year
> **mìhng lìhn** or **mìhng-lín** 明年 next year
> **gó(jahn)-sìh** or **gó(jahn)-sí** 嗰(陣)時 then
> **gauh(jahn)-sìh** or **gauh(jahn)-sí** 舊(陣)時 in the past
> **Méih yùhn** or **Méih yún** 美元 American dollar
> **lī pàaih/gó pàaih** or **lī páai/gó páai** 呢排/嗰排
> these days/in those days
> **mouh pàaih** or **mouh páai** 冒牌 fake brand
> **mìhng pàaih** or **mìhng páai** 名牌 name brand
> **mìhng páai** 名牌 name tag (with obligatory tone change)

The changed tone forms of these terms, such as currencies, are used especially by professionals to whom they are very familiar. This reflects the association of changed tones with familiarity.

Changed tone due to contraction

The high rising changed tone also occurs as a result of contraction:

- In expressions involving contraction of **yāt** 一 'one', the combination of a level tone and the high tone of **yāt** 一 results in the high rising tone:

> **si yāt si** 試一試 → **sí-si** 試試 have a try
> **bin yāt bin** 變一變 → **bín-bin** 變變 have a change
> **yāt go yāt go** 一個一個 → **yāt gó-go** 一個個 one at a time
> **yāt deui yāt deui** 一對一對 → **yāt déui-deui** 一對對 one pair at a time
> **yāt sìh yāt sìh** 一時一時 → **yāt sí-sìh** 一時時 occasionally
> **leng yāt leng** 靚一靚 → **léng-leng** 靚靚 nice and pretty

Go beisyū jeuk dou léng-leng gám heui hōi-wúi 個秘書著到靚靚咁去開會
(*lit.* The secretary dresses pretty-pretty thus go meeting)
The secretary goes to meetings dressed to the nines.

- The perfective marker **jó** 咗 is sometimes dropped, leaving behind its
  rising tone (and a lengthened vowel) on the preceding verb:

Fong-jó ga meih a? 放咗假未呀 → **Fóng' ga meih a?** 放假未呀?
Have you started your holiday yet?
Máaih-jó fēi meih a? 買咗飛未呀 → **Máai' fēi meih a?** 買飛未呀?
Have you bought the tickets?

Classifiers and changed tones

Here, there is a rather systematic alternation between a low tone for the classifier and the changed tone when the same word appears as a noun or part of a compound noun:

Classifier	*Noun*
yāt bohng yuhk 一磅肉 a pound of meat	**yāt go bóng** 一個磅 a scale
yāt dihp choi 一碟菜 a dish of vegetables	**jek díp** 隻碟 a plate
géi doih laahpsaap 幾袋垃圾 a few bags of rubbish	**sáu-dói** 手袋 handbag
léuhng hahp béng 兩盒餅 two boxes of cakes	**go háp** 個盒 the box
yāt pin tòhng 一片糖 a piece of sugar cane	**yùh-pín** 魚片 slices of fish **cheung-pín** 唱片 CD/record
sèhng pùhn séui 成盆水 a basinful of water	**mihn-pún** 面盆 wash basin (but **fā-pùhn** 花盆 container for plants)
tìuh yú 條魚 fish	**syùh-tíu** 薯條 potato chip **yàuh-tíu** 油條 (a savoury elongated doughnut eaten with rice congee)

The high level changed tone

A second kind of tone change, much less common than the first, produces a high level tone. As with the high rising changed tone, it is usually the last syllable in a compound expression which is affected. The most frequently encountered examples involve kinship terms:

múih 妹 younger sister → **mūi-mūi** 妹妹 little sister (as an address term)

síujé 小姐 Miss → **jèhjē** 姐姐 or **gājē** 家姐 big sister

daaih-ngáahn-mūi 大眼妹	big-eyed girl
dākyi-mūi 得意妹	cute girl, cutie
daaih-luhk mūi 大陸妹	mainland girl
bān-mūi 賓妹	domestic helpers, especially from the Philippines

These forms are colloquial and tend to be pejorative – they often occur with the classifier **tìuh** 條 as in **gó tìuh lēng-mūi** 嗰條嚹妹 'that lass'. Other sporadic cases include:

lìhng 靈 spritely, versatile → **jīng-līng** 精靈 shrewd, clever
méi 尾 last → **daih mēi** 第尾 the last, **bāau mēi** 包尾 come last (as in an exam)
láahng 冷 cold → **yehlāang** 夜冷 second-hand goods

In many cases, this change is optional:

yauh-paai or **yauh-pāai** 右派	right-wing party
yìhgā or **yīgā** 而家	now
gām-máahn or **gām-māan** 今晚	tonight

In a few cases, either the high rising or the high level changed tone may be used:

yāt go yàhn 一個人 one person, but **yāt go yán** or **yān** alone, all by oneself
Kéuih yāt go yān làuh hái Hēunggóng 佢一個人留喺香港
She stays in Hong Kong all on her own.

Further cases of the high level changed tone arise in baby talk:

hóu yáih 好曳 → **hóu yāi, yāi-yāi** 曳曳 naughty

When **daaih** 大 'big' changes to high level **dāai** 大, the opposite meaning is obtained:

Kéuih dāk gam dāai, jouh dāk dī māt a? 佢得咁大，做得啲乜呀? (from a
    Cantonese soap opera)
She's so small, what can she do?
Léih dāai-dāai go góján jauh heui gwo Méihgwok ge la
你大大個嗰陣有去過美國嘅喇
When you were little, you went to the United States.

Exercise 3.1

Apply reduplication to the following words, adding the tone change in the following forms where applicable.

1 **chau** 臭 smelly → _____ _____ -**déi** 哋
2 **laahn** 爛 broken → _____ _____ -**déi** 哋
3 **waaih** 壞 broken → _____ _____ -**déi** 哋
4 **guih** 劫 tired → _____ _____ -**déi** 哋
5 **lyuhn** 亂 messy → _____ _____ -**déi** 哋
6 **chèuhng** 長 long → _____ _____ -**déi** 哋
7 **lèuhng** 涼 cool → _____ _____ -**déi** 哋
8 **hàhn** 痕 itchy → _____ _____ -**déi** 哋
9 **làhm** 腍 tender, soft → _____ _____ -**déi** 哋
10 **lùhng** 聾 deaf → _____ _____ -**déi** 哋
11 **laaht** 辣 spicy hot → _____ _____ -**déi** 哋
12 **jī** 知 know → _____ _____ -**déi** 哋

Exercise 3.2

Apply the high rising tone change to the following:

Example: **gūng-tàuh** 工頭 head worker → **gūng-táu** 工頭 foreman

A: Obligatory tone change

1 **gong-tìuh** 鋼條 steel bar → _____ _____
2 **hói-meih** 海味 dry seafood → _____ _____
3 **gauh lìhn** 舊年 last year → _____ _____
4 **tói-mihn** 枱面 table surface → _____ _____
5 **ōnchyùhn-daai** 安全帶 safety belt → _____ _____
6 **tō-hàaih** 拖鞋 slippers → _____ _____
7 **goklōk-tàuh** 角落頭 corner → _____ _____
8 **máaih làuh** 買樓 buy a flat → _____ _____
9 **taaiyèuhng ngáahn-geng** 太陽眼鏡 sunglasses → _____ _____
10 **Hēunggóng-deih (yàhn dō, chē dō)** 香港地 (人多, 車多) (*lit.* Hong Kong land, many people, many cars) → _____ _____

B: Optional tone change

11 **sānmàhn** 新聞 news → _____ _____
12 **gójahn** 嗰陣 then → _____ _____
13 **gójahn-sìh** 嗰陣時 then → _____

14 **diht lohk deih** 跌落嚟 fall on the ground → _____

15 **yáuh yāt pàaih (móuh gin)** 有一排 (冇見) (I haven't seen you) for some
   time → _____

16 **sān-lèuhng** 新娘 bride → _____

17 **sān-lòhng** 新郎 bridegroom → _____

18 **sī-daih** 師弟 fellow student (of the same teacher) → _____

19 **dá màhjeuk** 打麻雀 play mahjong → _____

20 **boují tàuhtìuh** 報紙頭條 newspaper headline → _____

Exercise 3.3

Choose the appropriate pronunciation of classifier versus noun.

1 **Ngóh būn-jó géi go _____ (hahp/háp) heui sān ūk**
   我搬咗幾個 _____ 盒去新屋
   I moved a few boxes to the new house.

2 **Kéuih daai-jó yāt _____ (tìuh/tíu) jyunsehk génglín**
   佢戴咗一 _____ 條鑽石頸鍊
   She wore a diamond necklace.

3 **Jek māau dá laahn-jó géi jek _____ (dihp/díp)**
   隻貓打爛咗幾隻 _____ 碟
   The cat broke a few dishes.

4 **Léih kéih séuhng go _____ (bohng/bóng) bohng-háh lā**
   你企上個 _____ 磅磅下啦
   Stand on the scale to measure your weight.

5 **Ngóh jūngyi sihk sìhchoi yuhk _____ (pin/pín) faahn**
   我鍾意食時菜肉 _____ 片飯
   I like sliced pork with rice and seasonal vegetables.

6 **Ngóh giu-jó yāt _____ (dihp/díp) lóuh-ngó**
   我叫咗一 _____ 碟滷鵝
   I've ordered a dish of marinated goose (a Chiu Chow speciality)

7 **Cheui-bōk-bōk ge syùh _____ (tìuh/tíu) jeui hóu-sihk**
   脆卜卜嘅薯 _____ 條最好食
   Crispy chips taste the best.

8 **Liuh Síujé daai-jó géi _____ (hahp/háp) béng làih**
   廖小姐帶咗幾 _____ 盒餅嚟
   Miss Liu has brought a few boxes of cake along.

9 **Tói seuhngbihn yáuh _____ (pùhn/pún) séuisīn-fā**
   枱上便有 _____ 盆水仙花
   There are some daffodils in a basin on the table.

10 **Mgōi béi go _____ (pùhn/pún) ngóh ā**
   唔該畀個 _____ 盆我吖
   Please give me a tray (as in a fast food buffet).

Exercise 3.4

Apply the high level changed tone to the following:

A: Optional tone change

1 **tīng-máahn**   聽晚 tomorrow evening → _____
2 **pòhpó**   婆婆 grandma → _____
3 **séi-ngaahng-paai**   死硬派 die-hards → _____
4 **goklohk**   角落 corner → _____
5 **lèuih-léui**   女女 little girl → _____
6 **móuh géi loih**   冇幾耐 not too long → _____

B: Obligatory tone change

7 **hēunghá-múi**   鄉下妹 country girl → _____
8 **mòuh-*mòuh* gūngjái**   毛毛公仔 furry toy animal → _____
9 **ngáahn-yāp-mòuh**   眼泣毛 eyelashes → _____
10 **sáují-méih**   手指尾 last finger → _____

UNIT 4
Reduplication

Reduplication involves repeating a syllable according to a certain pattern. The effect depends on what is being reduplicated – nouns, adjectives etc. – sometimes making the meaning of the word more vivid, sometimes attenuating it. Many of the patterns involve a changed tone, like the reduplicated adjectives with **-déi** 啲 discussed in Unit 3 (see also *Basic Cantonese*, Unit 9). Intermediate learners should recognize the main patterns and their implications. At a more advanced stage, they may try to make up their own reduplicated forms, although this can be somewhat hit and miss since the processes of reduplication are not entirely predictable.

ABB adjectives

A number of adjectives are made more vivid by the addition of a reduplicated syllable (sometimes meaningful in its own right but often not):

(a) Colour terms:

hāk 黑 black, dark	**hāk-māng-māng** or **hāk-mā-mā** 黑媽媽 pitch dark
baahk 白 white	**baahk-syūt-syūt** 白雪雪 white as snow (**syut** 雪)
hùhng 紅 red	**hùhng-dōng-dohng** 紅噹噹 red (as in clothes) or **hùhng-bōk-bōk** 紅卜卜 rosy (as in cheeks)
chēng 青 light green	**chēng-bī-bī** 青**BB** too green, unripe
wòhng 黃 yellow	**wòhng-gàhm-gàhm** 黃淦淦 yellowed (as in lecture notes, skin)

(b) Size and dimension:

fèih 肥 fat	**fèih-tàhn-tàhn** 肥揗揗 fatty or **fèih-dyūt-dyūt** 肥嘟嘟 chubby
sau 瘦 thin	**sau-máang-máang** 瘦蜢蜢 slim (of people)
ngái 矮 short	**ngái-dāt-dāt** 矮腯腯 short, stocky (of people)
bohk 薄 thin	**bohk-chīt-chīt** 薄切切 thin (of clothes, paper etc.)
chèuhng 長 long	**chèuhng-làaih-làaih** 長癩癩 (over) long

bín 扁 flat	**bín-teht-teht** 扁踢踢 flat (surface)
maht 密 dense	**maht-jāt-jāt** 密質質 cramped, crowded
yùhn 圓 round	**yùhn-lūk-lūk/yùhn-dàhm-dàhm/yùhn-dàhm-dèuh** 圓碌碌/圓揉揉/ 圓揉墮 rounded

(c) Taste:

cheui 脆 crisp	**cheui-bōk-bōk** 脆卜卜 crispy
syūn 酸 sour	**syūn-mēi-mēi** 酸瞇瞇 on the sour side
tìhm 甜 sweet	**tìhm-yèh-yèh** 甜椰椰 too sweet, sickly
táahm 淡 bland	**táahm-mauh-mauh** 淡茂茂 too bland, tasteless

These forms are used as expressive adjectives:

Kéuih sé dī jih maht-jāt-jāt ge 佢寫啲字密質質嘅
The characters he writes are cramped.

Kéuih jyú dī sung táahm-mauh-mauh ge 佢煮啲餸淡茂茂嘅
The food he cooks is too bland.

Two or more such forms can be combined to paint a vivid picture, for example:

Go bìhbi hóu dākyi, fèih-dyūt-dyūt, baahk-syūt-syūt 個BB好得意，肥嘟嘟，白雪雪
The baby is pretty, chubby and white as snow.

Faai mihn yùhn-lūk-lūk hùhng-bōk-bōk 塊面圓碌碌紅卜卜
Her face is rounded and rosy.

AAB verbs and adverbs

Most of these expressions exist only in reduplicated form:

gáau-gáau-jan 搞搞震 meddle (*gáau-jan 搞震 does not exist)
tàhn-tán-jan 騰騰震 shake (*tàhn-jan 騰震 does not exist)
jihng-jíng-gāi 靜靜雞 or **jihng-gāi-gāi** 靜雞雞 quietly, secretly
kàhm-chēng 擒青 → **kàhmkám-chēng** 擒擒青 in a hurry

These forms serve as predicates and/or adverbs:

Ngóh gínggou léih, mhóu joi gáau-gáau-jan la
我警告你，唔好再搞搞震喇
I warn you, don't meddle any more.

Léih kàhmkám-chēng gwo máhlouh, gón-jyuh heui bīn a?
你擒擒青過馬路，趕住去邊呀？
You crossed the street in such a hurry, where are you going?

Kéuih meih hōi yùhn wúi jauh jihng-jíng-gái jáu-jó
佢未開完會就靜靜雞走咗
She quietly left before the end of the meeting.

AABB adjectives and adverbs

Words consisting of two syllables are reduplicated by repeating each syllable in the pattern AABB:

daaih-fōng 大方	graceful	→ **daaih-daaih-fōng-fōng** 大大方方	elegant, graceful(ly)
sī-màhn 斯文	refined	→ **sī-sī-màhn-màhn** 斯斯文文	gentlemanly
sei-fōng 四方	square	→ **sei-sei-fōng-fōng** 四四方方	rather square
sih-daahn 是但	indifferent	→ **sih-sih-daahn-daahn** 是是但但	rather indifferent(ly)
kàuh-kèih 求其	casual	→ **kàuh-kàuh-kèih-kèih** 求求其其	casually
faai-cheui 快趣	quickly	→ **faai-faai-cheui-cheui** 快快趣趣	nice and quickly

These forms may also serve as adverbs (see *Basic Cantonese*, Unit 10):

A-Lìhng kàuh-kàuh-kèih-kèih ga-jó go gwáijái
阿玲求求其其嫁咗個鬼仔
Ling casually got married to a foreign boy.

Ngóhdeih faai-faai-cheui-cheui gáau-dihm lī dāan sāangyi lā
我哋快快趣趣搞掂呢單生意啦
Let's get this business deal over and done with quickly.

Such reduplication applied to directional verbs gives a meaning of repetition:

séuhng-séuhng-lohk-lohk 上上落落	go up and down
héi-héi-dit-dit 起起跌跌	rise and fall
chēut-chēut-yahp-yahp 出出入入	come in and out

Kéuih ge yāt sāng héi-héi-dit-dit, haih paak hei ge hóu tàihchòih
佢嘅一生起起跌跌，係拍戲嘅好題材
Her life is full of ups and downs; it is good material for a film.

Lī go deihdím hóu fōngbihn; hóu dō yàuh-haak chēut-chēut-yahp-yahp
呢個地點好方便；好多遊客出出入入
This location is convenient, with many tourists coming in and out.

As with the ABB forms above, two or more AABB adjectives or adverbs can
be combined to give a particularly vivid impression:

gwōng-máahng bright → **gwōng-gwōng-máahng-máahng** nice and bright
光猛 → 光光猛猛
fut-lohk spacious → **fut-fut-lohk-lohk** pleasantly spacious
闊落 → 闊闊落落

Gāan sān ūk gwōng-gwōng-máahng-máahng fut-fut-lohk-lohk
間新屋光光猛猛闊闊落落
The new house is nice and bright and spacious.

Jūk léih gihn-gihn-hōng-hōng faai-faai-lohk-lohk
祝你健健康康快快樂樂
(*lit.* wish you healthy-healthy happy-happy)
Wishing you health and happiness.

Onomatopoeic expressions

Reduplication commonly appears in onomatopoeic expressions, with tone
change of the second syllable where applicable (see Unit 3). Typically these
include the noun **sēng** 聲 meaning 'voice' or 'sound':

kàh-ká-sēng 咔咔聲 or **hā-hā-sēng** 哈哈聲 (as in laughing)
mā-mā-sēng 媽媽聲 (as in scolding, rebuking)
mē-mē-sēng 咩咩聲 bleating (sheep)
wāng-wāng-sēng 嗡嗡聲 buzzing (bees)
guhk-gúk-sēng or **gohk-gók-sēng** 咯咯聲 crowing (cock)
gwàhng-gwáng-sēng 轟轟聲 (usually construction noise)
lòhm-lóm-sēng 浪浪聲 (any big noise as in a construction site)

Many of these onomatopoeic expressions are used as predicates or as adverbs:

jìh-jàhm 吱噚 → **jìhjī-jàhmjàhm** 吱吱噚噚 (usually in chatting secretly)
Kéuihdeih sèhngyaht jìhjī-jàhmjàhm; fàahn séi yàhn la
佢哋成日吱吱噚噚, 煩死人喇
They're always chatting in a low voice; it's very annoying.

jī-jā 吱喳 → **jījī-jājā** 吱吱喳喳 (talking noisily like birds chirping)
Dī hohksāang yātjóu jījī-jājā háidouh kīng-gái
啲學生一早吱吱喳喳喺度傾偈
The students are chatting away every morning.

Some of these forms have an adverbial meaning unrelated to sound, as in **lōk-lók-sēng** 咯咯聲 or **lāak-lāak-sēng** 嘞嘞聲 (fluently), **làh-lá-sēng** 嘑嘑聲 and **jàh-já-sēng** 吔吔聲 (quickly):

> **Kéuih Yīngmán hóu lēk ga; góng dou lāak-lāak-sēng**
> 佢英文好叻㗎, 講到嘞嘞聲
> Her English is very good; she can speak it fluently.

> **Ngóh séung làh-lá-sēng jouh saai dī yéh**
> 我想嘑嘑聲做晒啲嘢
> I want to finish the work quickly.

> **Kéuih jàh-já-sēng sé yùhn fūng seun, sahp fānjūng dōu msái**
> 佢吔吔聲寫完封信, 十分鐘都唔使
> She finished writing the letter quickly and it didn't even take ten minutes.

Reduplication in baby-talk register

As in other languages, reduplication is a feature of the baby talk used between parents and small children. The baby-talk forms often resemble the adult ones, as in the case of ABB forms with verb and reduplicated object:

yám-láaih 飲奶 drink milk → **yám-lāai-lāai** 飲奶奶
yám-séui 飲水 drink water → **yám-séui-séui** 飲水水
sái-mihn 洗面 wash one's face → **sái-mihn-mihn** 洗面面
maat-mihn 抹面 wipe one's face → **maat-mihn-mihn** 抹面面
baahn-leng 扮靚 make oneself up → **baahn-leng-leng** 扮靚靚
chūng-lèuhng 沖涼 have a shower → **chūng-lèuhng-lèuhng** 沖涼涼

Other baby-talk expressions are used only in ABB forms:

sihk 食 eat → **sihk-mūm-mūm** 食mum mum		eat
ō 痾 excrete → **ō-syùh-syùh/ō-syùh-syú** 痾殊殊		pee, go wee-wee
sái 洗 wash → **sái-baahk-baahk** 洗白白		wash oneself clean
buhk 伏 ambush → **buhk-lēi-lēi** 伏匿匿		play hide and seek

Exercise 4.1

Reduplicate the adjective to give a vivid impression (note that **hóu** 好 is not normally used with reduplicated adjectives).

Example:	**Kéuih go jéfū hóu sī-màhn** 佢個姐父好斯文	Her brother-in-law is gentlemanly.
→	**Kéuih go jéfū sī-sī-màhn-màhn** 佢個姐父斯斯文文	nice and gentlemanly

1 **Gāan ūk hóu kéihléih** 間屋好企理   The house is orderly.
2 **Go léui hóu baahk-jehng** 個女好   The daughter is fair. (in
   白淨   complexion)
3 **Tou hei hóu póutūng** 套戲好普通   The film was ordinary.
4 **Ngóhdeih ūkkéi hóu yihtlaauh**   Our home is lively.
   我哋屋企好熱鬧
5 **Gó gāan hohkhaauh hóu séi-báan**   The school is strict. (inflexible)
   嗰間學校好死板
6 **Lóuhbáan gāmyaht hóu mángjáng**   Today the boss is impatient.
   老闆今日好瘟瘤
7 **Go dīksí sīgēi hóu chōulóuh**   The taxi driver is rude.
   個的士司機好粗魯
8 **Kéuih go jái hóu gōudaaih** 佢個仔   Her son is big and tall.
   好高大
9 **Ngóh fahn gūng hóu ōndihng** 我份   My job is stable.
   工好安定
10 **Gó go móhngkàuh mìhngsīng hóu**   The tennis star is well-built.
   daaih-jek 嗰個網球明星好大隻

Exercise 4.2

Add a reduplicated adverb to the sentence based on the adjective provided.

Example: **Kéuihdeih lèih-fān** 佢哋離婚 (**chèuih-bín** 隨便) They got
           divorced (casual)
  →   **Kéuihdeih chèuih-chèuih-bín-bín lèih-fān** 佢哋隨隨便便離婚
           They casually got divorced

1 **Kéuih sailóu daapying wàahn chín** 佢細佬答應還錢 (**hàhm-wùh** 含糊 vague)
   His brother promised to return the money (vaguely).
2 **Kéuihdeih bouji sān ūk** 佢哋佈置新屋 (**gáandāan** 簡單 simple)
   They're decorating the new house (simply).
3 **Kéuih fuhmóuh yéuhng daaih kéuih** 佢父母養大佢 (**sānfú** 辛苦 endure
   hardship)
   His parents brought him up (with much hardship).
4 **Lī gāan gūngsī syūnbou pocháan** 呢間公司宣布破產 (**jingsīk** 正式 formally)
   This company declared itself bankrupt (formally).
5 **Ngóh hēimohng léih duhk-syū** 我希望你讀書 (**kàhnlihk** 勤力 diligently)
   I hope you will study (hard).
6 **Kéuih gói saai dī gyún** 佢改晒啲卷 (**hīngsūng** 輕鬆 relax)
   She marked all the papers (in a relaxed manner).
7 **Jūk léih ló dóu hohk-wái** 祝你攞到學位 (**seuhnleih** 順利 smooth)
   Hope you get the degree (smoothly).
8 **Dáng ngóh gáaisīk béi léih tēng** 等我解釋畀你聽 (**chèuhng-sai** 詳細 detailed)
   Let me explain to you (in a detailed manner).

Exercise 4.3

Choose a suitable onomatopoeic form to modify the verb phrase.

1 _____ **haam** 喊 cry

2 _____ **jihgéi tùhng jihgéi góng-yéh** 自己同自己講嘢 talk to oneself

3 _____ **siu** 笑 laugh

4 _____ **góng hàahn-wá** 講閒話 gossip

5 _____ **góng beimaht** 講秘密 talk secrets

6 _____ **jōngsāu** 裝修 remodel

7 _____ **laauh go jái** 鬧個仔 scold the son

8 _____ **sām tiu** 心跳 heart beating

9 _____ **heui tàuhsou** 去投訴 go to complain

10 _____ **làuh hyut** 流血 bleeding

a **gwàhng-gwáng-sēng** 轟轟聲 banging noise

b **jījī-jājā** 吱吱喳喳 chirping

c **buhk-búk-sēng** 卜卜聲 pulsing

d **jìh-jī-jàhm-jàhm** 吱吱噚噚 quietly chit-chatting

e **àhm-àhm-chàhm-chàhm** 喃喃噚噚 talking to oneself

f **wā-wā-sēng** 嘩嘩聲 crying noise

g **kàh-ká-sēng** 咔咔聲 chuckling noise

h **mā-mā-sēng** 媽媽聲 rebuking

i **bàh-bá-sēng** 吧吧聲 flowing out in great quantity

j **ngàhng-ngáng-sēng** 唉唉聲 mumbling

Exercise 4.4

Reduplicate both the adjectives to give a vivid impression of the situation.

Example: **Ngóh sèhngyaht dōu hóu hōisām, hóu gihnhōng** 我成日都好開心, 好健康
I'm always happy and healthy.
→ **Ngóh sèhngyaht dōu hōi-hōi-sām-sām,** 我成日都開開心心,
gihn-gihn-hōng-hōng 健健康康

1 **Kéuihdeih hóu chānmaht, hóu yīnngahn** 佢哋好親密, 好煙韌
They're very close and intimate.

2 **Gó go làahmyán hóu sàhnbei, hóu gwáisyú** 嗰個男人好神秘, 好鬼鼠
That guy is mysterious and stealthy.

3 **Ngóh lóuhgūng hóu sìhngsaht, hóu táanbaahk**
我老公好誠實, 好坦白
My husband is honest and frank.

4 **Lī go jokgā sé ge yéh hóu hūngduhng, hóu kèihgwaai**
呢個作家寫嘅嘢好空洞, 好奇怪
The stuff written by this author is empty and strange.

5 **Kéuih go yéung hóu yìhmsūk, hóu láahng-ngouh**
佢個樣好嚴肅, 好冷傲
He looks serious, cold and arrogant.

6 **Gāan ūk hóu gōnjehng, hóu jíngchàih**　間屋好乾淨, 好整齊
The house is nice and clean, neat and tidy.

7 **Léih go léuih-pàhngyáuh hóu sīmàhn, hóu daaih-fōng**
你個女朋友好斯文, 好大方
Your girlfriend is gentle and graceful.

8 **Kéuih gāan seuihfóng hóu syūfuhk, hóu hōiyèuhng**　佢間睡房好舒服,
好開揚
Her bedroom is cosy and open.

9 **Léih go beisyū hóu māfū, hóu fùhlūk**　你個秘書好馬虎, 好符碌
Your secretary is sloppy and irresponsible.

10 **Ngóh sailóu hóu gúwaahk, hóu gwái-máh**　你細佬好古惑, 好鬼馬
My brother is cunning and tricky.

Exercise 4.5

Choose one of the ABB adjectives/adverbs (or two where specified) for each
sentence.

1 **Kéuih dī tàuhfaat** 佢啲頭髮
Her hair _____

2 **Kéuih hàahng-louh** 佢行路
She walks _____

3 **Go bō** 個波 The ball _____

4 **Dī geijé mahn dou kéuih** 啲
記者問到佢 The reporters
questioned him till _____

5 **Léih sèhngyaht lyún góng-yéh**
你成日亂講嘢 You always talk
nonsense _____ **gám** 咁

6 **Gó go hohksāang sìhngjīk hóu
hóu, sèhngyaht** 嗰個學生成
績好好, 成日 That student's
marks are very good and he
often brags _____

7 **Dihp choi** 碟菜 The vegetables
_____,

a **yùhn-lūk-lūk** 圓碌碌 roundish

b **táahm-mauh-mauh** 淡茂茂
tasteless

c **waaht-lyūt-lyūt** 滑脟脟 soft

d **ngàh-chaat-chaat** 牙擦擦
proud, bragging

e **yiht-laaht-laaht** 熱辣辣 piping
hot

f **háu-ngá-ngá** 口啞啞 speechless

g **baahk-syūt-syūt** 白雪雪 white,
fair

8 **Gauh jyūyuhk** 舊豬肉 The
pork _____ , _____

9 **Kéuih dī pèihfū** 佢啲皮膚
Complexion _____ , _____

10 **Dī hóisīn** 啲海鮮 The seafood
_____ , _____

h **ngohng-gēui-gēui** 戇居居 stupid

i **wū-jēut-jēut** 烏卒卒 dark, shiny

j **fèih-tàhn-tàhn** 肥腍腍 fat

k **maahn-tān-tān** 慢吞吞 slowly

l **yàuh-lahm-lahm** 油淋淋 oily

m **gōn-jāng-jāng** 乾爭爭 very dry

n **hēung-pan-pan** 香噴噴
fragrant, smells nice

UNIT 5
Word formation

Apart from reduplication, new words are formed largely by compounding – juxtaposition of morphemes – and a small number of prefixes and suffixes.

Forming nouns

In forming compound nouns the modifying words come before the noun itself, much as they do in English:

People:

(a) Attributes modifying **yàhn** 人 'person':

hóu-yàhn 好人 good, nice person

waaih-yàhn 壞人 bad person, villain

kùhng-yàhn 窮人 poor person

yáuh-chín-yàhn 有錢人 rich person

chūngmìhng-yàhn 聰明人 clever person

chéun-yàhn 蠢人 stupid person

daaih-chìhng-yàhn 大情人 great lover

daaih-méih-yàhn 大美人 great beauty

Oujāu-yàhn 澳洲人 Australian (person)

Méihgwok-yàhn 美國人 American

Yidaaihleih-yàhn 意大利人 Italian

Sāijohng-yàhn 西藏人 Tibetan

(b) The suffix **-lóu** 佬 for males tends to have a pejorative connotation, referring prototypically to middle-aged, dishevelled, rough and rugged-looking men:

chāai-lóu 差佬 policeman

jōngsāu-lóu 裝修佬 decorator

chaahk-lóu 賊佬 thief

gēi-lóu 基佬 homosexual

fūngséui-lóu 風水佬 fung shui consultant

sāu-máaih-lóu 收買佬 collector of used goods

bintaai-lóu 變態佬 pervert

baahkfán-lóu 白粉佬 drug (e.g. heroin) addict

jeuijáu-lóu 醉酒佬 drunkard   **hàahmsāp-lóu** 鹹濕佬 lecherous man
chīsin-lóu 黐線佬 crazy guy   **sēui-lóu** 衰佬 bad guy
fèih-lóu 肥佬 fatty   **gwái-lóu** 鬼佬 foreigner

The suffix **-pòh** 婆 or its changed-tone form **pó** provide a female counterpart of **-lóu** 佬, though less widely used:

chāai-pòh 差婆 policewoman   **maaih-choi-pó** 賣菜婆 (woman)
vegetable vendor
baat-pòh 八婆 busybody   **mùih-yàhn-pòh** 媒人婆 matchmaker
gwái-pòh 鬼婆
foreign woman

-jái 仔 and its female counterparts **-léui** 女 and **-mūi** 妹 have a diminutive meaning, also denoting familiarity:

dá-gūng-jái 打工仔 worker   **suhkhaak-jái** 熟客仔 familiar customer
Yahtbún-jái 日本仔 Japanese guy   **Taai(gwok)-mūi** 泰(國)妹 Thai girl
fā-léui 花女 flower girl, bridesmaid   **fā-jái** 花仔 flower boy, page
gwái-jái 鬼仔 foreign boy   **gwái-mūi** 鬼妹 foreign girl

Food terms provide nice illustrations of how compound nouns are formed. Note how all modifiers precede the noun:

jyū-yuhk 豬扒 pork   **ngàuh-yuhk** 牛肉 beef
baahk-choi 白菜 pak choy   **tūng-choi** 通菜 water spinach
muhk-gwā 木瓜 papaya   **chēng-gwā** 青瓜 cucumber
chā-sīu-bāau 叉燒包 pork bun   **tàihjí-bāau** 提子包 raisin bun
Hóilàahm gāi-faahn 海南雞飯   **yuhk-sī cháau mihn** 肉絲炒麵
Hainanese chicken rice   fried noodles with shredded pork

Technical terminology follows a similar pattern:

jīseun fōgeih 資訊科技   information technology (IT)
yàhn-gūng jilàhng 人工智能   artificial intelligence (AI)
sou-máh séung-gēi 數碼相機   digital camera
hauh-yihndoih jyúyi 後現代主義   Postmodernism

A special set of compounds are formed by juxtaposing opposites:

dō 多 many + **síu** 少 few   → **dō-síu** 多少 amount
gōu 高 tall + **dāi** 低 low   → **gōu-dāi** 高低 height
chèuhng 長 long + **dyún** 短 short   → **chèuhng-dyún** 長短 length

For example:

Dohk-háh gōu-dāi tùhngmàaih chèuhng-dyún
度下高低同埋長短
Measure the height and length.

A similar type combines two kinship terms to form collective nouns:

jái 仔 son + **léui** 女 daughter   →   **jái-léui** 仔女 children
hing 兄 elder + **daih** 弟 younger brother   →   **hīngdaih** 兄弟 brothers
fuh 父 father + **jí** 子 son (formal)   →   **fuhjí** 父子 father and son
lóuhgūng 老公 husband + **lóuhpòh** 老婆 wife   →   **(léuhng) gūngpó** (兩) 公婆 husband and wife (colloquial)

Note how these forms are used with **léuhng** 兩 'two' or other numerals:

Kéuihdeih léuhng fuhjí hóu chíh-yéung 佢哋兩父子好似樣
The two of them, father and son, look very much alike.
Ngóhdeih léuhng gūngpó chaang tói-geuk 我哋兩公婆撐枱腳
The two of us, husband and wife, are having a private meal.
Kéuihdeih sāam hīngdaih háidouh jāang yuhng dihnlóuh 佢哋三兄弟喺度爭用電腦
The three brothers are fighting for the use of the computer.

Abbreviations

Longer names of companies, etc., are often abbreviated by combining the first syllable of each component word:

Yīng-gwok Hòhng-hūng Gūngsī 英國航空公司	British Airways → **Yīng-Hòhng** 英航 BA
Sīng-ga-bō Hòhng-hūng Gūngsī 新加坡航空公司	Singapore Airlines → **Sīng-Hòhng** 新航 SIA
Fō-geih daaih-hohk 科技大學	The University of Science and Technology → **Fō-daaih** 科大 HKUST
Hàhngsāng jísou 恆生指數	The Hang Seng index (Hong Kong stock index) → **Hàhng-jí** 恆指 the HSI
Jūngwàh dihnlihk 中華電力	China Light and Power → **Jūng-dihn** 中電 China Light

Sometimes, however, the second syllable is selected to give a more satisfactory abbreviation, as with **Hēunggóng** 香港 becoming **Góng** 港:

Hēunggóng titlouh 香港鐵路	Mass Transit Railway → **Góng-tit** 港鐵 MTR
Hēunggóng daaih-hohk 香港大學	Hong Kong University → **Góng-daaih** 港大 HKU

Hēunggóng síu-jé 香港小姐   Miss Hong Kong
                                    → **Góng-jé** 港姐 Miss HK

hūng-jūng síu-jé 空中小姐   female flight attendant
                                    → **hūng-jé** 空姐

Forming adjectives

A number of adjectives form compounds:

tāam-X 貪-**X** greedy for X:
tāam-sām 貪心 greedy   **tāam-pèhng** 貪平 greedy for bargains
tāam-leng 貪靚 vain   **tāam-chín** 貪錢 avaricious, miserly

dái-X 抵-**X** worthy, deserving of X
dái-sek 抵錫 lovable   **dái-máaih** 抵買 worth buying, good
dái-tái 抵睇 worth seeing   value
dái-wáan 抵玩 worth playing   **dái-laauh** 抵鬧 in need of a scolding
dái-séi 抵死 deserving to die   **dái-sihk** 抵食 worth eating, good value
                                     (food)
                                     dái-cháau 抵炒 deserving to be fired
                                     (sacked)

ngāam-X 啱-**X** right for X
ngāam-sihk 啱食 good to eat   **ngāam-tēng** 啱聽 good-sounding, good
ngāam-yám 啱飲 good to drink   to hear
                                     ngāam-tái 啱睇 good to look at (or read)

X-dāk X-得 capable of X
dá-dāk 打得 good at fighting   **sihk-dāk** 食得 can eat a lot
yám-dāk 飲得 can drink a lot   **wáan-dāk** 玩得 capable of playing to
fan-dāk 瞓得 can sleep a lot   the full
                                     ngàaih-dāk 挨得 able to endure hardship

Adjectives can readily be formed with **yáuh** 有 and **móuh** 冇 (see *Basic Cantonese*, Unit 6):

yáuh-méng 有名 famous, renowned   **móuh-tīnfahn** 冇天份 untalented
yáuh-seunsām 有信心 confident   **móuh-hēimohng** 冇希望 hopeless

Forming verbs

Reflexive verbs and adjectives are formed with **jih** 自 (as in **jihgéi** 自己 oneself):

jih-saaht 自殺   commit suicide   **jih-jin** 自薦   recommend oneself
jih-duhng 自動 automatic   **jih-yihng**   confess, admit
                                      自認

A number of these verbs appear in the following example:

Kéuih lī tou hei jih-pīn, jih-douh jih-yín, ló-jó Ousīkā gāmjeuhng-jéung
佢呢套戲自編，自導自演，擺咗奧斯卡金像獎
(*lit.* he this film self-script self-direct self-act got Oscar award)
He wrote, directed and acted in this film himself and received an Oscar.

tāu 偷 'steal' forms verbs denoting surreptitious activities:

tāu-tēng 偷聽 eavesdrop	**tāu-sihk** 偷食 snatch something to eat
tāu-tái 偷睇 peep	**tāu-yan** 偷印 copy (books, etc.) illegally
tāu-wahn 偷運 smuggle	**tāu-paak** 偷拍 take secret photographs
tāu-siu 偷笑 smile secretly	**tāu-douh** 偷渡 cross illegally (into a country)
tāu-gāi (jáu) 偷雞(走) sneak away early, shirk	**tāu-láahn** 偷懶 snatch the opportunity to be lazy

See also Unit 6 on verb-object compounds.

Exercise 5.1

Add a modifier to specify the kind of food you prefer.

Example: **tōng** 湯 soup → **syūn-laaht-tōng** 酸辣湯 hot and sour soup

1 **faahn** 飯 rice
2 **sāléut** 沙律 salad
3 **mihn** 麵 noodles
4 **yuhk** 肉 meat
5 **láaih** 奶 milk
6 **fán** 粉 (rice) noodles

7 **chàh** 茶 tea
8 **yàuh** 油 oil

9 **béng** 餅 cake

10 **bāau** 包 bun

a **gōukoi** 高鈣 high calcium; **dāijī** 低脂 low fat
b **fèih** 肥 fat; **sau** 瘦 lean
c **luhk** 綠 green; **lìhngmūng** 檸檬 lemon
d **sūkmáih** 粟米 corn; **fāsāng** 花生 peanut
e **yuht** 月 moon; **sāi** 西 western
f **chāsīu** 叉燒 barbecued pork; **lìhn-yùhng** 蓮蓉 lotus paste
g **cháau** 炒 fried; **lohmáih** 糯米 sticky rice
h **sāanggwó** 生果 fruit; **jaahp-choi** 雜菜 mixed vegetable
i **yùhdáan** 魚蛋 fishball; **ngàuhyún** 牛丸 beef ball
j **chōu** 粗 broad; **yau** 幼 thin; **cháau** 炒 fried

Exercise 5.2

Form adjectives with **yáuh/móuh** 有/冇 to give the meaning specified.

Example: **haauhléut** 效率 efficiency → **yáuh-haauhléut** 有效率 efficient

1 **yiyih** 意義 meaning → _____ meaningful
2 **líu** 料 substance → _____ vacuous
3 **mahntàih** 問題 problem → _____ problematic
4 **loihsing** 耐性 patience → _____ impatient
5 **bánmeih** 品味 taste → _____ tasteful
6 **lèuhngsām** 良心 conscience → _____ unscrupulous
7 **leih** 利 profit → _____ advantageous
8 **yùhnjāk** 原則 principle → _____ unprincipled
9 **haahn** 限 boundary → _____ limited
10 **jaakyahm-gám** 責任感 responsibility → _____ irresponsible

Exercise 5.3

Form abbreviations from the following:

1 **Jūnggwok ngàhnhòhng** 中國銀行 Bank of China
2 **Dahkkēui Sáujéung** 特區首長 Chief Executive of the Special Administrative Region
3 **Máh-lòih-sāi-a Hòhng-hūng-gūngsī** 馬來西亞航空公司 Malaysian Airlines
4 **Ajāu Dihnsih** 亞洲電視 Asia Television (ATV)
5 **Sāi-kēui Seuihdouh** 西區隧道 Western Harbour Tunnel
6 **Bākgīng Daaih-hohk** 北京大學 Beijing University
7 **Deih-hah Titlouh** 地下鐵路 Underground Railway
8 **Hēunggóng Dihndāng** 香港電燈 Hong Kong Electric

UNIT 6
Verb-object compounds

An important set of phrases are known as verb-object compounds. They are considered compounds because they behave in some way as a single unit. Although containing an object, they often correspond to intransitive verbs in English:

gaau-syū 教書	teach	**sihk-faahn** 食飯	eat (a meal)
duhk-syū 讀書	study	**jyú-faahn** 煮飯	cook (food)
jouh-yéh 做嘢	work	**jā-chē** 揸車	drive (a car)
yàuh-séui 游水	swim	**waahk-wá** 畫畫	draw/paint (a picture)
dá-jih 打字	type	**cheung-gō** 唱歌	sing (a song)
dá-dihnwá 打電話	telephone	**béi-chín** 畀錢	pay (money)

With these verbs the object is usually not translated:

Ngóh m̀h sīk jā-chē 我唔識揸車	I don't know how to drive (a car).
Yáuh yàhn háidouh cheung-gō 有人喺度唱歌	Someone's singing (songs).
Dáng ngóh béi-chín lā 等我畀錢啦	Let me pay (the money).
Ngóh go jái jūngyi waahk-wá 我個仔鍾意畫畫	My son likes to draw (pictures).
Gāmmáahn bīngo jyú-faahn a? 今晚邊個煮飯呀?	Who's cooking (the food) tonight?
Léih yiu sé-seun heui seui-gúk 你要寫信去稅局	You have to write (a letter) to the tax office.

The word **yéh** 嘢 (thing, stuff) comes in handy here as a generic object which can be used with many verbs:

Ngóhdeih heui yám-yéh 我哋去飲嘢	We're going for a drink.
Léih mhóu góng-yéh jyuh 你唔好講嘢住	Don't speak yet.
Kéuih yauh háidouh baahn-yéh 佢又喺度扮嘢	He's pretending again.
Mhóu hái ngóh mihn chìhn wáan-yéh 唔好喺我面前玩嘢	Don't put on a show in front of me (*lit.* play things).

With some verbs of this kind, there is no way to translate the object at all:

git-fān 結婚	get married	**fan-gaau** 瞓覺	sleep
dihng-fān 訂婚	become engaged	**tiu-móuh** 跳舞	dance
lèih-fān 離婚	get divorced	**tiu-síng** 跳繩	skip

The aspect marker or verbal particle comes between the verb and the object, just as it would in the case of a regular object:

Kéuih lóuhbáan chìh-*jó*-jīk
佢老闆辭咗職
His boss has resigned.

Go beisyū dá-*gán*-dihnwá
佢秘書打緊電話
The secretary is talking on the phone.

Ngóh dī pàhngyáuh kīng-*gán*-gái
我哋朋友傾緊偈
My friends are chatting.

Kéuih meih duhk-*gwo*-syū
佢未讀過書
He has not studied before.

Ngóh juhng meih gaau-*yùhn*-syū
我仲未教完書
I have not finished teaching.

This contrasts with other verbs which happen to have two syllables (but do not contain an object), where the aspect marker comes at the end:

Ngóh gáaisīk-*jó* hóu loih
佢解釋咗好耐
I explained for a long time.

Lī go gaiwaahk faatjín-*jó* géi lìhn
呢個計劃發展咗幾年
This project has developed for some years.

Kéuih wàaihyìh-*gwo* jihgéi ge làhnglihk
佢懷疑過自己嘅能力
He has doubted his own ability.

Kéuih tùhng yàhn-haak gaaisiuh-*gán* dī syū
佢同人客介紹緊啲書
He's introducing the books to the guests.

Directional verb compounds

The directional verbs (see *Basic Cantonese*, Unit 15) also form verb-object compounds:

séuhng-chē 上車	get on (a bus, etc.)	**lohk-chē** 落車	get off (a bus, etc.)
séuhng-tòhng 上堂	go to class	**lohk-tòhng** 落堂	finish class
fāan-gūng 返工	go to work	**fāan-hohk** 返學	go to school
chēut-fo 出貨	sell goods, shares	**yahp-fo** 入貨	buy goods, shares etc.
héi-sān 起身	get up	**gwo-sān** 過身	pass away

Modifying the object

It is often possible to insert a modifier between the verb and its object:

fan-gaau 瞓覺 sleep   **Go bìhbī yiu fan ngaan gaau** 個**BB**要瞓晏覺
The baby has to have an afternoon nap.
Ngóh fan fāan go leng gaau sīn 我瞓返個靚覺先
I'm going to have a nice sleep.

chūng-lèuhng 沖涼   **Léih yiu chūng go yiht séui lèuhng** 你要沖個熱水涼
shower   You need to take a hot shower.

fa-jōng 化妝 put on   **Kéuih yauh fa-jó go lùhng jōng** 佢又化咗個濃妝
make-up   She's put on loud make-up again.

This can be puzzling since **gaau** 覺 in **fan-gaau** 瞓覺, for example, is not meaningful on its own, while **lèuhng** 涼 meaning 'cool' can hardly be modified by 'hot water'. In effect, the modifier applies to the whole action, in this case taking a shower. A classifier can also be added to indicate a specific event:

sihk *chāan* faahn 食餐飯   have a meal
dá dō *go* dihnwá 打多個電話   make another call
tiu géi *jek* móuh 跳幾隻舞   have a few dances

In the phrase **wàhn-lohng** 暈浪 (*lit.* dizzy-wave), there is normally a modifier:

wàhn-syùhn-lohng 暈船浪   get seasick
wàhn-chē-lohng 暈車浪   get carsick
wàhn-gēi-lohng 暈機浪   get airsick
wàhn-(saai)-daaih-lohng 暈(晒)大浪   faint, go weak at the knees

Inverted verb-object compounds

In several situations, the verb-object 'compounds' may appear in inverted form or separated from each other. In such cases, they preserve the meaning of the original compound:

(a) With **yáuh/móuh** 有/冇 (see *Basic Cantonese*, Unit 6):

jouh-yéh 做嘢 work → **yáuh yéh jouh** 有做嘢   have work to do
tiu-móuh 跳舞 dance → **yáuh móuh tiu** 有跳舞   there is dancing
(to be done)
duhk-syū 讀書 study → **móuh syū duhk** 冇讀書   have no opportunity
to study
fan-gaau 瞓覺 sleep → **móuh gaau hóu fan**   be unable to sleep
冇覺好瞓   properly

(b) With topicalization (see *Basic Cantonese*, Unit 22), for example, given
the verb-object compounds **duhk-syū** 讀書 (study) and **fāan-hohk** 返學
(attend school), we can topicalize the objects:

> **Syū yauh m̀h duhk, hohk yauh m̀h fāan** 書又唔讀, 學又唔返
> He doesn't study and doesn't go to school.

Similarly, based on **git-fān** 結婚 (to get married), the object **fān** 婚 can be made
the topic of the sentence:

> **Fān chìh jóu dōu yiu git ge la** 婚遲早都要結嘅啦
> (*lit.* marriage sooner or later still have to close)
> You have to get married sooner or later.

(c) With **lìhn ... dōu** 連 ... 都 'even' (see Unit 9) to emphasize the object of
the verb-object compound:

> **Kéuih yìhgā lìhn gāai dōu m̀h séung hàahng** 佢而家連街都唔想行
> Now she doesn't even want to go out. (**hàahng-gāai** 行街)
> **Ngóh go jái behng dou lìhn wá dōu m̀h séung waahk** 我個仔病到連畫都唔
> 想畫
> My son is so sick that he doesn't even want to draw. (**waahk-wá** 畫畫)
> **Léih mòhng dou lìhn faahn dōu móuh sìhgaan sihk àh?** 你忙到連飯都冇時
> 間食呀?
> Are you so busy that you have no time to eat? (**sihk-faahn** 食飯)

Exercise 6.1

Add the missing object where required:

1 **Ngóhdeih yìhgā heui sihk ____**   We're going to eat now.
　我哋而家去食 ____

2 **Dī yāmngohk lihng dou ngóh séung tiu ____**   The music makes me want to
　啲音樂令到我想跳 ____   dance.

3 **Ngóh go jái jeui lēk haih waahk ____**   My son is best at drawing.
　我個仔最叻係畫 ____

4 **Léih jeui hóu sé ____ béi kéuih**   You'd better write to him.
　你最好寫 ____ 畀佢

5 **Léih géisìh béi ____ a?**   When are you going to pay?
　你幾時畀 ____ 呀?

6 **Ngóh juhng meih chūng ____**   I haven't taken a shower yet.
　我仲未沖 ____

7 **Sīngkèih-yaht msái fāan ____**   No need to go to school on
　星期日唔使返 ____   Sunday.

8 **Kéuih hóu jūngyi kīng** ___   He likes to chat.
  佢好鍾意傾 ___
9 **Ngóh yiu yaht-yaht yàuh** ___   I need to swim every day.
  我要日日游 ___
10 **Kéuih sèhngyaht daaih-sēng cheung** ___   She always sings loudly.
   佢成日大聲唱 ___

Exercise 6.2

Add a suitable aspect marker or particle such as **jó** 咗, **gán** 緊, **gwo** 過 or **yùhn** 完 to modify the verb-object phrase.

Example:

      Kéuih hái Gānàhdaaih gaau-syū   He teaches in Canada.
      佢喺加拿大教書
→   **Kéuih hái Gānàhdaaih gaau-gwo-syū**   He has taught in Canada.
      佢喺加拿大教過書

1 **Kéuih māmìh hái chyùhfóng jyú-faahn**   His mother is cooking in
  佢媽咪喺廚房煮飯   the kitchen.
2 **Léih taai-táai haih-mhaih faat-pèihhei a?**   Is your wife throwing her
  你太太係唔係發脾氣呀?   temper tantrums?
3 **Seuhng go láihbaai ngóh fong-ga**   Last week I took leave.
  上個禮拜我放假
4 **Kéuih hái Gimkìuh duhk-syū**   He has studied at
  佢喺劍橋讀書   Cambridge before.
5 **Ngóh hàahng-gūngsī jīhauh gokdāk hóu guih**   I felt tired after shopping.
  我行公司之後覺得好劫
6 **Léih géisìh yám-jáu lèih a?**   When did you have a
  你幾時飲酒嚟呀?   drink?
7 **Ngóh hóu loih móuh háau-síh la**   It's been a long time since I
  我好耐冇考試喇   took an exam.
8 **Dá-dihnwá fāan ūkkéi meih a?**   Have you called home yet?
  打電話返屋企未呀?

†Exercise 6.3

Separate the object from the verb by making it the topic or focus of the sentence (see Unit 9).

Example: **Yātdihng yiu jéunsìh gāau-seui**   One must pay taxes on time.
        一定要準時交稅
→   **Seui yātdihng yiu jéunsìh gāau**
        稅一定要準時交

1 **Kéuih m̀h sīk gaau-syū** 佢唔識教書
He doesn't know how to teach.

2 **Syúga ngóhdeih dōu móuh dāk fong-ga** 暑假我哋都冇得放假
Even in summer we have no opportunity to take a holiday.

3 **Kéuih taai-táai yauh msái chau-jái, yauh msái fāan-gūng**
佢太太又唔使湊仔, 又唔使返工
His wife doesn't need to take care of the kids or go to work.

4 **Chìh jóu dōu yiu sāang-jái** 遲早都要生仔
Sooner or later one has to have children.

5 **Yauh m̀h daap-fēigēi yauh m̀h jā-chē** 又唔搭飛機又唔揸車
He won't take a plane or drive.

6 **Kéuih sāmchìhng m̀h hóu, yauh m̀h sihk-faahn yauh m̀h fan-gaau**
佢心情唔好, 又唔食飯又唔瞓覺
He's not in a good mood, doesn't eat or sleep.

7 **Léih yauh m̀h sé-seun, yauh m̀h dá-dihnwá** 你又唔寫信, 又唔打電話
You don't write or call.

8 **Kéuih yauh m̀h fa-jōng yauh m̀h chēui-tàuh** 佢又唔化妝又唔吹頭
She doesn't put on make-up or style her hair.

UNIT 7
Adjectives and stative verbs

Adjectives as verbs

Adjectives in Cantonese share several features with verbs. They can be used with aspect markers such as **jó** 咗, **gwo** 過 and **háh** 下 (Unit 12) as well as verbal particles such as **fāan** 返, **saai** 晒, **màaih** 埋 to indicate a change in the situation:

Ngóh go jái jeuigahn hōisām-jó 我個仔最近開心咗	My son has become happier lately.
Kéuih yìhgā hōisām fāan 佢而家開心返	She's happy again now.

The ways adjectives and verbs are questioned and negated are also alike:

Adjective	Verb
Gwai-m̀h-gwai a? 貴唔貴呀? It's expensive?	**Léih jáu-m̀h-jáu a?** 你走唔走呀? Are you leaving?
m̀h gwai 唔貴 It's not expensive.	**Ngóh m̀h jáu** 我唔走 I'm not leaving.

Stative verbs

A number of words which describe a state of affairs are intermediate between verbs and adjectives. These are generally known as stative verbs. Some of the most common are:

gánjēung 緊張 anxious
gēng 驚 afraid
ngāam 啱 right
sihnmouh 羨慕 envious

suhk 熟 familiar
chīngchó 清楚 clear
mòhng 忙 busy
douhgeih 妒忌 jealous

Like adjectives, stative verbs enter into a range of comparative constructions (see Unit 13):

Jeui gánjēung haih léih 最緊張係你	You're the most nervous.
Léih juhng chīngchó gwo ngóh 你仲清楚過我	You know even more than I do.
Ngóh tùhng kéuih suhk dī 我同佢熟啲	I know her better.
Gám yéuhng ngāam dī 咁樣啱啲	This way is more appropriate.

They also behave like adjectives in other respects, such as reduplication (see Unit 4):

chīng-chó 清楚 clear	→ **chīng-chīng-chó-chó** 清清楚楚	nice and clear
suhk 熟 familiar	→ **suhk-súk-déi** 熟熟哋	somewhat familiar

Although behaving in many ways like adjectives, some stative verbs can nevertheless take an object like transitive verbs:

Kéuih hóu gánjēung dī jáiléui 佢好緊張啲仔女	She's anxious about the children.
Ngóh hóu chīngchó lī gihn sih 我好清楚呢件事	I understand this matter well. (*lit.* I am very clear about this matter)
Ngóhdeih hóu suhk kéuihdeih 我哋好熟佢哋	We know them well. (*lit.* We are very familiar with them)
Ngāam saai dī léuihjái 啱晒啲女仔	Just right for the girls.
Léih jeuigahn mòhng mātyéh a? 你最近忙乜嘢呀?	What have you been busy with recently?
Ngóh sihnmouh léih, yauh douhgeih léih 我羨慕你，又妒忌你	I'm both envious and jealous of you.

This transitive use of what appear to be adjectives is especially prevalent in colloquial language:

Kéuih mtóh léih 佢唔妥你	He finds you disagreeable.
Kéuih sèhngyaht yùh jihgéi dī pàhngyáuh 佢成日瘀自己啲朋友	He always embarrasses his own friends.
Lóuhbáan hàahmsāp-gwo kéuih 老闆鹹濕過佢	The boss has sexually harassed her.
Go léui yauh chyun ngóh 個女又寸我	My daughter is giving me an attitude again.

Like other verbs and adjectives, they can take aspect markers such as **jó** 咗 to indicate a change in the situation described:

Ngóhdeih maahn-máan suhk-jó 我哋慢慢熟咗
We gradually got to know each other (*lit.* became familiar).

Līgo yuht mòhng-jó dī 呢個月忙咗啲
This month has gotten busier.

Similarly, stative verbs combine with particles such as **saai** 晒 'all' and **màaih** 埋 'in addition' (see Unit 15):

Kéuih suhk saai dī baatgwa sānmán 佢熟晒啲八卦新聞
She's familiar with all the gossip.
Ngóh mòhng màaih līgo yuht jauh msái jouh 我忙埋呢個月就唔使做
I'll be busy for this (one more) month, then I won't have to work.

Easy and difficult

The words **yùhngyih** 容易 'easy' and **làahn** 難 'difficult' pose some difficulty. When followed by a verb, the meaning is literally 'easy to . . . ' but actually means that something happens easily.

Ngóh hóu yùhngyih wán dóu jinggeui   It's easy for me to find evidence.
我好容易搵到證據
(*lit*. I'm very easy to find evidence)
Līdī yéh hóu yùhngyih cho   It's easy to get these things wrong.
呢啲嘢好容易錯
(*lit*. these things are easy to be wrong)
Ngóh hóu làahn séungjeuhng   I have difficulty imagining it.
我好難想像

The literal translations are often reflected in Chinese learners' English (as in 'I'm easy to make mistakes'). Colloquially, **yùhngyih** 容易 is often shortened to **yih** 易, as in:

Hóu yih wán ge jē 好易搵嘅啫
It's easy to find it.

Idiomatically, **māt** 乜 'what' is inserted to give **yùhng-māt-yih** 容乜易, a form of rhetorical question (see Unit 17):

Yùhng-māt-yih gūng dōu móuh màaih ga! 容乜易工都冇埋㗎!
(One) could easily lose one's job as well!

A few other adjectives work the same way as 'easy' and 'difficult', notably **fōngbihn** 方便 'convenient' and **hólàhng** 可能 'possible':

Léih fōng-m̀h-fōngbihn sīngkèih-yaht làih a? 你方唔方便星期日嚟呀?
Is it convenient for you to come on Sunday?
Kéuihdeih m̀h hólàhng gou léih ge 佢哋唔可能告你嘅
There's no way they can sue you.

43

Exercise 7.1

Add a suitable object to the stative verb.

> Example: **Ngóh gin dóu dī hàaih ngāam saai *léih*** 我見到啲墓啱晒你
> I saw some shoes that were just right (for you).

1 **Ngóh hóu dāamsām** _____ I'm worried (about....)
   我好擔心 _____
2 **Kéuih hóu sihnmouh** _____ He's envious of....
   佢好羨慕 _____
3 **Ngóh m̀h gēng** _____ **ga** I'm not scared (of....)
   我唔驚 _____ 㗎
4 **Kéuih làahmpàhngyáuh dahkbiht gánjēung** _____
   佢男朋友特別緊張 _____
   Her boyfriend is particularly anxious (about....)
5 **Kéuih séung chyun** _____ (street language) He wants to show an attitude (to....)
   佢想寸 _____
6 **Léih suhk** _____ **a?** Which ... are you familiar with?
   你熟 _____ 呀?
7 **Ngóh m̀h jī kéuih mòhng** _____ **wo** I don't know what he's busy with.
   我唔知佢忙 _____ 喎
8 **Hóu dō yàhn douhgeih** _____ A lot of people are jealous (of....)
   好多人妒忌 _____

Exercise 7.2

Add an aspect marker or verbal particle such as **jó** 咗, **gwo** 過, **saai** 晒, **màaih** 埋
or **fāan** 返 to the adjective or stative verb to give the meaning specified.

> Example: **Léih fèih-jó wo!** 你肥咗喎! You've put on weight!

1 **Kéuih jouh yùhn sáuseuht yìhgā leng** ___   After the operation, she got
   佢做完手術而家靚 ___   her looks back.
2 **Kéuih yíhchìhn chàhnggīng leng** ___   She was beautiful once.
   佢以前曾經靚 ___
3 **Léih hóuchíh leng** ___ **bo**   You seem to have become
   你好似靚 ___ 噃   more beautiful.
4 **Jeuk-jyuh gihn sān sāam, léih sèhng go** You're looking completely
   leng ___   beautiful with the new clothes
   著住件新衫, 你成個靚 ___   on.
5 **Ngóh mòhng** ___ **gām chi jē**   I'll be busy just one more time.
   我忙 ___ 今次啫
6 **Ngóh jeuigahn mòhng** ___   I've become busy lately.
   我最近忙 ___

7

Adjectives
and stative
verbs

7 **Ngóh gām-lín meih mòhng** ___
我今年未忙 ___

I haven't been busy this year.

8 **Ngóh hōichí mòhng** ___ ___
我好似忙 ___ ___

I'm starting to be busy again.

9 **Lī pàaih tīnhei lyúhn** ___
呢排天氣暖 ___

The weather has become
warmer lately.

10 **Yìhgā lyúhn** ___ ___
而家暖 ___ ___

It's all warm again now.

Exercise 7.3

Insert **hóu yùhngyih/hóu làahn** 好容易/好難 'easy/difficult' in the following
sentences to give the meaning specified.

1 **Ngóh tùhng kéuih hahpjok** 我同佢合作
   It's difficult for me to collaborate with him.
2 **Kéuih lám dóu daapngon** 佢諗到答案
   It's easy for her to think of the answer.
3 **Kéuihdeih yèhng-jó lī chèuhng béichoi** 佢哋贏咗呢場比賽
   It was easy for them to win this competition.
4 **Lī go yúhn-gín sailouhjái yuhng dóu** 呢個軟件細路仔用到
   It's difficult for children to use this software.
5 **Kéuihdeih béi yàhn ngāak** 佢哋畀人呃
   It's easy for them to be cheated.
6 **Chín múhnjūk yāt go yàhn jānjing ge sēuiyiu** 錢滿足一個人真正嘅需要
   It's hard for money to satisfy a person's real need.
7 **Yīgā ge tīnhei, go-go dōu sēungfūng** 而家嘅天氣, 個個都傷風
   In the current weather, it's easy for everyone to catch a cold.
8 **Dī yāmngohk lihng ngóh lám fāan yíhchìhn ge sih** 啲音樂令我諗返以前嘅事
   It's easy for the music to make me think of past events.
9 **Léih yíhwàih ngóh yīngsìhng yàhn jouh-yéh àh?** 你以為我應承人做嘢呀?
   You thought it's easy for me to promise people to do things?
10 **Lī júng yàhn hái līdouh sāngchyùhn** 呢種人喺呢度生存
   It's difficult for this kind of people to survive here.

45

UNIT 8
Classifiers revisited

Classifiers as articles

Classifiers play several important roles in Cantonese grammar (see *Basic Cantonese*, Unit 8). One of the distinctive grammatical features of Cantonese is the way in which the classifier acts like a definite article, as in **ga chē** 架車 'the car' referring to a particular car known to the speaker. This is especially so when the classifier goes with the subject or topic of the sentence:

Gāan ūk héi hóu la 間屋起好喇	The house is finished.
Fahn boují tái yùhn la 份報紙睇完喇	I've finished reading the newspaper.

Compare a 'bare' noun used without a classifier, which refers to things belonging to a certain category in general:

Páau-chē gwai dī 跑車貴啲	Sports cars are more expensive.
Hùhng-jáu hóu yáuh-yīk 紅酒好有益	Red wine is good for you.

Now contrast the 'generic' meaning of a noun used alone and the 'specific' meaning of the same noun with a classifier:

Gauh ūk pèhng hóu dō 舊屋平好多	Old houses are much cheaper.
Gāan gauh ūk pèhng hóu dō 間舊屋平好多	The old house is much cheaper.

When the classifier goes with an object coming after the verb, the noun phrase may be indefinite – indicating something which is not already known to the hearer – but usually still refers to a specific entity:

Kéuihdeih máaih-jó ga sān chē 佢買咗架新車	They've bought a new car.
Kéuih sīk-jó go léuih-yīsāng 佢識咗個女醫生	He's gotten to know a female doctor.

That is classifiers help to pick out a particular item or individual. In this respect, they serve like articles in English and other European languages.

Possessive classifiers

Classifiers are often used to indicate possession in preference to the particle **ge** 嘅 (see *Basic Cantonese*, Unit 5), especially when referring to a particular possessed item:

Léih tìuh fu taai dyún; m̀h ngāam jeuk 你條褲太短; 唔啱著
Your trousers are too short for you; they don't fit.
Kéuihdeih gāan ūk hóyíh mohng dóu Chīng Máh Daaih Kìuh
佢哋間屋可以望到青馬大橋
(From) their house, one can see the Tsing Ma Suspension Bridge.

This may be seen as a natural extension of the use of classifier + noun to refer to specific things as described above. These usages are characteristic of Cantonese as opposed to Mandarin and most other Chinese languages. Another extension is to add a demonstrative, **lī** 呢 'this' or **gó** 嗰 'that' before the classifier:

léih lī gihn sāam 你呢件衫   this shirt of yours
léuih gó júng singgaak 佢嗰種性格   that personality of his
ngóhdeih gó chàhng láu 我哋嗰層樓   that flat of ours

Dī 啲 as plural classifier

dī 啲 works like a rather special classifier. It serves not only to indicate plurality but also, with mass nouns, a certain quantity:

(a) With countable nouns:

Dī hohksāang gāmyaht m̀h làih   The students are not coming today.
啲學生今日唔嚟
Dī wá hái bīndouh máaih ga?   Where did you buy the pictures?
啲畫喺邊度買㗎?
Ngóhdeih gin dóu dī doihsyú   We saw some kangaroos.
我哋見到啲袋鼠

(b) With mass nouns:

Dī tōng bōu lūng-jó 啲湯煲燶咗   The soup has burnt (as a result of overcooking).

Dī yāmngohk taai chòuh 啲音樂太嘈   The music is too noisy.
Ngóh séung máaih dī sāang-gwó   I want to buy some fruit.
我想買啲生果

47

It is also used generically:

Dī làuhga hóuchíh sīng fāan
啲樓價好似升返

House prices seem to be going up again.

Jeuigahn dī choi hóu gwai
最近啲菜好貴

Vegetables have been expensive recently.

A peculiar use of **dī** 啲 is in questions with **mātyéh** 乜嘢:

Yáuh dī mātyéh yàhn háidouh a?
有啲乜嘢人喺度呀?

What people are there?

Sihk dī mātyéh hóu a? 食啲乜嘢好呀?

What (things) shall we eat?

The use of **dī** 啲 here indicates that the answer to the question is expected to be in the plural.

Classifiers as quantifiers

Another feature of Cantonese classifiers is reduplication used to give the meanings 'all' or 'every':

Go-go léuihjái dōu jūngyi kéuih
個個女仔都鍾意佢

All the girls like him.

Léih tìuh-tìuh fu dōu haih hāk-sīk
你條條褲都係黑色

All your trousers are black.

Here two rules apply, as with other quantifiers meaning 'all' and 'every' (see Unit 15):

(a) **dōu** 都 is added before the verb.
(b) The object with reduplicated classifier comes before the verb:

Kéuih *bún-bún syū* dōu tái-gwo
佢本本書都睇過

He's read every book.

Ngóhdeih gāan-gāan poutáu dōu heui-gwo
我哋間間舖頭都去過

We've been to every shop.

When there is an auxiliary or other combination of verbs, the reduplicated classifier phrase comes before both:

Ngóh sīnsāang *tou-tou sāam* dōu yìhm gwai 我先生套套衫都嫌貴
My husband thinks every suit is expensive.

Kéuih *jek-jek pàaihjí* dōu wah m̀h jūngyi 佢隻隻牌子都話唔鍾意
He says he dislikes every brand.

Once the classifier is reduplicated, the noun itself can readily be omitted when the meaning is clear from the context:

Kéuih yeuhng-yeuhng (sung) dōu jūngyi sihk 佢樣樣(餸)都鍾意食
He likes everything (every dish).
Ngóhdeih gāan-gāan (poutáu) dōu heui-gwo 我哋間間(舖頭)都去過
We've been to them all (every shop).

Nouns as collective classifiers

Collective classifiers are those such as **bāan** 班 'group' or 'class', which refer to a grouping (see *Basic Cantonese*, Unit 8). Many nouns can be pressed into service as classifiers with a collective sense. The word **ūk** 屋 'house', for example, is normally a noun but can serve as a classifier meaning 'house full':

yāt ūk ngahm dāng 一屋暗燈 (from a song sung by Faye Wong)	a house full of dim lights (*lit.* one house dim light)
yāt tóuh hei 一肚氣	a belly full of air (*lit.* one stomach air)
Tīn-lohk wáan dou sèhng mihn sā 天樂玩到成面沙	Tin-lok played till his whole face was covered in sand.

Generic classifiers

Words for 'kinds' also behave as classifiers:

gó júng taaidouh 嗰種態度	that kind of attitude
lī leuih yàhn 呢種人	this kind of person

They may also be treated as nouns, hence one can also add the possessive **ge** 嘅, especially in more formal contexts such as broadcasting:

gó júng ge gámgok 嗰種感覺	that kind of feeling
lī leuih ge jitmuhk 呢類嘅節目	this kind of programme

The classifier **jek** 隻, in addition to classifying animals, serves as a generic classifier:

Lī jek jáu gwai-m̀h-gwai a? 呢隻酒貴唔貴呀?	Is this (brand of) wine expensive?
Kéuih sihk bīn jek láaih-fán a? 佢食邊隻奶粉呀?	What (brand of) milk powder did he take?
Ngóh jūngyi wān-wān-yàuh-yàuh tēng-tēng-wah-wah gó jek 我鍾意溫溫柔柔聽聽話話嗰隻	I like the tender, compliant kind (of man/woman).

Alternative classifiers

As the more thorough dictionaries will show, a given noun may take more than one classifier, often with a subtle difference in meaning.

Kéuih go háu gam daaih 佢個口咁大	Her mouth is so big (physically).
Kéuih bá háu hóu sāileih 佢把口好犀利	She has a formidable mouth (in terms of speaking).
Léih séung tái bīn tou (hei) a? 佢想睇邊套(戲)呀?	Which film do you want to see?
Léih séung tái bīn chèuhng (hei) a? 佢想睇邊場(戲)呀?	Which screening (of the film) do you want to see?

The classifier **chèuhng** 場 treats the noun as an event taking place in time:

Entity		Event	
yāt go behng 一個病	a disease	**yāt chèuhng daaih behng** 一場大病	an illness
kéuih go bíuyín 佢個表演	her performance	**kéuih līi chèuhng bíuyín** 佢呢場表演	this performance of hers

For example:

Kéuih gīnglihk-gwo yāt chèuhng daaih behng jūngyū gaai-jó yīn
佢經歷過一場大病終於戒咗煙
After experiencing a (period of) serious illness he finally gave up smoking.

The classifier **chèuhng** 場 is used here because the verb **gīnglihk** 經歷 'experience' indicates an event. Similarly:

Wòhng Fēi hōi-jó sāamsahp chèuhng yín-cheung-wúi
王菲開咗三十場演唱會
Wong Fei gave thirty concerts.

Other alternative classifiers appear in slang expressions (Unit 24).

Adjective + classifier compounds

The adjectives **daaih** 大 and **sai** 細 combine with classifiers to form compounds which work like predicative adjectives:

hóu daaih dēui 好大堆	a big pile (of papers, etc.)
hóu sai wún 好細碗	a small bowl (of rice, etc.)
hóu daaih gāan (gūngsī) 好大間(公司)	very big (company)
hóu sai jek (māau) 好細隻(貓)	very small (cat)

Several expressions of this form have idiomatic meanings:

hóu daaih-jek 好大隻	well-built
hóu sai-lāp 好細粒	small (in physique)
hóu daaih-dáam 好大膽	brave
hóu sai-dáam 好細膽	timid
hóu daaih-wohk 好大鑊	big trouble (*lit.* big wok)
hóu daaih-jāi 好大劑	big trouble (*lit.* big dose)
hóu daaih-beih 好大鼻	snobbish (*lit.* big-nose)
hóu daaih-páai 好大牌	putting on airs (*lit.* big label)

Classifiers after the noun

While the classifier phrase normally comes before the noun, there are some specialized contexts in which it may follow:

(a) Enumerating, as in a shopping list:

máih sāam bāau, sih-yàuh yāt jēun, tóng léuhng hahp
米三包, 豉油一樽, 糖兩盒
three bags of rice, a bottle of soy sauce and two boxes of sweets

(b) Advertising:

Tàuh jéung sung gēipiu léuhng jēung 頭獎機票兩張
The first prize is two free air tickets.

Verbal classifier phrases

A classifier phrase (consisting of numeral + classifier) can come after a verb to specify some aspect of the action described, much as a noun classifier specifies the noun. These phrases are thus termed verbal classifier phrases. There are two main types:

(a) Indicating the frequency or duration of the action:

dá sāam háh 打三下	knock three times
dáng yāt jahn 等一陣	wait a moment

(b) Referring to the part of the body or instrument used:

tái yāt ngáahn 睇一眼	take a look (*lit.* look one eye)
sihk yāt daahm 食一啖	take a bite (*lit.* eat one mouthful)

A point to note here is that the object comes between the verb and the classifier phrase:

tek kéuih yāt geuk
踢佢一腳
give him a kick

sek ngóh yāt daahm
錫我一啖
give me a kiss

laauh kéuih jāt chāan
鬧佢一餐
give him a scolding
(*lit.* scold him a mealful)

Such phrases are useful for quantifying actions. While **yāt** 一 is used for single actions, the quantity can be varied, for example with **dō** 多 'more' to mean 'another':

tái dō yāt ngáahn 睇多一眼   take another look
láam màaih yāt gauh 攬埋一舊   hug one another closely
yám dō léuhng daahm 飲多兩啖   drink a couple more mouthfuls
go dihnwá héung-jó géi chi   the phone rang a few times
個電話響咗幾次

The verbal classifier phrase can also come at the beginning of the clause like a topic:

Yāt háh jauh dá séi jek mān 一下就打死隻蚊
One swipe and the mosquito was dead.
Yāt daahm jauh sihk saai 一啖就食晒
One mouthful and it's all gone.
Ngóh yāt ngáahn tái dóu saai yahpbihn yáuh géi dō yàhn
我一眼睇到晒入便有幾多人
In one look, I saw how many people were inside.

Exercise 8.1

Add a classifier to give the meaning indicated.

Example: **Chyùhfóng hóu gányiu** 廚房好緊要 → **Go chyùhfóng hóu gányiu**
The kitchen is important. 個廚房好緊要

1 **Séjihlàuh hóu dung** 寫字樓好凍   The office is cold.
2 **Baahk-jáu hóu dái-máaih**   (The bottle of) white wine is a good
 白酒好抵買   value.
3 **Sāi-jōng taai gwai** 西裝太貴   The suit is too expensive.
4 **Sān syū maaih saai la**   The (pile of) new books have all sold.
 新書賣晒喇
5 **Sósìh mgin-jó** 鎖匙唔見咗   The keys are lost.

6 **Sānfánjing wán fāan la**
身份證 搵返喇
The ID card has been found.

7 **Gaaisiuh seun hóu làahn sé**
介紹信好難寫
The recommendation letter is hard to write.

8 **Hohksāang háidouh sihwāi**
學生喺度示威
The (class of) students are demonstrating.

9 **Páau-chē gwai dī** 跑車貴啲
The sports car is more expensive.

10 **Lùhnghā hóu sānsīn** 龍蝦好新鮮
The lobster is nice and fresh.

Exercise 8.2

Reduplicate the classifier to give the meaning 'all'/'every', adding the adverb **dōu** 都 before the verb (see also Unit 15).

Example: **Gāan ūk hóu leng → Gāan-gāan (ūk) dōu hóu leng**
間屋好靚   間間(屋)都好靚
The house is lovely.   All the houses are lovely.

1 **Go hohksāang jáu-jó** 個學生走咗
The student has left.

2 **Tou hei hóu muhn** 套戲好悶
The film was boring.

3 **Tìuh tàihmuhk m̀h làahn**
條題目唔難
The question was not hard.

4 **Ga gēi baau saai** 架機爆晒
The plane was full.

5 **Kéuih bún syū hóu hóu-maaih**
佢本書好好賣
His book sells well.

6 **Kéuih gihn sāam hóu gwai**
佢件衫好貴
Her dress is expensive.

7 **Hahp tóng bāau dāk hóu leng**
盒糖包得好靚
The box of sweets was beautifully wrapped.

8 **Ngóhdeih giu-jó yeuhng dím-sām**
我哋叫咗樣點心
We ordered a kind of dim sum.

Exercise 8.3

Match the verbal classifier phrase with the verb or verb phrase provided.

1 **yám** 飲 drink
2 **mohng** 望 watch
3 **tek** 踢 kick
4 **mīt léih** 搣你 pinch you
5 **laauh kéuih** 鬧佢 scold him
6 **dóu** 賭 gamble

a **yāt chāan** 一餐 one mealful
b **géi geuk** 幾腳 a few feet
c **yāt háh** 一下 one time
d **yāt daahm** 一啖 one mouthful
e **yāt pōu** 一舖 one game
f **yāt ngáahn** 一眼 one eye

UNIT 9
Topic and focus

Making something the topic of the sentence by putting it at the beginning of a sentence is known as topicalization (see *Basic Cantonese*, Unit 22). In particular, this is used for:

(a) Making the object of the verb the topic of the sentence:

> ***Lī go yuht ge yàhn-gūng* kéuih yíhgīng sái saai** 呢個月嘅人工佢已經洗晒
> (*lit.* this month's salary he already spend all)
> He's already spent all of this month's salary.
> ***Yīnggwok* hóu dō yàhn séung heui** 英國好多人想去
> (from a film about 1997)
> (*lit.* England many people want to go)
> A lot of people want to go to England.
> ***Léihyàuh* jí yáuh yāt go** 理由只有一個 (TV advertisement)
> (*lit.* reason only have one)
> There's only one reason.

In each case, one could leave the object after the verb as usual, for example:

> **Hóu dō yàhn séung heui *Yīnggwok*** 好多人想去英國
> A lot of people want to go to England.
> **Jí yáuh yāt go *léihyàuh*** 只有一個理由
> There's only one reason.

In many cases, the 'topicalized' versions are preferred for stylistic and other reasons: the advertisement, for example, puts the emphasis on 'one' (relative clauses are another case in point: see Unit 18).

(b) Setting a topic about which a statement is made:

> ***Tái yīsāng* léih m̀h hóyíh tō ge** 睇醫生你唔可以拖嘅
> (*lit.* see doctor you cannot drag)
> You can't put off seeing the doctor.

Gúdín yāmngohk **ngóh béigaau jūngyi gongkàhm duhkjauh**
古典音樂我比較鍾意鋼琴獨奏
(*lit.* classical music I rather like piano solo)
As far as classical music is concerned I prefer solo piano.

An alternative way to make an element the topic is to place it between the subject and the verb:

Kéuih *Dākmán* **góng dāk hóu hóu** 佢德文講得好好
(*lit.* she German speaks manner very good)
She speaks German very well.
Léih *Jūnggwok lihksí* **sīk dāk dò gwo ngóh** 你中國歷史識得多過我
(*lit.* you Chinese history know manner more than me)
You know more about Chinese history than I do.
Kéuih *síu-tàih-kàhm* **lāai dāk géi hóu** 佢小提琴拉得幾好
(*lit.* he violin plays manner quite good)
He plays the violin quite well.

Focusing with lìhn 連 'even'

While topicalization makes an element the 'topic' which the sentence is about, focusing involves putting an element 'in focus' as something to be emphasized. Using **lìhn** 連 'even', the pattern is: **lìhn** 連 (item in focus) **dōu** 都 (verb):

Lìhn kéuih taai-táai dōu m̀h jīdou 連佢太太都唔知道	Even his wife didn't know.
Lìhn ngóh go léui dōu bōng ngóh sáu 連我個女都幫我手	Even my daughter is helping me.

Note two essential features of this construction (which generally go together – see Unit 15):

(a) **dōu** 都 is inserted before the verb.
(b) The object of a verb, when so focused, comes in front of the verb:

Léih lìhn lī dī yéh dōu yiu! 你連呢啲嘢都要!
(*lit.* you even these things still want)
You even want these things!

The same pattern also occurs without **lìhn** 連, especially in the negative:

Ngóh yāt geui dōu móuh góng-gwo 我一句都冇講過
(*lit.* I one phrase still didn't say)
I didn't say a word.
Kéuih gam leng ge gāsī dōu m̀h yiu 佢咁靚嘅傢俬都唔要
(*lit.* she such nice furniture still not want)
She doesn't even want such nice furniture.

lìhn 連 goes naturally together with the particle **màaih** 埋 (see Unit 15), one meaning of which is 'including . . . ':

Kéuih lìhn pèih dōu sihk màaih   He even eats the skin.
佢連皮都食埋
Lìhn fahn gūng dōu móuh màaih   (He) even lost his job.
連份工都冇埋

Sīn 先, jauh 就 and focus

The particles **sīn** 先 'only' and **jauh** 就 'then' are also used to express focus:

Léih sīn haih jyūn-gā 你先係專家   *You're* the expert (not me).
Lī go jauh haih ngóh séung wán gó go   *This* is the one I wanted to find.
呢個就係我想搵嗰個

The two particles **sīn** 先 and **jauh** 就 contrast in a systematic way:

(a) In the domain of time:

    Kéuih bun yé sahp-yih dím *sīn* **fāan ūkkéi** 佢半夜十二點先返屋企
    He doesn't return home until 12 midnight.
    Kéuih bun yé sahp-yih dím *jauh* **fāan ūkkéi** 佢半夜十二點就返屋企
    He returns home as early as 12 midnight.

Here, **sīn** 先 implies that the returning is later than expected while **jauh** 就 implies the opposite, namely, earlier than expected.

(b) In the domain of quantity:

    Ngóh dī pàhngyáuh yám sāam jēun jáu *sīn* **gau hàuh**
    我哋朋友飲三樽酒先夠喉
    (*lit.* my friends drink three bottles of wine then enough throat)
    My friends don't get enough until they have drunk three bottles of wine.
    Ngóh dī pàhngyáuh yám sāam jēun jáu *jauh* **gau hàuh** 我哋朋友飲三樽酒
    就夠喉
    (*lit.* my friends drink three bottles of wine then enough throat)
    My friends drink three bottles of wine and that's enough.

The sentence with **sīn** 先 implies that three bottles is more than expected while **jauh** 就 implies that three bottles is less than expected. A similar contrast appears in conditional sentences (see also Unit 20), where **sīn** 先 typically marks the antecedent clause as a necessary condition while **jauh** 就 marks it as a sufficient condition:

    Dī sailouhjái fan ngóhdeih *sīn* **fan** 啲細路仔瞓我哋先瞓
    (*lit.* the children sleep we then sleep)

We won't sleep unless the children sleep.

Dī sailouhjái fan ngóhdeih *jauh* fan 啲細路仔瞓我哋就瞓
(*lit.* the children sleep we then sleep)
We'll sleep as long as the children sleep.

Exercise 9.1

A: Make the object of the verb the sentence topic by putting it in initial position.

Example: **Kéuih m̀h jūngyi sihk laaht yéh**   He doesn't like (to eat)
佢唔鍾意食辣嘢   hot food.
Laaht yéh kéuih m̀h jūngyi sihk   Hot food he doesn't like
辣嘢佢唔鍾意食   to eat.

1 **Dī hohksāang meih tái-gwo lī bún síusyut**   The students have not read
   啲學生未睇過呢本小說   this novel.
2 **Kéuih jeui sek go sai léui**   He loves the youngest
   佢最錫個細女   daughter the most.
3 **Kéuih hóu m̀h sé dāk maaih gāan ūk**   She is loath (unwilling) to sell
   佢好唔捨得賣間屋   the house.
4 **Ngóh m̀h sīk yānséung gúdín yāmngohk**   I don't know how to
   我唔識欣賞古典音樂   appreciate classical music.
5 **Ngóh hóu suhk kéuih ūkkéi yàhn**   I'm familiar with his family.
   我好熟佢屋企人

B: Put the object in the second position (after the subject).

Example: **Ngóh meih heui-gwo Sāmjan**   I've not been to Shenzhen.
我未去過深圳
Ngóh Sāmjan meih heui-gwo   I've not been to Shenzhen.
我深圳未去過

6 **Ngóh m̀h dākhàahn tái gāmyaht ge sānmán**   I'm too busy to read
   我唔得閒睇今日嘅新聞   today's news.
7 **Ngóhdeih sīk síu-síu Yahtmán**   We know a little
   我哋識少少日文   Japanese.
8 **Kéuih hohk-jó sāam l̀ihn gongkàhm**   She's taken piano
   佢學咗三年鋼琴   lessons for three years.
9 **Kéuih m̀h wúih jouh gam làahn ge yéh**   He won't do such
   佢唔會做咁難嘅嘢   difficult things.
10 **Léih yīnggōi dō dī jouh wahnduhng**   You should do more
   你應該多啲做運動   exercise.

Exercise 9.2

Use **lìhn . . . dōu** 連...都 and/or **màaih** 埋 to put the italicized element in focus,

e.g. **Kéuih m̀h sihk máahn-faahn** 佢唔食晚飯
He doesn't eat *dinner*.

→ **Kéuih lìhn máahn-faahn dōu m̀h sihk** 佢連晚飯都唔食
He doesn't even eat dinner.

Go bìhbī haam dou gihn sāam sāp-jó 個BB喊到件衫濕咗
The baby cried such that *the clothes* got wet.

→ **Go bìhbī haam dou lìhn gihn sāam dōu sāp màaih** 個BB喊到連件衫都濕埋
The baby cried such that even the clothes got wet as well.

1 **Ngóh daai jīpiu-bóu làih** 我帶支票簿嚟	I bring (along) *the cheque book* (as well).
2 **Kéuih m̀h sīk jīng yú** 佢唔識蒸魚	He doesn't (even) know how to steam *fish*.
3 **Kéuihdeih meih heui-gwo Chín Séui Wāan** 佢哋未去過淺水灣	They haven't (even) been to *Repulse Bay*.
4 **Gíngchaat m̀h seun go yīsāng** 警察唔信個醫生	The police don't trust (even) *the doctor*.
5 **Kéuih je ga chē béi ngóh** 佢借架車畀我	He (even) loans me *his car*.
6 **Ngóh gēng dou bīu láahnghohn** 我驚到瀄冷汗	I'm so scared that I (even) came out in *a cold sweat*.
7 **Kéuih yiu maaih go gúdúng fājēun** 佢要賣個古董花樽	He (even) has to sell *the antique vase* (as well).
8 **Ngóh lóuhgūng hohk Chìuhjāu-wá** 我老公學潮州話	My husband (even) studies *Chiu Chow* (as well).
9 **Kéuih ngoh dou sihk gaakyeh sung** 佢餓到食隔夜餸	She's so hungry that she ate (even) *the left-overs* (as well).
10 **Lóuhbáan hāan dou m̀h hōi láahnghei** 老闆慳到唔開冷氣	The boss is so frugal that he doesn't (even) turn on *the air conditioner*.

Exercise 9.3

Fill in the blank with **sīn** 先 or **jauh** 就 in accordance with the English translation.

1 **Ngóh fong-jó-gūng, luhk dím ___ fāan dou ūkkéi**
我放咗工, 六點 ___ 返屋企
After I get off work, I don't get home until six (later than expected).

2 **Go daaih-jek-lóu sihk sāam wún faahn ___ báau**
個大隻佬食三碗飯 ___ 飽
The well-built man isn't full until he's eaten three bowls of rice.

3 **Kéuih sé-seun béi ngóh, ngóh ___ sé-seun béi kéuih**

佢寫信畀我，我 ___ 寫信畀佢

I'll write to him as long as he writes to me.

4 **Kéuih heui Bākgīng gūnggon, yāt go yuht ___ fāan làih**

佢去北京公幹，一個月 ___ 返嚟

She's on a business trip to Beijing and won't come back for at least a month.

5 **Go bìhbī sahpyāt yuht ___ chēut-jó-sai**

個**BB**十一月 ___ 出咗世

The baby was born in November (earlier than expected).

6 **Léih chīm-méng, ngóh ___ chīm**

你簽名，我 ___ 簽

I won't sign unless you sign.

7 **Kéuih yāt chi gwo tái sāam tou hei ___ gau péi**

佢一次過睇三套戲 ___ 夠皮

She doesn't get enough unless she watches three movies in a row.

8 **Kéuih sāam lìhn ___ ló dóu go boksih hohk-wái**

佢三年 ___ 攞到個博士學位

It took her three years to get the doctoral degree (earlier than expected).

UNIT 10
Using jēung 將

jēung 將 is one of the 'empty' functional words (**hēui-chìh** 虛詞 in Cantonese) whose role is an essentially grammatical one. Its function is to take a direct object and place it before the verb:

verb-object → **jēung** 將 – object-verb

This resembles a serial verb construction (Unit 11) except that **jēung** 將 is not used by itself as a verb.

Jēung 將 vs. ba 把

For learners with some knowledge of Mandarin, **jēung** 將 is the nearest counterpart to **ba** 把 and is broadly similar in function, though the use of **jēung** 將 is more restricted: in many cases, where **ba** 把 might be used **jēung** 將 would not. For example:

Mandarin		Cantonese
Ba shu fang zai nabian 把書放在那邊	Put the book there.	**Jēung bún syū fong hái gódouh** 將本書放喺嗰度
Ba deng guan diao 把燈關掉	Turn off the light but not:	***Jēung dāng sīk-jó** 將燈熄咗
Ba wo de shu na zhe 把我的書拿著	Hold my books but not:	***Jēung ngóh dī syū līng-jyuh** 將我啲書拎住

jēung 將 retains a sense of displacement and, in colloquial usage at least, is most typically used when the object of the sentence is literally moved from one place to another:

Ngóhdeih jēung dī gauh gāsī būn jáu 我哋將啲舊傢俬搬走
We're moving the old furniture away.
Kéuih jēung dī laahn sāam dám-jó 佢將啲爛衫扰咗
She threw the torn clothes away.

Kéuih jēung fūk wá gwa hái chèuhng douh 佢將啲褲掛喺牆度
She hung the picture on the wall.

One advantage of using the construction in such cases is that the vacant position after the verb can then be used for another element of the sentence, such as a prepositional phrase indicating where the object is moved to. It is possible to say:

Báai go fājēun hái chēutbihn   Put the vase outside.
擺個花樽喺出便

Gwa dī sāam hái tīntói douh   Hang up the clothes on the roof.
掛啲衫喺天台度

Nevertheless, the version with **jēung** 將 is preferred:

Jēung go fājēun báai hái chēutbihn   Put the vase outside.
將個花樽擺喺出便

Jēung dī sāam gwa hái tīntói douh   Hang the clothes up on the roof.
將啲衫掛喺天台度

Similarly, with duration and frequency phrases following the verb it is convenient to use **jēung** 將 and put the object before the verb:

Sīnsāang jēung pīn mán gōi-jó sāam chi 先生將篇文改咗三次
The teacher has reviewed the composition three times.
Ngóh jēung go beimaht sāu-màaih hái sām yahpbihn sahp lìhn
我將個秘密收埋喺心入便十年
I've been hiding the secret in my heart for ten years.

Jēung 將 in High Cantonese

Apart from the sense of literal displacement, more abstract uses are possible. For example, **jēung** 將 can be used in cases of transfer of ownership or possession:

Ngóh jēung lī gihn sih gāau béi léih 我將呢件事交畀你
I turn this matter over to you.
Ngóhdeih jēung bāt wàihcháan fān sāam fahn 我哋將筆遺產分三份
We divide the legacy into three parts.

Still more abstract senses of transfer include the following:

Kéuih jēung gá ge dong haih jān ge 佢將假嘅當係真嘅
He treats what is false as if it were true.
Dímgáai léih jēung pàhngyáuh dong jouh dihkyàhn ga?
點解你將朋友當做敵人㗎?
Why do you treat friends as foes?

Such extended uses of **jēung** 將 are a feature of High Cantonese, perhaps under the influence of Mandarin and written Chinese where **ba** 把 would be used in such cases. They can be heard in public announcements, for example:

Chéng jēung yāmleuhng sāu-sai 請將音量收細
Please turn your volume down.
Chéng jēung gwaijuhng mahtbán kwàihdaai hái sānbīn
請將貴重物品攜帶喺身邊
Please carry your valuable belongings with you.

Similarly, transitive verbs with the suffix – **fa** 化, a High Cantonese feature, are often used together with **jēung** 將:

Jingfú dásyun jēung Hēunggóng sou-máh-fa
政府打算將香港數碼化
The government is planning to digitalize Hong Kong.
Léihdeih m̀h yīnggōi jēung mahntàih fūkjaahp-fa
你哋唔應該將問題複雜化
You should not complicate the problems.

Jēung . . . kéuih 將 . . . 佢 and imperatives

A rather idiomatic combination uses the pronoun **kéuih** 佢 to represent the object already mentioned as the object of **jēung** 將:

Ngóh jēung dī yin-wō dahn-jó kéuih 我將啲燕窩燉咗佢
I've stewed the birds' nests (for soup).

Léih yiu jēung yíhchìhn ge sih mòhng-gei saai (kéuih) 你要將以前嘅事忘
記(佢)
You need to forget about things that happened before.

Note the regular use of the aspect marker **-jó** 咗 in this combination, which is used especially in imperative sentences:

Léih jēung dī wūjōu sāam sái-jó kéuih lā 你將啲污糟衫洗咗佢啦
Clean the dirty clothes.
Léih jēung dī yin-wō sihk-jó kéuih lā! 你將啲燕窩食咗佢啦!
(Why don't you) eat up the bird's nest soup!

In contrast to those discussed above, this is quite a colloquial usage (compare other colloquial uses of **kéuih** 佢 in Unit 24).

Exercise 10.1

Form sentences with **jēung** 將 as alternatives to those given.

Example: **Ngóh sailóu béi fāan dī chín ngóh**
我細佬畀返啲錢我
My brother is giving me the money back.

→ **Ngóh sailóu jēung dī chín béi fāan ngóh**
我細佬將啲錢畀返我

1 **Ngóh gāau gūngfo béi sīnsāang**
我交功課畀先生

I handed in the homework
to the teacher.

2 **Kéuih wuhn-jó go mahtmáh**
佢換咗個密碼

She has changed the code.

3 **Ngóh chéuisīu-jó go wuhháu**
我取消咗個戶口

I've cancelled the account.

4 **Ngóh séung gwa héi fūk wá**
我想掛起幅畫

I want to hang up the
picture.

5 **Tīn-waih gói-jó go yahtkèih**
天慧改咗個日期

Tin-wai has changed the
date.

6 **Kéuih jūngyū jāp hóu gāan fóng**
佢終於執咗間房

He has finally tidied up the
room.

7 **Ngóh yiu ló fāan dī syū heui hohkhaauh**
我要攞返啲書去學校

I have to take the books
back to school.

8 **Mùihmúi chaap dī fā hái fājēun douh**
妹妹插啲花喺花樽度

My little sister put the
flowers in the vase.

9 **Kéuih sāu-màaih saai dī seun**
佢收埋晒啲信

She hid away all the letters.

10 **Lóuhbáan chyùhn-jó dī chín yahp
ngàhnhòhng** 老闆存咗啲錢入銀行

The boss has deposited the
money in the bank.

Exercise 10.2

Add a resultative, duration or frequency complement in the following **jēung** 將
constructions.

Example: **Kéuih jēung dī seun sāu-màaih** 佢將啲信收埋 _____
She hid the letters away for ten years.

→ **Kéuih jēung dī seun sāu-màaih sahp lìhn** 佢將啲信收埋十年

1 **Kéuih jēung gāan fóng maat dāk** 佢將間房抹得 _____
He wiped the room clean.

2 **Gūngsī jēung go gachìhn gói-jó** 公司將個價錢改咗 _____
The company has changed the price many times.

3 **Ngóh jēung bún syū yàuh tàuh dou méih tái-jó** 我將本書由頭到尾睇咗

I read the book twice from beginning to end.

4 **Kéuih jēung dī tàuhfaat jín dāk** 佢將啲頭髮剪得 _____
He cut the hair very short.

5 **Kéuih jēung fahn láihmaht sāu-màaih-jó** 佢將份禮物收埋咗 _____
She hid the gift away for two days.

6 **Kéuih jēung tìuh yú jīng-jó** 佢將條魚蒸咗 _____
She steamed the fish for ten minutes.

7 **Dī gūngyàhn jēung chyùhn ūk yàuh-jó** 啲員工將全屋油咗 _____
The workers painted the whole house once.

8 **Ngóh jēung sáu gō fāanyihk-jó** 我將首歌翻譯咗 _____
I translated the song a few times.

9 **Lóuhbáan jēung go gwónggou dāng-jó** 老闆將個廣告登咗 _____
The boss has put up the advertisement for three days.

10 **Kéuih jēung go léui baahn dou** 佢將個女扮到 _____
She adorned her daughter beautifully.

Exercise 10.3

Form imperative sentences with **jēung** 將 as alternatives to those given, paying attention the use of the pronoun **kéuih** 佢.

> Example: **Léih maaih saai dī gúpiu kéuih lā** 你賣晒啲股票佢啦 Sell all the shares.
>
> → **(Léih) jēung dī gúpiu maaih saai kéuih lā** (你)將啲股票賣晒佢啦

1 **Léih ló gihn sāam lohk làih ā**   Bring the dress down.
   你攞件衫落嚟吖

2 **Ngóhdeih dám-jó dī laahpsaap kéuih lā**   Let's throw away the
   我哋扰咗啲垃圾佢啦   rubbish.

3 **Léih faai dī gói saai dī gyún kéuih**   Hurry up and finish
   你快啲改晒啲卷佢   marking the scripts.

4 **Jīkhāk wuhn-jó go dihnchìh kéuih**   Change the battery
   即刻換咗個電池佢   immediately.

5 **Faai-faai-cheui-cheui jāp hóu gāan fóng** Tidy up the room quickly.
   kéuih 快快脆脆執好間房佢

6 **Chan yiht yám-jó dī Jūng yeuhk kéuih**   Drink the Chinese
   趁熱飲咗啲中藥佢   medicine while it's hot.

7 **Fong dāi go syū bāau hái deihhá**   Put the school bag down
   放低個書包喺地下   on the floor.

8 **Jeui hóu dihn-jó dī tàuhfaat kéuih**   It's best to perm your hair.
   最好電咗啲頭髮佢

9 **Sái saai dī wūjōu sāam kéuih**   Wash all the dirty clothes.
   洗晒啲污糟衫佢

10 **Jōngsāu hóu gāan ūk kéuih** 裝修好間屋佢   Decorate the house well.

UNIT 11
Serial verbs

A class of words in Chinese are known as 'coverbs' because of the way they co-occur with another verb.

Kéuih gān ngóh hohk jyú-sung   He's learning to cook from me.
(COVERB)   (VERB)
佢跟我學煮餸

Kéuih waih-jó ngóh béi lóuhbáan laauh   He was told off by the boss for
(COVERB)   (VERB)   my sake.
佢為咗我畀老闆鬧

In Cantonese, these include a number of words which serve both as independent verbs and as coverbs:

	As verb	*As coverb*
hái 喺	be at	at
tùhng 同	accompany	with
gān 跟	follow	with
dou 到	reach	until
deui 對	face	towards
heung 向	face	towards (direction)
waih (jó) 為(咗)	–	for (the sake of)

Given that their meanings have to do with spatial relationships, it is tempting to equate the coverbs with prepositions, as the English translations suggest. However, the coverbs behave like verbs in taking aspect markers such as **jó** 咗, **gwo** 過, **gán** 跟, **jyuh** 住 etc. and verbal particles such as **saai** 晒 and **fāan** 返:

Ga chē heung-*jó* gó bihn hàahng 架車向咗嗰邊行
The car went off in that direction.

Go BBC geijé tùhng-*gwo* kéuih jouh fóngmahn 個BBC記者同過佢做訪問
The BBC reporter has done an interview with her.

Ngóh lóuhgūng tùhng-*gán* go jái wáan Daaihfuyūng 我老公同緊個仔玩大
富翁
My husband is playing Monopoly with my son.
Go-go gúdūng hái *saai* douh hōi-wúi 個個股東喺晒度開會
All the shareholders are here having a meeting.
Kéuihdeih jūngyū hái *fāan* màaih yātchàih jouh-yéh 佢哋終於喺返埋一
齊做嘢
They're finally back working together again.

In this respect, coverbs behave like serial verbs, a series of verbs in the same
clause without a conjunction linking them. This is a characteristic feature of
Cantonese, together with many languages of southeast Asia, but not generally
found in European languages – the closest counterpart being the American
English 'Let's go eat'. A typical example is the following:

Ngóh sīnsāang wúih bōng ngóh wán chē-sìh 我先生會幫我搵車匙
(*lit.* my husband will help me find car keys)
My husband will look for the car keys for me.

Notice how the additional verb typically takes the place of a preposition. The
meaning which results often seems to be that of a preposition rather than
a verb, e.g. **bōng** 幫 literally means 'help' but in a serial verb construction it
means to do something for another's benefit, not to help the person to accom-
plish something:

Léih bōng ngóh dá go dihnwá ā 你幫我打個電話吖
(*lit.* you help me dial a telephone)
Make a call for me.
Faai dī bōng go bìhbī wuhn liuhpín lā 快啲幫個BB換尿片啦
(*lit.* quickly help the baby change nappy)
Change the nappy for the baby quickly.

Clearly one cannot 'help' a baby to change a nappy and the intended meaning
is to change it for him or her. Similarly, the verb **wán** 搵 by itself means 'look
for' but in the serial verb construction this meaning is attenuated to the point
where it means 'with' or 'use':

Léih wán faai bouh maat háh kéuih lā 你搵塊布抹下佢啦
(*lit.* you look for sheet cloth wipe a little it)
Give it a wipe with a cloth.
Léih wán go goi kám-jyuh go wohk ā 你搵個蓋冚住個鑊啦
Use the lid to cover the wok.

Since chances are that the cover of the wok is lying within reach of the cook,
this need not entail any actual searching. Similarly, it is hardly necessary to look
for one's own hands:

Wán jek sáu jē-jyuh deui ngáahn 搵隻手遮住對眼
Cover one's eyes with one hand.

Common meanings expressed by serial verbs include:

- With – instrument
  Léih m̀h hóyíh sèhngyaht yuhng chín gáaikyut mahntàih
  你唔可以成日用錢解決問題
  You can't always solve problems with money.
- Together with – accompanying
  Ngóh pùih léih sihk-faahn lā 我陪你食飯啦
  (*lit.* I accompany you eat rice)
  I'll have lunch with you.
- For, on one's behalf
  Léih doih ngóh gūnghéi Rowena ā 你代我恭喜**Rowena**吖
  (*lit.* you replace me congratulate Rowena)
  Send my congratulations to Rowena.
  Ngóh dahng kéuihdeih gōuhing 我戥佢哋高興
  I feel happy for them.
  Mgōi léih waih-háh yàhndeih jeuhkséung 唔該你為下人哋著想
  Please try to show consideration for others.
  Lī go haih waih léih dohk sān dehng jouh ge 呢個係為你度身訂造嘅
  This is tailor made for you.

Simultaneous actions

A series of verbs can express simultaneous actions, especially with the continuous aspect marker **jyuh** 住 attached to the first verb (see *Basic Cantonese*, Unit 19):

> **Jā-jyuh fahn boují dáng yàhn** 揸住份報紙等人
> Wait for someone (while) carrying a newspaper.
> **Go léui láam-jyuh go gūngjái fan-gaau** 個女攬住個公仔瞓覺
> The daughter sleeps hugging a soft toy.
> **Yán-jyuh ngáahnleuih góng joi gin** 忍住眼淚講再見
> Say goodbye (while) holding back one's tears.

Sequence of actions

A sequence of verbs can express a sequence of actions:

> **Báau tóuh sihk yeuhk** 飽肚食藥
> (*lit.* fill stomach eat medicine)
> Eat before taking the medicine; take the medicine on a full stomach.

Gei-jyuh chèuih hàaih yahp fóng 記住除鞋入房
Remember to take off one's shoes before going into the room.
Chūng yùhn lèuhng fan-gaau 沖完涼瞓覺
Go to sleep after taking a shower.

Notice how these sentences express the sequence of events in time without using a conjunction meaning 'before' or 'after' (see also Unit 19). The order in which the verbs come reflects the sequential order of events in real time. This is a characteristic of serial verbs (often not reflected in the English translation), which is especially clear in the constructions expressing sequence and purpose.

Purpose

When one action is done for the purpose of another, the verbs appear as a series:

Ngóh yiu chēut heui saan-bouh 我要出去散步
I have to go out to take a walk.
Kéuih yeuk ngóh heui gāai 佢約我去街
She arranged with me to go out.
Ngóhdeih yuhng chín máaih sìhgaan 我哋用錢買時間
We use money to buy time.

The verb **jouh** 做 'do' can indicate the purpose for which something is done (acquired, used etc.):

Ngóh chéng léih jouh ngóh ge bóubīu　I'll hire you as my bodyguard.
我請你做我嘅保鏢
Gíngchaat wán ngóh jouh jing-yàhn　The police asked me to be a witness.
警察搵我做證人
Lī go sung béi léih jouh geilihm-bán　This is for you as a souvenir.
呢個送界你做紀念品

The verbs of motion **làih** 嚟 'come' and sometimes **heui** 去 'go' are used similarly:

Ló làih/heui maaih　Take them to sell.
攞嚟/去賣

Máaih làih sung béi yàhn 買嚟送界人
Buy to give to someone.

Note how the object of the main verb is omitted, being understood as 'it' or 'them' according to the context.

jouh 做 and làih 嚟 can be combined in this function:

Ló làih/heui jouh chāamháau 攞嚟/去做參考
Take it as a reference.
Līdī sé-jó yuhng làih jouh gaau-chòih 呢啲寫咗用嚟做教材
When these are written up we can use them as teaching material.

Verbs of communication

Describing an act of communication typically involves two verbs – **góng** 講 or **wah** 話 expressing what the speaker does, and **tēng** 聽 'hear' or **jī** 知 'know' the effect on the hearer:

Ngóh góng-jó go sīusīk béi kéuihdeih tēng   I told them the news.
我講咗個消息畀佢哋聽
Ngóh m̀h wah léih jī 我唔話你知   I won't tell you.

See also Unit 21 on indirect speech.

Combining serial verbs

By combining two or more of the serial verb types we can easily end up with three or more verbs in a series:

Bōng ngóh wán jīlíu sé bougou 幫我搵資料寫報告
(*lit.* help me find material write report)
Get some material for me to write my report.
Doih ngóh sé-seun mahnhauh kéuih 代我寫信問候佢
(*lit.* replace me write letter ask after her)
Write a letter on my behalf to ask how she is.
Chàhng láu héi hóu yuhng làih jouh séjihlàuh 層樓起好用嚟做寫字樓
(*lit.* the flat build finish use come do office)
When the flat is finished it will be used as an office.

Exercise 11.1

Insert a verb from the list provided – **wán** 搵, **bōng** 幫, **yuhng** 用, **doih** 代:

Example: **Ngóh go jái *bōng* ngóh sái ga chē** 我個仔幫我洗架車
           My son washes the car for me.

1 **Ngóh hóyíh ___ léih sé gaaisiuh seun**
   我可以 ___ 你寫介紹信

   I can write a recommendation letter for you.

2 **Léih yiu ___ lihk dá go bō**
   你要 ___ 力打個波

   You have to hit the ball with strength.

3 **___ ngóh gahm jūng ā?**
   ___ 我撳鐘吖？

   Would you press the bell for me?

4 **Léih ___ jek yauh sáu gahm-jyuh jēung jí lā**
   你 ___ 隻右手撳住張紙啦

   Use your right hand to press the sheet down.

5 **Chéng léih ___ lóuh lám-háh yéh**
   請你 ___ 腦諗一下

   Please use your brain to think a little.

6 **Kéuih móuh sìhgaan ___ léih séuhng-tòhng**
   佢冇時間 ___ 嚟上堂

   He doesn't have time to do relief teaching for you.

7 **Ga páau-chē ___ làih béichoi ge**
   架跑車 ___ 嚟比賽嘅

   The sports car is used for competition.

8 **Léih hó-m̀h-hóyíh ___ ngóh mahnhauh kéuih a?**
   你可唔可以 ___ 我問候佢呀？

   Could you send greetings on my behalf?

Exercise 11.2

Formulate a serial verb construction by adding a verb phrase:

> Example: **Ngóh doih kéuih** 我代佢   I'm taking his place.
> →   **Ngóh doih kéuih gaau yāt tòhng**   I'm teaching a class for him.
>   我代佢教一堂

1 **Dáng ngóh bōng léih** 等我幫你....   Let me ... for you.
2 **Kéuih heung ngóh** 佢向我....   He ... to me.
3 **Dī chānchīk doih kéuih** 啲親戚代佢....   The relatives ... on his behalf.
4 **Yīsāng bōng ngóh** 醫生幫我....   The surgeon ... for me.
5 **Gó go hohksāang gān ngóh**
   嗰個學生跟我....   That student ... with me.
6 **Lī jēung hóibou yuhng làih**
   呢張海報用嚟....   This poster is for....
7 **Fuhmóuh waih-jó jáiléui**
   父母為咗仔女....   Parents ... for their children's sake.
8 **Ngóh dī tùhngsih dahng ngóh**
   我啲同事戥我....   My colleagues are ... for me.
9 **Kéuih sèhngyaht deui-jyuh ngóh**
   佢成日對住我....   He always ... to my face.
10 **Kéuih pùih ngóh** 佢陪我....   He accompanies me....

Exercise 11.3

Add a second verb phrase to specify the purpose of the action (**jouh** 做, **làih** 嚟 or **heui** 去 may be added):

> **Ngóhdeih yuhng chín (*làih/heui*) máaih sìhgaan** 我哋用錢(嚟/去)買時間
> We use money (to buy time).

1 **Kéuih wán jek geuk** 佢搵隻腳....
   He uses his foot....
2 **A-Yīng yuhng sānsīn séuigwó** 阿英用新鮮水果....
   Ying uses fresh fruit....
3 **Gaausauh béi sìhgaan ngóhdeih** 教授畀時間我哋....
   The professor gave us time....
4 **Kéuihdeih heui leuhtsī-làuh** 佢哋去律師樓....
   They went to the solicitors....
5 **Dī geijé làih Hēunggóng** 啲記者嚟香港....
   The reporters came to Hong Kong....
6 **Léih m̀h hóu yuhng sāp bou** 你唔好用濕布....
   Don't use a wet cloth....
7 **Go behngyàhn múih go láihbaai dōu heui yīyún** 個病人每個禮拜都去醫院....
   The patient goes to the hospital every week....
8 **Dī chānchīk làih ngóhdeih ūkkéi** 啲親戚嚟我哋屋企....
   The relatives came to our house....
9 **Kéuih tēuijin ngóh heui daaih-hohk** 佢推薦我去大學....
   He recommended for me to go to the university....
10 **Ngóh fuhmóuh làih ngóh sūkse** 我父母嚟我宿舍....
    My parents are coming to my hall of residence....

UNIT 12
Aspect markers

Cantonese has a rich system of aspect markers which describe how events take place in time, offering different perspectives even on the same event. The major aspect markers **jó** 咗 and **gwo** 過, **gán** 緊 and **jyuh** 住 have been introduced in *Basic Cantonese* (Units 18–19). Here we focus on some other aspect markers which express further nuances of time and action.

The delimitative aspect: háh 下

The aspect **háh** 下 (sometimes termed delimitative or tentative) means to do something 'for a little while':

Mgōi béi ngóh tái-háh 唔該畀我睇下	Please let me have a look.
Ngóh chēut heui hàahng-háh 我出去行下	I'm going out for a walk.
Léih si-háh yuhng lī jek sái-tàuh-séui ā 你試下用呢隻洗頭水吖	Try using this shampoo (for a while).

This meaning is idiomatically reinforced by the particle **sīn** 先, which literally means 'first':

Ngóh yiu táu-háh sīn 我要唞下先	I need to take a little rest.
Dáng ngóh lám-háh sīn 等我諗下先	Let me think for a moment.

Some verbs can also be reduplicated together with **háh** 下 to express an even more tentative action:

wáan 玩 play	→	**wáan-háh** 玩下 play for a while	→	**wáan-wáan-háh** 玩玩下 just play around
gú 估 guess	→	**gú-háh** 估下 have a guess	→	**gú-gú-háh** 估估下 have a (tentative) guess
si 試 try	→	**si-háh** 試下 have a try	→	**si-si-háh** 試試下 have a (tentative) try

These forms can be used, for example, with the 'downplaying' particle **je** 啫:

Lī go baahnfaat ngóh si-si-háh ge je 呢個辦法我試試下嘅啫
I'm just trying out this method.
Kéuih tùhng go léuihyán wáan-wáan-háh ge ja 佢同個女人玩玩下嘅啫
He's just playing around with that woman.

Such reduplicated forms (verb-verb-**háh** 下) are also used in subordinate clauses, followed by another clause expressing a consequence or subsequent event:

Ngóh lám-lám-háh, dōu haih mhóu la 我諗諗下，都係唔好喇
After thinking about it for a while, it's not a good idea.
Kéuih hàahng-hàahng-háh gāai, faatgok mgin-jó go sáu-dói
佢行行下街，發覺唔見咗個手袋
After walking for a while, she discovered she had lost her handbag.
Kéuihdeih kīng-kīng-háh, sīn jīdou yùhnlòih daaihgā haih jūnghohk tùhnghohk
佢哋傾傾下，先知道原來大家係中學同學
Only after chatting for a while did they find out they were secondary-school classmates.
Ngóh fan-fan-háh jauh séng-jó 我瞓瞓下就醒咗
After sleeping for a while, I woke up.

A third format repeats both the verb and the suffix **háh** 下, where the reduplication reflects a meaning of repetition:

Kéuih góng-yéh jaht-háh-jaht-háh   When he talks, he keeps stuttering.
佢講嘢窒下窒下
Jáan dāng jáam-háh jáam-háh   The light keeps flickering.
盞燈䀹下䀹下

There are also some idiomatic expressions of this form, like **saahp-háh-saahp-háh** 煠下煠下 (which cannot be reduced to **saahp-háh** 煠下):

Léih sèhng jīu saahp-háh-saahp-háh, haih-maih fan m̀h séng a?
你成朝煠下煠下，係咪未瞓醒呀？
You have been in a muddle all morning. Haven't you woken up yet?

Verb-yāt 一-verb

This combination with **yāt** 一 'one' (corresponding to verb-yi-verb in Mandarin) resembles the verbal classifier phrase (Unit 8) except that the verb here serves as its own classifier.

tái 睇 look → **tái-yāt-tái** 睇一睇 take a look
jáam ngáahn 䀹眼 blink → **jáam-yāt-jáam ngáahn** 䀹一䀹 blink for a moment

The meaning is similar to that of **háh** 下 as illustrated above:

Līdouh yāt chīn mān, léih sóu-yāt-sóu ā
呢度一千蚊，你數一數吖 (or **léih sóu-háh** 你數下)
Here's a thousand dollars; you can count it.
Kéuih jāang yàhn hóu dō chín, lám-jyuh heui Oumún bok-yāt-bok
佢爭人好多錢，諗住去澳門搏一搏
He owes people a lot of money, so he's thinking of going to Macau to gamble.

In fast speech, this sequence is often contracted so that **yāt** 一 is not audible, resulting in a high rising tone on the first verb (see Unit 3):

bok-yāt-bok 搏一搏 → **bók-bok** 搏搏 gamble, take a risk
chaat-yāt-chaat 擦一擦 → **cháat-chaat** 擦擦 rub for a while

Verb-léuhng 兩-verb

A variant with **léuhng** 兩 'two' instead of **yāt** 一 'one', this tends to have a negative or dismissive connotation:

Kéuih m̀h gwaan chau-jái; chau-léuhng-chau jauh m̀h chau
佢唔慣湊仔，湊兩湊就唔湊
She's not used to taking care of children; she tries for a while then gives up.
Bún syū tái-léuhng-tái jauh móuh sām-gēi tái-lohk-heui
本書睇兩睇就冇心機睇落去
After reading this book for a while, one has no inclination to go on.

The same construction can also describe accomplishing something with a minimum of time and effort:

Lī go jái gam síng, duhk-léuhng-duhk jauh yahp saai lóuh
呢個仔咁醒，讀兩讀就入晒腦
This child is so bright, he studies a bit and it's all there in his head.
Kéuih cháau-léuhng-cháau jauh jaahn-jó géi baak maahn
佢炒兩炒就賺咗幾百萬
After a brief bout of speculation, she earned a few million dollars.

The habitual aspect: hōi 開

The aspect **hōi** 開 generally has a habitual meaning:

Ngóhdeih jouh-hōi lī hòhng
我哋做開呢行
We've been in this profession for some time.
Kéuih yuhng-hōi gó jek pàaihjí
佢用開嗰隻牌子
He regularly uses that brand.

This sense commonly appears in relative clauses (see Unit 18):

Ngóhdeih wán-hōi gó go jōngsāu sīfu taai mòhng
我哋搵開嗰個裝修師傅太忙
The decorator we usually deal with is too busy.
Kéuihdeih jyuh-hōi gódouh hóu fōngbihn 佢哋住開嗰度好方便
Where they've been living is very convenient.

Less commonly, in subordinate clauses, **hōi** 開 may have a progressive meaning, indicating continuation of an activity that has already begun:

Ngóhdeih hàahng-hōi lībihn, bātyùh heui màaih Sìhdoih Gwóngchèuhng lo
我哋行開呢便，不如去埋時代廣場囉
Now that we're already walking this way, let's go on to Times Square.
Góng-hōi kéuihdeih léuhng go, gaugíng yáuh-móuh lèih-fān a?
講開佢哋兩個，究竟有冇離婚呀？
Talking of these two, have they actually gotten divorced?
Góng-hōi yauh góng ā, . . . 講開又講吖，. . . (idiom)
Talking of that, . . .

The inchoative héi-séuhng-làih 起上嚟

The phrase **héi-séuhng-làih** 起上嚟 literally means 'rise up', but after a verb, it denotes the beginning of an action (an inchoative meaning, corresponding fairly closely to **qǐlái** 起來 in Mandarin).

Go bìhbī daht-yìhn-gāan haam héi-séuhng-làih 個BB突然間喊起上嚟
The baby suddenly started to cry.

It is most characteristically used in subordinate clauses, for example with **yāt** 一 meaning 'as soon as':

Ngóh yāt lāu héi-séuhng-làih jauh lyún gam laauh yàhn
我一嬲起上嚟就亂咁鬧人
As soon as I get angry I scold people indiscriminately.

When used with a transitive verb or verb-object compound (Unit 6), the sequence **héi** 起 . . . **séuhng-làih** 上嚟 is split up, with **héi** 起 coming between the verb and object:

Ngóh go jái (yāt) faat-héi-pèihhéi séuhng-làih hóuchíh jek lóuhfú gám
我個仔(一)發起脾氣上嚟好似隻老虎咁
Once my son gets angry, he's like a tiger.
Kéuih dá-héi móhngkàuh séuhng-làih sèhng go Jēung Dāk-pùih gám
佢哋打起網球上嚟成個張德培咁
Once he's playing tennis, he's a real Michael Chang.

The continuative lohk-heui 落去

The combination **lohk-heui** 落去 literally means 'go down', as when it is used following a verb of motion:

hàahng lohk-heui 行落去 walk down   **dit lohk-heui** 跌落去 fall down

Much as **héi-séuhng-làih** 起上嚟 'come up' can indicate inception of an action, **lohk-heui** 落去 'go down' (like **xiàqù** 下去 in Mandarin) following a verb can express continuation:

Msái joi góng lohk-heui la
唔使再講落去喇
Joi siht lohk-heui jauh m̀h dihm la
再蝕落去就唔掂喇

There's no need to go on talking.

If we go on losing (money) we'll be in trouble.

This combination can combine with the potential **m̀h dóu** 唔到:

Ngóh ngàaih m̀h dóu lohk-heui la 我挨唔到落去喇
I can't go on suffering.
Ngóhdeih gám yéung jouh m̀h dóu lohk-heui 我哋咁樣做唔到落去
We can't go on working like this.

The particle chān 親

The particle **chān** 親 also has two distinct meanings:

(a) Habitual: 'every time' (only in subordinate clauses):

Kéuih làih chān ngóh ūkkéi dōu daai màaih jek gáu
佢嚟親我屋企都帶埋隻狗
Every time she comes to my house, she brings the dog along.
Lī go beisyū hōi-chān-wúi dōu jóu jáu
呢個秘書開親會都早走
Whenever there's a meeting, this secretary leaves early.

Because it involves quantification (meaning 'every time'), this requires the adverb **dōu** 都 before the main verb (see Unit 15).

(b) Adversative (to one's misfortune, whether physical or psychological):

dit chān 跌親 fall over   **láahng chān** 冷親 catch a cold
Ga chē jong chān jek gáu   The car bumped into a dog.
架車撞親隻狗
Kéuih cháai chān ngóh 佢踩親我   He stepped on me (my foot).

Verbs with **chān** 親 can typically be used as either transitive or intransitive verbs:

Transitive	Intransitive
Lóuhbáan haak chān kéuih 老闆嚇親佢	**Kéuih haak chān** 佢嚇親
The boss scared him.	He was scared.
Tou hei muhn chān kéuih 套戲悶親佢	**Kéuih hóu faai muhn chān** 佢好快悶親
The film bored her.	She quickly became bored.

Also with the affected body part as object:

Ngóh hám chān go tàuh　　　　I bumped my head.
我扰親個頭

Kéuih jíng chān jek geuk　　　　He hurt his leg/foot.
佢整親隻腳

Léih dan chān tìuh méih-lùhng-gwāt àh?　　Did you hurt your spine?
你撳親條尾龍骨呀?

With its adversative meaning, **chān** 親 goes naturally with the passive (see *Basic Cantonese*, Unit 21):

Active	Passive
Lóuhbáan gīk chān kéuih 老闆激親佢	**Kéuih béi lóuhbáan gīk chān** 佢畀老闆激親
The boss angered him.	He was angered by the boss.
Jek mān ngáauh chān ngóh 隻蚊咬親我	**Ngóh béi jek mān ngáauh chān** 我畀隻蚊咬親
The mosquito has bitten me.	I've been bitten by a mosquito.

Exercise 12.1

Add an aspect marker (**háh** 下 or **hōi** 開) to the sentences given to produce the meaning specified in the translation.

Example:　**Ngóhdeih ūkkéi jyú Jūnggwok choi** 我哋屋企煮中國菜
　　　　　We (regularly) cook Chinese food at home.
→　　　　**Ngóhdeih ūkkéi jyú-hōi Jūnggwok choi** 我哋屋企煮開中國菜

1　**Ngóh yiu kāp ___ sānsīn hūnghei**　　I need to get some fresh air
　我要吸 ___ 新鮮空氣　　　　　　　(for a while).

2 **Ngóh sīnsāang chē ___ ngóh fāan-gūng**
我先生車 ___ 我返工

My husband (normally) drives me to work.

3 **Léih yiu jyuyi ___ léih ge gihnhōng**
你要注意 ___ 你嘅健康

You need to pay attention to your health (for a while).

4 **Ngóh jyuh ___ lītàuh, m̀h séung būn**
我住 ___ 呢頭, 唔想搬

I'm (used to) living here and don't want to move.

5 **Ngóhdeih heui Hói-yèuhng Gūngyún wáan ___** 我哋去海洋公園玩 ___

We're going to have (a bit of) fun at Ocean Park.

6 **Léih gú ___ ngóh géi dō seui ā**
你估 ___ 我幾多歲

(Have a) guess how old I am.

7 **Kéuih jā ___ Yidaaihleih páau-chē**
佢揸 ___ 意大利跑車

He (regularly) drives an Italian sports car.

8 **Léih yīnggōi gói ___ léih ge waaih jaahpgwaan** 你應該改 ___ 你嘅壞習慣

You should change your habits (a bit).

9 **Kéuih jeuk ___ mìhng pàaih sāam**
佢著 ___ 名牌衫

She (normally) wears designer clothes.

10 **Ngóhdeih heui tòuhsyūgwún chāamgwūn ___ sìn**
我哋去圖書館參觀 ___ 先

Let's go to the library to (have a) look around.

Exercise 12.2

Use **háh** 下 to express the same idea as the reduplicated forms given.

Example: **Dáng ngóh wán-yāt-wán sīn** 等我搵一搵先 Let me take a quick look.

→ **Dáng ngóh wán-háh sīn** 等我搵下先

1 **Léih yiu lihn-yāt-lihn lī sáu gō**
你要練一練呢首歌

You need to practise this song.

2 **Léih heui mahn-yāt-mahn lā**
你去問一問啦

Go and ask.

3 **Léih si-yāt-si gihn sāam sīn**
你試一試件衫先

Try on this blouse.

4 **Ngóh yiu lám-yāt-lám sīn**
我要諗一諗先

I need to think about it for a while.

5 **Mgōi léih dáng-yāt-dáng sīn lā**
唔該你等一等先啦

Please wait a moment.

6 **Ngóhdeih táu-yāt-táu sīn**
我哋唞一唞先

Let's have a rest.

7 **Léih màhn-yāt-màhn dī hēungséui ā**
你聞一聞啲香水吖

Smell the perfume.

8 **Faai dī maat-yāt-maat faai mihn lā**
快啲抹一抹塊面啦

Wipe your face quickly.

Exercise 12.3

Use reduplication and **háh** 下 or **léuhng** 兩 to express the meaning suggested.

Example: **Kéuih fan ___ ___ dihnwá jauh héung laak**
佢瞓 ___ ___ 電話就響嘞
She'd been sleeping for a while when the phone rang.
→ **Kéuih fan-fan-háh dihnwá jauh héung laak** 佢瞓瞓下電話就響嘞

1 **Ga gēi yuhng ___ ___ jauh waaih-jó**
架機用 ___ ___ 就壞咗
The machine broke down after being used once or twice.
2 **Pīn mán gói ___ ___ jauh gói hóu la**
篇文改 ___ ___ 就改好啦
The essay was corrected in a jiffy.
3 **Kéuih góng ___ ___ dihnwá, yáuh yàhn hāau-mùhn**
佢講 ___ ___ 電話, 有人敲門
Somebody knocked on the door while he was talking on the phone.
4 **Kéuih sihk ___ ___ faahn dahtyìhn wàhn-jó**
佢食 ___ ___ 飯突然暈咗
She suddenly fainted while eating.
5 **Kéuih sé ___ ___ jauh sé hóu la**
佢寫 ___ ___ 就寫好喇
He wrote it up in no time.
6 **Gihn baahk sēutsāam jeuk ___ ___ jauh wūjōu-jó**
件白恤衫著 ___ ___ 就污糟咗
The white shirt got dirty after being worn once or twice.
7 **Go hohksāang séuhng ___ ___ tòhng fan-jeuhk-jó**
個學生上 ___ ___ 堂瞓著咗
The student fell asleep while attending a class.
8 **Jēung chòhng fan ___ ___ jauh laahn-jó**
張床瞓 ___ ___ 就爛咗
The bed broke after being slept in a few times.
9 **Ngóhdeih jyuh ___ ___ faatgok gāan ūk lauh séui**
我哋住 ___ ___ 發覺間屋漏水
Having lived here for a while, we discovered that the house leaks.
10 **Síu-tàih-kàhm, kéuih lāai ___ ___ jauh m̀h lāai**
小提琴, 佢拉 ___ ___ 就唔拉
She played the violin for a while, then gave up.

Exercise 12.4

Use **héi . . . séuhng-làih** 起 . . . 上嚟 or **lohk-heui** 落去 to give the meaning suggested in brackets.

Example: **Ngóhdeih juhng hóyíh kīng** 我哋仲可以傾
We can still (carry on) chat(ting).
→ **Ngóhdeih juhng hóyíh kīng lohk-heui** 我哋仲可以傾落去

1 **Kéuih siu góján go yéung hóu tìhm** 佢笑嗰陣個樣好甜
Once (she starts) smiling, she looks sweet.

2 **Ngóh m̀h hóyíh joi ngàaih** 我唔可以再捱
I can't (go on) suffer(ing) any more.

3 **Tīnhei jyun, hóu yùhngyih behng** 天氣轉, 好容易病
(Once) the weather (starts to) change, it's easy to get ill.

4 **Léihdeih joi chòuh ngóh jauh giu gíngchaat làih** 你哋再嘈我就叫警察嚟
If you (carry on) making so much noise, I'll call the police.

5 **Seui-gúk chàh-seui jauh màhfàahn** 稅局查稅就麻煩
(Once) the tax office starts investigating one's taxes, it's troublesome.

6 **Gám yéung aau móuh yuhng** 咁樣拗冇用
It's no use (to continue) arguing this way.

7 **Ngóhdeih kyutdihng m̀h dáng** 我哋決定唔等
We decided not to (go on) wait(ing).

8 **Kéuih yāt chīsin māt dōu jouh dāk chēut** 佢一黐線乜都做得出
Once he becomes crazy, he's capable of doing anything.

Exercise 12.5

Form sentences using **chān** 親 with an adversative or habitual sense.

   Example: He angered (**gīk** 激) me.
   →   **Kéuih gīk chān ngóh** 佢激親我
              Whenever we go to Guangzhou, we stay in this hotel.
   →   **Ngóhdeih heui chān Gwóngjāu, dōu jyuh lī gāan (jáudim)**
              我哋去親廣州, 都住呢間(酒店)

1 She fell over (**dit** 跌) again.
2 I twisted (**láu** 扭) my foot.
3 Whenever it rains (**lohk-yúh** 落霉), the house gets very wet (**sāp** 濕).
4 I got trodden on (**cháai** 踩).
5 The child tripped up (**pūk** 仆).
6 Every time he drinks (**yám-jáu** 飲酒) he gets drunk (**jeui** 醉).
7 We got burnt (**saai** 曬) in the sun.
8 Every time he takes the exam (**háau-síh** 考試), he fails (**m̀h hahpgaak** 唔合格).
9 Don't starve (**ngoh** 餓) the baby.
10 Whenever he sees (**tái** 睇) that film, he cries (**haam** 喊).

UNIT 13
Comparisons

In *Basic Cantonese* (Unit 12), we introduced comparisons using **gwo** 過 and **béi** 比 with adjectives:

Kéuih lēk gwo ngóh 佢叻過我	She's cleverer than me. (colloquial)
Kéuih béi ngóh chūngmìhng 佢比我聰明	She's cleverer than me. (formal)
Ngóh taai-táai jaahn dāk dō gwo ngóh 我太太賺得多過我	My wife earns more than me.
Ngóh taai-táai béi ngóh jaahn dāk dō 我太太比我賺得多	My wife earns more than me.

Here we look at more complicated cases such as:

- comparisons based on verbs
- negating and questioning comparisons
- comparisons of similarity

We also look at expressions of excess for both adjectives and verbs.

Comparisons with verbs

While comparisons with adjectives use **gwo** 過, those with verbs generally require **dō gwo** 多過 'more than':

Ngóh sihk dō gwo léih 我食多過你	I eat more than you.
Ngóh jūngyi léih dō gwo (jūngyi) kéuih 我鍾意你多過(鍾意)佢	I like you more than (I like) her.

This pattern can also be used to contrast two different activities:

Léih tái hei juhng dō gwo ngóh tái syū 你睇戲仲多過我睇書
You watch films even more than I read books.

Ngóh oi kéuih dō gwo hahn kéuih 我愛佢多過恨佢
I love him more than I hate him.

81

Similarly, **síu gwo** 少過 after a verb phrase gives the meaning 'less than':

Ngóh sihk síu gwo léih 我食少過你   I eat less than you.

Gūngsī gām-lín siht dāk síu gwo gauh-lín   The company lost less this year than
公司今年蝕得少過舊年   last year.

Negative and interrogative comparisons

Comparisons in the form of negative statements and questions, respectively, can be formed with **móuh** 冇 and its question form, **yáuh-móuh** 有冇, together with **gam** 咁 'as':

> **Ngóh móuh léih gam yáuh-seunsām** 我冇你咁有信心
> I'm not as confident as you (are).

> **Kéuih yáuh-móuh léih gam lengjái a?** 佢有冇你咁靚仔呀?
> Is he as good-looking as you?

This pattern also works for stative verbs (see Unit 7):

> **Ngóh móuh léih gam jūngyi yàuh-séui** 我冇你咁鍾意游水
> I don't like swimming as much as you do.

> **Yáuh-móuh léih mùihmúi gam gēng háau-síh a?** 有冇你妹妹咁驚考試呀?
> Are you as afraid of exams as your sister?

For interrogative comparisons, a simpler structure is often preferred, using **dihng** 定 'or' (see Unit 17) and the comparative **dī** 啲 (see *Basic Cantonese*, Unit 12):

> **Wàihjān pèhng dī dihng Gwoktaai pèhng dī a?** 維珍平啲定國泰平啲呀?
> Which is cheaper, Virgin or Cathay?

> **Sān haauh-yùhn dihng gauh haauh-yùhn fōngbihn dī a?** 新校園定舊校園方
> 便啲呀?
> Which is more convenient, the old campus or the new one?

Béihéi 比起

The word **béihéi** 比起 is required when adding a comparison as an afterthought to a statement that has already been made:

> **Kéuih gaau dāk géi hóu, béihéi kèihtā yàhn** 佢教得幾好, 比起其他人
> He teaches quite well, compared with the others.

> **Gām chi syun faai . . . béihéi seuhng chi làih góng** 今次算快...比起上次嚟講
> This time it went quickly . . . compared to last time.

Note the addition of **làih góng** 嚟講, literally 'come to speak (of it)'. See also Unit 24 for similar afterthoughts.

Comparisons of similarity

yāt yeuhng 一樣, literally 'one and the same' can be used to express similarity:

Kéuih (tùhng léih) yāt yeuhng gam kùhng 佢(同你)一樣咁窮
He's just as hard up (as you are).

chā-m-dō 差唔多, literally 'differing not much', is used generically to make approximations:

Kéuih tùhng léih chā-m-dō (gam gōu) 佢同你差唔多(咁高)
He's about the same (height) as you.

Note the use of **tùhng** 同 'with' specifying the standard of comparison in these constructions; **hóuchíh** 好似 is a verb meaning 'resemble' (or 'seem') which works together with **gam** 咁 in expressions of similarity:

Yùhgwó hóuchíh léih gam hahngfūk jauh hóu la!
如果好似你咁幸福就好啦!
If (I) were as fortunate as you that would be fine!

Léih gwú ngóh hóuchíh lóuhbáan gam gūhòhn mē?
你估我好似老闆咁孤寒咩?
Do you think I'm as miserly as the boss?

Jeuhn 盡 'as . . . as possible'

The word **jeuhn** 盡 (*lit.* 'exhaust') forms adverbial phrases with a superlative sense:

jeuhn faai 盡快	as quickly as possible
jeuhn jóu 盡早	as soon as possible
jeuhn lihk 盡力	with as much effort as possible
jeuhn leuhng 盡量	as far as possible, to the best of one's ability

These serve as adverbs:

Ngóhdeih wúih jeuhn faai tūngjī léih 我哋會盡快通知你
We'll let you know as quickly as possible.

Ngóh wúih jeuhn leuhng bōng-sáu 我會盡量幫手
I'll do my best to help.

Excess

The most straightforward expression of excess is **taai** 太, which corresponds closely to Mandarin **tài** 太 and English 'too':

Dī tōng taai yiht 啲湯太熱	The soup is too hot.
Léih jā dāk taai faai 你揸得太快	You're driving too fast.

Another alternative is **taai-gwo** 太過, which gives emphasis by combining **taai** 太 and **gwo** 過:

taai-gwo gáandāan 太過簡單   much too simple

While **taai** 太 is neutral in terms of register as well as intensity, other idiomatic and more distinctively Cantonese terms are **dāk jaih** 得滯 and **gwotàuh** 過頭:

Kéuih góng dāk faai dāk jaih   He's speaking a bit too fast.
佢講得快得滯

Dī tōng yiht gwotàuh   The soup is too hot.
啲湯熱過頭

With verbs, the corresponding expression is **gwolùhng** 過龍:

fan gwolùhng 瞓過龍   oversleep
jyú gwolùhng 煮過龍   overcook
sek gwolùhng 錫過龍   spoil (a child) to death

gihk douh 極度 'exceedingly' is a formal expression:

gihk douh fūkjaahp 極度複雜   exceedingly complicated
gihk douh húnggeuih 極度恐懼   exceedingly fearful

Exercise 13.1

Refute the following comparisons by using a negative comparison.

Example:	**Háaih gwai gwo lùhnghā** 蟹貴過龍蝦	Crab is more expensive than lobster.
→	**Háaih móuh lùhnghā gam gwai** 蟹冇龍蝦咁貴	Crab is not as expensive as lobster.

1   **Héi-kehk hóu-tái gwo bēi-kehk**   Comedy is more fun to watch
    喜劇好睇過悲劇   than tragedy.

2   **Hahtīn chèuhng gwo dūngtīn**   Summer is longer than winter.
    夏天長過冬天

3   **Yīsāng mòhng gwo wuhsih**   Doctors are busier than nurses.
    醫生忙過護士

4   **Láuyeuk jitjau faai gwo Hēunggóng** New York's pace is faster than
    紐約節奏快過香港   Hong Kong's.

5   **Lihksí-haih yùhngyih yahp gwo**   The history department is
    jithohk-haih   easier to get into than the
    歷史系容易入過哲學系   philosophy department.

6   **Wohnggok bīk-yàhn gwo Jīmsājéui**   Mongkok is more crowded
    旺角迫人過尖沙咀   than Tsimshatsui.

Exercise 13.2

Ask questions to compare the elements stated.

A: Using **dī** 啲

Example: **hùhng sīk** 紅色 red vs. **wòhng sīk** 黃色 yellow: **seuhn-ngáahn** 順眼 pleasing to the eyes

Hùhng sīk dihng wòhng sīk seuhn-ngáahn dī a? 紅色定黃色順眼啲呀？
Is red or yellow more pleasing to the eyes?

1 **dīksí** 的士 taxi vs. **fóchē** 火車 train: **faai** 快 fast
2 **gātìhng** 家庭 family vs. **sihyihp** 事業 career: **juhngyiu** 重要 important
3 **Jūng yeuhk** 中藥 Chinese medicine vs. **sāi yeuhk** 西藥 Western medicine: **yáuh-haauh** 有效 effective
4 **daap-fēigēi** 搭飛機 flying vs. **daap-syùhn** 搭船 taking the boat: **syūfuhk** 舒服 comfortable
5 **duhk-syū** 讀書 study vs. **jouh-yéh** 做嘢 work: **sānfú** 辛苦 demanding

B: Using **yáuh-móuh** 有冇

Example: **yúhyìhnhohk** 語言學 linguistics vs. **màhnhohk** 文學 literature: **làahn** 難 difficult

Yúhyìhnhohk yáuh-móuh màhnhohk gam làahn a? 語言學有冇文學咁難呀？
Is linguistics as difficult as literature?

6 **go léui** 個女 the daughter vs. **go jái** 個仔 the son: **pa-cháu** 怕醜 shy
7 **tái dihnsih** 睇電視 watch television vs. **hàahng-gūngsī** 行公司 shopping: **sāai-sìhgaan** 嘥時間 time-consuming
8 **Seuhnghói** 上海 Shanghai vs. **Bākgīng** 北京 Beijing: **yúhn** 遠 far
9 **Jūngdaaih** 中大 Chinese University vs. **Góngdaaih** 港大 Hong Kong University: **yáuh-méng** 有名 famous
10 **fōwaahn pín** 科幻片 science fiction films vs. **húngbou pín** 恐怖片 horror films: **chigīk** 刺激 thrilling

Exercise 13.3

Add an appropriate expression of excess in place of **hóu** 好:

Example:	**Kéuih ūkkéi hóu yúhn** 佢屋企好遠	It's a long way to his house.
→	**Kéuih ūkkéi yúhn dāk jaih** 佢屋企遠得滯	It's a bit far to his house.

1	**Dī gāsī hóu pèhng** 啲傢俬好平	The furniture is (too) cheap.
2	**Chau-jái hóu sānfú** 湊仔好辛苦	Taking care of children is (exceedingly) hard work.
3	**Kéuih jyú ge sung hóu hàahm** 佢煮嘅餸好鹹	The dishes she cooks are (too) salty.
4	**Yìuhgwán ngohk hóu chòuh** 搖滾樂好嘈	Rock music is (too) noisy.
5	**Kéuih hàahng dou hóu guih** 佢行到好劫	He gets (too) tired as a result of walking.
6	**Hēunggóng bin dāk hóu faai** 香港變得好快	Hong Kong changes (too) quickly.
7	**Jingfú taaidouh hóu kèuhng-ngaahng** 政府態度好強硬	The government's attitude is (excessively) firm.
8	**Kéuih làaih-láai hóu làahn fuhksih** 佢奶奶好難服侍	Her mother-in-law is (too) hard to please
9	**Ngóh ūkkéi ge mahntàih hóu fūkjaahp** 我屋企嘅問題好複雜	My family's problems are (too) complicated.
10	**Sīnsāang góng ge yéh hóu sām-ou** 先生講嘅嘢好深奧	What the teacher said is (exceedingly) profound.

UNIT 14
Resultative and causative sentences with dou 到

Resultative sentences denote the state resulting from an action (usually a verb) or the extent of a certain state (usually an adjective). They are formed with **dou** 到, one of the grammatical words with many functions which are crucial to Cantonese grammar. As a verb in its own right, **dou** 到 means 'arrive' or 'reach' and also goes with other verbs to form verb-particle units like **sāu dou** 收到 'receive'. **dou** 到 also serves to introduce the state of affairs resulting from an event, which may be seen as an extension of the core meaning of 'getting to', 'reaching a certain state or point'. The nearest equivalent of this **dou** 到 in English is 'until', and indeed in some cases, **dou** 到 simply means 'until':

Yāt dím jūng dáng dou sāam dím 一點鐘等到三點 (from one of Faye Wong's songs)
Wait from one until three o'clock.

Ngóh góng dou móuh saai hei 我講到冇晒氣
I talked till I had no breath left.

The resultative meaning of **dou** 到 is 'to the point of . . . ' as we see here:

A-Lìhng sēui dou yàhn-yàhn dōu ngāak 阿玲衰到人人都呃
Ling is so bad that she'll cheat anyone.

In the clause following **dou** 到, the subject is omitted if it is the same as that of the main verb:
Same subject:

Kéuih guih dou hàahng m̀h yūk 佢攰到行唔郁
S/he was so tired that s/he couldn't move.

Different subject:

Kéuihdeih chòuh dou ngóh jouh m̀h dóu yéh 佢哋嘈到我做唔到嘢
They're making so much noise that I can't get any work done.

Dou 到 with adjectives

Since adjectives and verbs generally behave alike in Cantonese (see Unit 7), it is no surprise that we can use **dou** 到 with adjectives as well as with verbs. Especially productive is (adjective) **dou séi** 到死 'to death' with adjectives of emotive evaluation, typically where negative evaluation is involved:

gēng dou séi 驚到死	scared to death
wahtdaht dou séi 核突到死	really ugly, gross
lyuhn dou séi 亂到死	really messy
gwai dou séi 貴到死	really expensive
tìhm/syūn/fú/laaht dou séi 甜/酸/苦/辣到死	really sweet/sour/bitter/spicy

While the emphatic meaning of **dou séi** 到死 is also applicable to positive evaluation, others such as **dou fēihéi** 到飛起 ('to the point of taking off') and **dou wàhn** 到暈 ('to the point of dizziness') are often more idiomatic:

Go sailouh-léui dākyi dou séi 個細路女得意到死	The little girl is dead cute.
Gihn sāam leng dou séi/dou wàhn 件衫靓到死/到暈	The blouse is dead gorgeous.
Kéuih go jái lēk dou séi/dou fēihéi 佢個仔叻到死/到飛起	His son is fiendishly smart.

. . . **dou jeuhn** 到盡 'to the full', 'to the limit' often appears in colloquial expressions:

bok dou jeuhn 搏到盡	do one's utmost, e.g. win the game, work hard
je dou jeuhn 借到盡	borrow to the limit
syū/yèhng dou jeuhn 輸/贏到盡	win/lose everything
wáan dou jeuhn 玩到盡	play to the full
wāi dou jeuhn 威到盡	super cool

For example:

Gām chi kéuihdeih ló saai sei go jéung jānhaih wāi dou jeuhn la
今次佢哋攞晒四個獎真係威到盡啦
This time they got all four prizes; they're super cool.

A common use of these phrases is as an answer to questions of the type . . . **sèhng dím a?** 成點呀? 'to what extent?'

A: **Lóuhbáan lāu sèhng dím a?** 老闆嬲成點呀?
How angry is the boss? (i.e. what's the extent of the boss's anger?)

B: **Lāu dou sihk m̀h lohk faahn lō** 嬲到食唔落飯囉
So angry that he can't eat anything.

A: **A-Lìhng lēk sèhng dím a?** 阿玲叻成點呀?
How smart is Ling?

B: **Lēk dou léih m̀h seun** 叻到你唔信
(*lit.* smart till you not believe)
Incredibly smart.

Finally, **dou** 到 can be left 'stranded' with the complement clause omitted but implied:

Kéuih faai dou ā 佢快到吖....   He's so fast.
Kéuih lēk dou lē 佢叻到吖....   She's so smart, you know.

This gives the effect of being left speechless, with the particle drawn out for emphasis.

Verb copying with transitive verbs

If the verb has an object, the verb has to be repeated before the **dou-phrase**:

Ngóh laauh kéuih laauh dou bá sēng dōu sā-jó 我鬧佢鬧到把聲都沙咗
I scolded him till my voice was hoarse.

Kéuih gēng lóuhpòh gēng dou m̀h gám fāan ūkkéi 佢驚老婆驚到唔敢返屋企
He's so afraid of his wife that he dare not go home.

Kéuih jouh-yéh jouh dou waih tung 佢做嘢做到胃痛
She worked so hard that she got a stomach ache.

This verb copying also applies to adverbial constructions with **dāk** 得 (see *Basic Cantonese*, Unit 10).

Dou 到 with causative verbs

The main causative constructions use **dou** 到 as used in resultative sentences. **dou**-phrases combine with a number of causative verbs such as **jíng** 整 'make'. These have almost the same meaning but are given here in increasing order of formality: **gáau** 搞 and **jíng** 整 are colloquial, while **ling** 令 and **sái** 使 are more formal.

Dímgáai gāan fóng gáau dou gam lyuhn ga? 點解間房搞到咁亂㗎?
(*lit.* why the room make till so messy)
Why is the room so messy (as a result of somebody's wilful action)?

Kéuihdeih sèhngyaht dá màh-jéuk jíng dou ngóh fan m̀h dóu
佢哋成日打麻雀整到我瞓唔到
Their playing mahjong prevents me from sleeping.

Syūbaahkdahk ge yāmngohk lihng dou yàhn sām kong sàhn yìh
舒伯特嘅音樂令到人心曠神怡
Schubert's music is uplifting to the human heart and spirit.

Sīusīk sái dou tàuhjī-jé yahp síh 消息使到投資者入市 (financial report)
The news has led investors to enter the market.

These causative constructions are used to express several concepts which are expressed by transitive verbs in English, such as 'please', 'excite', 'embarrass' and 'disappoint':

Kéuih séung lihng dou lóuhbáan hōisām jē 佢想令到老闆開心啫
He just wants to please his boss (make her happy).

Go bougou lihng dou ngóh hóu hīngfáhn 個報告令到我好興奮
The report excited me (made me excited).

Kéuih góng ge yéh jíng dou ngóh hóu mhóuyisi 佢講嘅嘢令到我好唔好意思
The things he said embarrassed me (made me embarrassed).

Ngóh m̀h séung lihng dou kéuih sātmohng 我唔想令到佢失望
I don't want to disappoint her (make her disappointed).

†Inverted resultative sentences

A particular version of the resultative/causative construction with **dou** 到 involves a kind of inversion of the verb and its logical subject. As an alternative to (a) we can have (b):

(a) **Kàhm-máahn ngóh góng dou hóu gīkhei** 琴晚我講到好激氣
    (*lit.* last night I talked till very angry)
    Last night, I talked and (as a result) got very angry.
(b) **Kàhm-máahn góng dou ngóh hóu gīkhei** 琴晚講到我好激氣
    (*lit.* last night talked till I very angry)
    Last night, I talked and (as a result) got very angry.

This amounts to making **ngóh** 我 the subject of the **dou**-clause rather than the main clause. Based on the inverted construction (b), we can even have the logical object of the verb at the beginning of the sentence. This object is then seen as the cause of the event:

Pīn mán tái dou Mìhng-jái ngáahn tung 篇文睇到明仔眼痛
(*lit.* the paper read till Ming boy's eyes hurt)
Reading the paper makes Ming's eyes hurt.

Gām jīu dī Yīng-sīk jóuchāan sihk dou ngóhdeih bāau saai
今朝啲英式早餐食到我哋飽晒
This morning's English breakfast filled us all up.

Dī gúpiu siht dou ngóh pā háidouh 啲股票蝕到我趴喺度
Losing on shares has brought me to the ground.

Some similar sentences are also possible without **dou** 到:

Dī gāsī sái-jó ngóh sahp maahn mān 啲傢俬洗咗我十萬蚊
This furniture cost me one hundred thousand dollars.

Lī tiuh sósìh wán-jó ngóh sèhng máahn 呢套鎖匙搵咗我成晚
(*lit.* this key search me an entire evening)
It took me an entire evening to look for this key.

Bún baatgwa jaahpji tái-jó kéuih sèhng go hahjau 本八卦雜誌睇咗佢成個下晝
(*lit.* the gossip magazine read her whole afternoon)
Reading the gossip magazine took up her whole afternoon.

Lī go jōng fa-jó ngóh léuhng go jūng 呢個妝化咗我兩個鐘
(*lit.* this make-up spent me two hours)
This make-up session took two hours.

Gāmmáahn chāan faahn jyú-jó kéuihdeih sèhng yaht 今晚餐飯煮咗佢哋成日
(*lit.* tonight dinner cook them whole day)
It took a whole day to cook tonight's dinner.

Dī hùhngchàuh-gú siht-jó kéuih yāt baak maahn 啲紅籌股蝕咗佢一百萬
(*lit.* the red chip shares lost him a million)
The red chip shares made him lose a million.

Exercise 14.1

Form sentences using **dou** 到:

A: To indicate the extent of the following psychological states:

Example:
Emotion: **gámduhng dou** 感動到 . . . **haam héi séuhng-làih** 喊起上嚟
so moved . . . that (she) began to cry

1 Happiness: **hōisām dou** 開心到 . . .
2 Fear: **gēng dou** 驚到 . . .
3 Anger: **lāu dou** 嬲到 . . .
4 Frustration: **mángjáng dou** 瘟瘤到 . . .
5 Comfort: **syūfuhk dou** 舒服到 . . .

B: To describe things:

1 The sea view: **Go hói-gíng leng dou** 個海靚到 . . .
2 A house: **Gāan ūk gōnjehng dou** 間屋乾淨到 . . .
3 A picture: **Fūk wá daaih dou** 幅畫大到 . . .
4 Summer in Hong Kong: **Hēunggóng hahtīn yiht dou** 香港夏天熱到 . . .
5 A rich person: **Kéuih dī chín dō dou** 佢啲錢多到 . . .

Exercise 14.2

Advertise your products as follows:

Example: **Lī go sān chitgai gūnglàhng dō dou sóu m̀h saai**
呢個新設計功能多到數唔晒
This new design has too many functions to count.

1 A new medicine: **Lī jek yeuhk lihng dou** 呢隻新藥令到
                         (makes you)....

2 Prizes in a raffle: **Ngóhdeih ge jéungbán** (prize) **dō dou**
                         我哋嘅獎品多到....

3 A television programme: **Lī go jitmuhk jīngchói** 呢個節目精彩
                         (this programme is so fabulous) **dou** 到....

4 A restaurant: **Ngóhdeih jáulàuh ge dím-sām** 我哋酒樓嘅點心
                         (our restaurant's dim sum) **sihk dou** 食到....

5 A book: **Sung Fūyàhn** 宋夫人 (Madam Sung) **dī syū
                         maaih** 啲書賣 (are selling) **dou** 到....

Exercise 14.3

Answer the question using **dou** 到 to indicate the extent of the situation.
Try to be as informative and detailed as possible in elaborating the extent
clause.

Example: **Jēung gēipiu pèhng sèhng dím a?** 張機票平成點呀?
         Just how cheap is the air ticket?
         Pèhng dou léih m̀h seun! 平到你唔信!
         So cheap that you wouldn't believe it!

1 **Jáan dāng gwai sèhng dím a?**   Just how expensive is the
   盞燈貴成點呀?   lamp?

2 **Kéuihdeih go yéung chíh sèhng dím a?** Just how alike are they?
   佢哋個樣似成點呀?

3 **Jek gáu behng sèhng dím a?**   How sick is the dog?
   隻狗病成點呀?

4 **Go yīsāng yī kéuih yī sèhng dím a?** How's the doctor's treatment
   個醫生醫佢醫成點呀?   going?

5 **Kéuih ga chē béi ga fochē johng sèhng** How badly was her car
   dím a? 佢架車畀架貨車撞成點呀?   damaged by the lorry?

6 **Léih hohk Jūngmán hohk sèhng dím a?** How's your Chinese doing?
你學中文學成點呀?

7 **Léih taai-táai lāu sèhng dím a?** How angry is your wife?
你太太嬲成點呀?

8 **Léih gú kéuih mòhng sèhng dím a?** Guess how busy he is?
你估佢忙成點呀?

†Exercise 14.4

Use **dou** 到 to show that the second clause expresses a result of the first. Begin
the sentence with the italicized object.

> **Ngóh yám *dī tōng* I drank the soup . . . sèhng sān hohn** sweat all over
> 我飲啲湯 . . . 成身汗
>
> → **Dī tōng yám dou ngóh sèhng sān hohn** 啲湯飲到我成身汗
> Drinking the soup made me sweat all over.

1 **Ngóh tái *fūng seun* I read the letter . . . hóu lāu** got angry
我睇封信 . . . 好嬲

2 **Ngóh sé *pīn mán* I wrote the paper . . . ngāau saai tàuh** got confused
我寫篇文 . . . 搲晒頭

3 **Kéuih yám *jēun jáu* he drank the bottle of wine . . . jeui-jó** got drunk
佢飲樽酒 . . . 醉咗

4 **Ngóh jouh go *sahtyihm* I did the experiment . . . jauhlèih chīsin** almost
crazy
我做個實驗 . . . 就嚟黐線

5 **Ngóh fan *jēung chòhng* I slept on the bed . . . hóu msyūfuhk** uncomfort-
able
我瞓張床 . . . 好唔舒服

6 **Ngóh tái *go dihnsih* I watched the television . . . ngáahn fā** couldn't see
clearly
我睇個電視 . . . 眼花

7 **Kéuih tēng *gó dī gwái-gú* He listened to those ghost stories . . . fan m̀h
dóu** can't sleep
佢聽嗰啲鬼故 . . . 瞓唔到

8 **Kéuih sihk *lī dī yeuhk* He took this medicine wàhn-tòh-tòh** became dizzy
佢食呢啲藥 . . . 暈陀陀

UNIT 15
Quantification

Quantifiers express relative quantities such as 'all', 'many' and 'few'. In Cantonese, they involve some special syntactic patterns and an important set of particles including **dōu** 到, **saai** 晒, **màaih** 埋, **dāk** 得 and **tīm** 添.

All and every

The concept 'all' (universal quantification) can be expressed by:

(a) A reduplicated classifier, with or without the noun (see Unit 8):

gāan-gāan ūk 間間屋	every house	**jek-jek duhngmaht** 隻隻動物	every animal
go-go (yàhn) 個個(人)	everyone	**douh-douh** 度度	everywhere

(b) **múih** 每 'each':

múih (go) yàhn 每(個)人	each person	**múih ga chē** 每架車	each car
múih gāan ūk 每間屋	each house	**múih bún syū** 每本書	each book

(c) **só yáuh ge** 所有嘅 'all' (a formal alternative: see Unit 25):

só yáuh (ge) yàhn 所有(嘅)人	everyone
só yáuh (ge) sihkmaht 所有(嘅)食物	all the food there is

When these expressions are used, two general rules should be observed:

(a) The adverb **dōu** 都 is added before the verb:

Go-go dōu jaan kéuih 個個都讚佢	Everyone praises her.
Múih gāan ūk dōu yáuh láahnghei 每間屋都有冷氣	Each house has air conditioning.
Só yáuh (ge) tùhngsih dōu yiu jéunsìh dou 所有(嘅)同事都要準時到	All colleagues need to arrive on time.

(b) When the object of the sentence is quantified it must come before the verb:

Kéuih *douh-douh* dōu séung heui
佢度度都想去

He wants to go
everywhere.

Gíngchaat *múih ga chē* dōu gímchàh-gwo
警察每架車都檢查過

The police have inspected
every car.

Haauhjéung *só yáuh ge sīnsāang* dōu gin-gwo
校長所有嘅先生都見過

The principal has met all
the teachers.

The resulting word order (subject-object-verb) resembles that of the focus construction in Unit 9.

In addition to the quantifiers (a–c) above, numerals may be used together with **dōu** 都 to mean 'both', 'all three' etc.

Ngóhdeih *léuhng go* dōu heui
我哋兩個都去

We're both going.

Ngóh *sāam gihn* dōu jūngyi
我三件都鍾意

I like all three (pieces of clothing).

Note again the position of the object before the verb.

Any

A question word such as **bīngo** 邊個 'who' together with the adverb **dōu** 都 gives the meaning 'any' or 'every':

bīngo 邊個	who	**bīngo dōu** 邊個都	anyone
māt(yéh) 乜(嘢)	what	**māt(yéh) dōu** 乜(嘢)都	anything, everything
bīndouh 邊度	where	**bīndouh dōu** 邊度都	anywhere

For example:

Bīngo dōu làih dāk 邊個都嚟得

Anyone can come.

Mātyéh dōu hóyíh faatsāng ge
乜嘢都可以發生嘅

Anything can happen.

Again notice the position of the object, which comes before the verb:

Gīngléih bīngo dōu háng gin
經理邊個都肯見

The manager is willing to see anyone.

Hēunggóng mātyéh yàhn dōu yáuh
香港乜嘢人都有

There are all sorts of people in
Hong Kong.

yahmhòh 任何 is a more formal expression for 'any':

Yahmhòh yīsāng dōu hóyíh jouh lī go sáuseuht 任何醫生都可以做呢個手術
Any doctor can do this operation.

Yahmhòh jaahn chín ge gēiwuih dōu m̀h hóyíh fonggwo
任何賺錢嘅機會都唔可以放過
(*lit.* any earn money opportunity also can't let go)
One can't let go of any opportunity to make money.

None

To express 'none', 'nothing' etc., we basically add a negative word to the constructions given above meaning 'every' and 'any':

Dúng Sāang bīngo dōu sīk 董生邊個都識	Mr Tung knows everyone.
Dúng Sāang bīngo dōu m̀h sīk 董生邊個都唔識	Mr Tung doesn't know anyone.
Ngóh māt(yéh) dōu jī 我乜(嘢)都知	I know everything.
Ngóh māt(yéh) dōu m̀h jī 我乜(嘢)都唔知	I don't know anything.
Kéuih mātyéh choi dōu sihk 佢乜嘢菜都食	She eats any kind of vegetable.
Kéuih mātyéh choi dōu m̀h sihk 佢乜嘢菜都唔食	She doesn't eat any kind of vegetable.

Many and much: dō/síu 多/少

The words **dō** 多 and **síu** 少 have several uses:

- With nouns:

Hóu dō yàhn lihn taaigihk 好多人練太極	Many people practise tai chi.
Béigaau síu yīsāng sīk yī lī go behng 比較少醫生識醫呢個病	Relatively few doctors know how to treat this disease.

- As predicative adjectives:

Ngóhdeih ge mahntàih hóu dō 我哋嘅問題好多	Our problems are many.
Dī gau jīgaak ge sīnsāang taai síu 啲夠資格嘅先生太少	The qualified teachers are too few.

- As verbs, when they can take the aspect marker **jó** 咗 to indicate a change
  in quantity, or even a meaning of excess (too many or too few):

Gāmyaht dō-jó géi go haak　　There were a few more clients today.
今日多咗幾個客

Jeuigahn síu-jó hóu dō yàuh-haak　There have been many fewer tourists lately.
最近少咗好多人客

Dō-jó léuhng go hohksāang　　There were two students too many.
多咗兩個學生

Síu-jó yāt go léihyàuh　　There was one reason too few.
少咗一個理由

These combinations can also be added to a verb, with a similar effect:

Ngóh waihháu m̀h hóu, sihk-síu-jó hóu dō yéh 我胃口唔好，食少咗好多嘢
My appetite is not good, and I have been eating a lot less.

Kéuih hyut-ngaat gōu, yám-síu-jó hóu dō jáu 佢血壓高，飲少咗好多酒
He has high blood pressure and drinks a lot less.

Léih chēut-dō-jó tìuh tàihmuhk 你出多咗條問題
You set one question too many.

Gūngsī sung-síu-jó yāt yeuhng yéh làih 公司送少咗一樣嘢嚟
The company delivered one thing too few.

When used as adverbs, **dō dī** 多啲 'more' and **síu dī** 少啲 'less' typically come
before the verb like other adverbs:

Ngóhdeih yīnggōi dō dī wahnduhng 我哋應該多啲運動
We should exercise more.

Léih bātyùh síu dī màaihyun lā! 你不如少啲埋怨啦!
Why don't you complain less?

Particles of quantification saai 晒 and màaih 埋, dāk 得 and tīm 添

The particle **saai** 晒 offers an idiomatic alternative way to express the idea 'all'.
It follows the verb like other verbal particles:

* With transitive verbs (referring to the object):

Léih giu gam dō sung dím sihk dāk saai a?
你叫咁多餸點食得晒呀?
You order so many dishes, how can we eat them all?

Yīsāng gām-jīu góng saai béi kéuih tēng la
醫生今朝講晒畀佢聽喇
The doctor told him everything this morning.

Kéuih béi yàhn ngāak saai dī chín
佢畀人呃晒啲錢
He got cheated and as a result lost all the money.

- With intransitive verbs (referring to the subject):

Dī geijé jáu saai la 啲記者走晒喇   The reporters have all left.
Dī sailouhjái yātjóu jauh fan saai   The children have all gone to
啲細路仔一早就瞓晒   sleep early.
Dī yú hóu faai séi saai 啲魚好快死晒   The fish all died quickly.

- With adjectives (emphasizing quality):

Móuh gin gam loih, léih sèhng go leng saai wo
冇見咁耐，你成個靚晒喎
Haven't seen you for a long time; you've become prettier.
Dī fūng yāt chēui, léih dī tàuhfaat jauh lyuhn saai
啲風一吹，你啲頭髮就亂晒
Once the wind blows, your hair becomes all messy.

- With verb-object compounds and idioms (usually indicating a change of state):

ngāau-saai-tàuh 搲晒頭 (*lit.* scratch one's head) rack one's brain
lyuhn saai hāang 亂晒坑 make a complete mess of things
lèih-póu 離譜 outrageous →   **lèih-saai-póu** 離晒譜 totally outrageous
lé-he chaotic →   **lé-saai-he** totally chaotic

Like other particles, **saai** 晒 can be used in combination with:

(a) The aspect markers **gwo** 過 and **jyuh** 住 (but not **jó** 咗):

Ngóh wán-gwo saai lī tàuh ge daaih síu syū-dim ge la
我搵過晒呢頭嘅大小書店嘅喇
I've searched all the big and small bookshops around here.
Daaih-hohk kám-jyuh saai dī cháumàhn
大學冚住晒啲醜聞
The university is covering up all the scandals.
Dī sailouh chòuh-jyuh saai ngóhdeih jouh-yéh
啲細路阻住晒我哋做嘢
The children are preventing us from doing any work (by making a noise).

(b) The comparative **gwo** 過 (see Unit 13) and other particles such as **dóu** 到,
hóu 好 and **fāan** 返:

lēk gwo saai kèihtā hohksāang   cleverer than all the other students
叻過晒其他學生
Léih dī jīlíu ngóh sāu dóu saai   I received all your data.
你啲資料我收到晒
Go bougou sé hóu saai la   The report is all done.
個報告寫好晒喇
Go behngyàhn hóu fāan saai la wo   The patient has recovered completely.
個病人好返晒喇喎

(c) The potential construction in which the negative **m̀h** 唔 or the potential **dāk** 得 is inserted between the verb and the particle (see *Basic Cantonese*, Unit 17):

Ngóhdeih sihk m̀h saai 我哋食唔晒   We can't eat it all.
Ngóhdeih sihk dāk saai 我哋食得晒   We can eat it all.
Ngóhdeih sihk m̀h sihk dāk saai a?   Can we eat it all?
我哋食唔食得晒呀?

saai 晒 can also combine with other quantifiers such as **go-go dōu** 個個都 and **māt(yéh) dōu** 乜(嘢)都, thereby emphasizing the idea of totality:

Yùhgwó go-go dōu jáu saai, bīngo léih Hēunggóng a? 如果個個走晒, 邊個 理香港呀?
(from a pre-handover television advertisement)
If everyone leaves, who will care about Hong Kong?
Hēunggóng māt dōu bin saai sīk 香港乜嘢都變晒色
(from a film set in 1997)
Everything in Hong Kong is changing colour.

The particle **màaih** 埋, which resembles **saai** 晒 in several respects, has a number of meanings. As a verb it means 'to approach', as in **màaih ngohn** 埋岸 'approach the shore' and **màaih làih** 埋嚟 'come closer'. As a particle (following another verb), it can mean:

(a) 'close'; 'together':

Sāan màaih douh mùhn 閂埋道門   Close the door.
Yeuk màaih dī pàhngyáuh heui yám-chàh   Gather the friends together to
約埋啲朋友去飲茶   have dim sum.

(b) 'in addition to all the rest':

Sihk màaih dī sung lā! 食埋啲餸啦!
Let's eat up the food (in addition to what has already been eaten)!
Ngóh taai-táai béi màaih ngóh ge wúifai 我太太畀埋我嘅會費
My wife paid my membership fees too (apart from her own fees).
Kéuihdeih daai màaih dī sailouh heui taam pàhngyáuh 佢哋帶埋啲細路去探朋友
They bring the children along to visit some friends.

Often either **saai** 晒 or **màaih** 埋 can be used, with a subtle difference in meaning:

Ngóh yiu jouh saai dī yéh sīn fāan ūkkéi 我要做晒啲嘢先返屋企
I have to finish doing everything before I go home.

Ngóh yiu jouh màaih dī yéh sīn fāan ūkkéi 我要做埋啲嘢先返屋企
I have to finish up a few more things before I go home.

dāk 得 'only' applies to the following noun phrases in subject and object positions, usually with numerals:

Dāk sāam go hohksāang yáuh-hingcheui 得三個學生有興趣
Only three students are interested.
Dāk kéuih geidāk sung sāangyaht láihmaht béi ngóh 得佢記得送生日禮物
畀我
Only she remembers to send me a birthday gift.
Ngóh chàhmmáahn fan dāk yāt go jūng 我琴晚瞓得一個鐘
I slept only one hour last night.
Kéuih yāt go yuht jaahn dāk gó yāt maahn mān, síu-m̀h-síu dī a?
佢一個月賺得嗰一萬蚊，少唔少啲呀？
(from a film)
He earns only ten thousand dollars a month; isn't that too little?

If the verb has two objects, **dāk** 得 comes after the verb, even when its meaning of 'only' applies to the second object:

Yihp gaausauh gaau dāk ngóh yāt go hohkkèih ja 葉教授教得我一個學
期咋
Professor Yip taught me for only one term.

Note that the particle **je/ja** 啫/咋 with its meaning of 'playing down' goes naturally with **dāk** 得 (see Unit 23).
While **dāk** 得 indicates that expectations have not been reached, **tīm** or **tìm** 添 suggests that they have been exceeded. The high falling tone **tìm** 添 is used at the end of a sentence (see Unit 2).

Dī tōng gam hóu meih, ngóh séung yám dō yāt wún tìm
啲湯咁好味，我想飲多一碗添
The soup's so tasty, I'd like to have another bowl.

The meaning is often reinforced by the adverb **juhng** 仲 and/or the verbal particle **màaih** 埋:

Kéuih yauh yáuh-jó, juhng wah mhaih yi-ngoih tìm!
佢又有咗，仲話唔係意外添！
She's pregnant again, and she says it's not an accident either!
Kéuih chéng ngóh sihk-faahn, juhng sung màaih ngóh fāan ūkkéi tìm
佢請我食飯，仲送埋我返屋企添
He took me to dinner and brought me back home too.

Exercise 15.1

The following sentences are incomplete. Insert **dōu** 都 before the verb as follows:

> Example: **Kéuih go-go hoksāang béi 'A' ge** 佢個個學生畀A嘅
> → **Kéuih go-go hoksāang dōu béi 'A' ge** 佢個個學生都畀A嘅
> He gives every student an 'A'.

1 **Kéuih mātyéh beimaht jī ge**
佢乜嘢秘密知嘅
She knows every secret.

2 **Gāan-gāan gūngsī móuh sīusīk**
間間公司冇消息
There's no news from any of the companies.

3 **Ngóh go-go jih m̀h sīk duhk**
我個個字唔識讀
I don't know how to read every word.

4 **Ngóh fuhmóuh go-go jáiléui gam sek**
我父母個個仔女咁錫
My parents love all their children.

5 **Kéuih fún-fún sān chē m̀h múhnyi**
佢款款新車唔滿意
He is dissatisfied with all the new car models.

6 **Lóuhbáan tìuh-tìuh sou gai dāk hóu chīngchó**
老闆條條數計得好清楚
The boss calculates every sum accurately.

7 **Kéuih go-go yuht jéunsìh gāau-jōu**
佢個個月準時交租
He pays the rent on time every month.

8 **Kéuih chi-chi jāang-jyuh màaih-dāan**
佢次次爭住埋單
Every time, he fights to foot the bill.

Exercise 15.2

Quantify the noun with a classifier in the Cantonese sentence and make the necessary changes to the sentence to express the meaning in the English translation given.

> Example: **Ngóh tong-jó tìuh fu la**
> 我熨咗條褲喇
> I've ironed the trousers.
>
> **Ngóh tìuh-tìuh fu dōu tong-jó la**
> 我條條褲都熨咗喇
> I've ironed all the trousers.
> or
> **Tìuh-tìuh fu ngóh dōu tong-jó la**
> 條條褲我都熨咗喇

1 **Go sīgēi yáuh tūnghàhng-jing**
個司機有通行證
Every driver has the permit.

2 **Ngóh jūngyi jek māau** 我鍾意隻貓
I like every cat.

3 **Gāan jáulàuh ngóhdeih heui-gwo**
間酒樓我哋去過

We've been to every restaurant.

4 **Kéuih sīk daap tìuh tàihmuhk**
佢識答條題目

She knows how to answer every question.

5 **Ngóh jek sáují tung dou séi**
我隻手指痛到死

All my fingers hurt like mad.

6 **Fūng seun tái saai la** 封信睇晒喇

I've finished reading all the letters.

7 **Fūk wá hóu yáuh-yisī** 幅畫好有意思

Every picture is full of meaning.

8 **Sáu gō hóu ngāam-tēng** 首歌好啱聽

All the songs are good to listen to.

9 **Pō syuh yáuh jeukjái jyuh ge**
棵樹有雀仔住嘅

Every tree has birds living in it.

10 **Dihp choi hóu hēung** 碟菜好香

Every dish of vegetables smells good.

Exercise 15.3

Use **dō/síu** 多/少, **dō/síu dī** 多/少啲 or **dō-jó/síu-jó** 多咗/少咗 as appropriate to add the meaning 'more' or 'less'.

Example: **Ngóh séung chēut gāai** 我想出街 I want to go out (less) → **Ngóh séung síu dī chēut gāai** 我想少啲出街 or

Ngóh séung chēut síu dī gāai 我想出少啲街

1 **Léih yiu tùhng jáiléui kīng-gái**
你要同仔女傾偈

You need to talk to your children (more).

2 **Ngóhdeih chéng-jó yāt wàih tói ge yàhn**
我哋請咗一圍枱嘅人

We've invited one (more) table of people.

3 **Gāmyaht làih-jó go gúdūng**
今日嚟咗個股東

One shareholder (too few) came today.

4 **Léih hó-m̀h-hóyíh góng dī, jouh dī a?**
你可唔可以講啲, 做啲呀?

Could you talk a bit (less) and do a bit (more)?

5 **Léih jeui hóu dá màh-jéuk**
你最好打麻雀

You had better play (less) mahjong.

6 **Chéng léih gwāansām háh ūkkéi yàhn**
請你關心下屋企人

Please take (more) care of your family.

7 **Ngóh séung làuh hái ūkkéi yāusīk háh**
我想留喺屋企休息下

I'd like to stay at home to rest (more).

8 **Jeuigahn sihk-jó Sāigung dī hóisīn**
最近食咗西貢啲海鮮

Recently we've been eating (less) Sai Kung seafood.

9 **Gām-lín syúga hóu dō yàuh-haak**
今年暑假好多遊客

This summer there have been many (more) tourists.

10 **Gāan ūk yāt go fóng, yāt go gūngyàhn**
間屋一個房, 一個工人

The house has one (more) room and one (less) maid.

Exercise 15.4

Add **saai** 晒 or **màaih** 埋 as appropriate.

> Example: **Ngóhdeih daai *màaih* dī sailouh heui douh-ga**
> 我哋帶埋啲細路去渡假
> We're taking the children (along) on holiday.
> **Ngóhdeih daai *saai* dī sailouh heui douh-ga**
> 我哋帶晒啲細路去渡假
>
> We're taking (all) the children on holiday.

1 **Yám ___ dī tōng kéuih lā** 飲 ___ 啲湯佢啦
  Drink up (all) the soup.
2 **Jáu jīchìhn yiu tái ___ fahn bougou** 走之前要睇 ___ 份報告
  I have to read (the whole of) the report before leaving.
3 **Léih yiu béi ___ gām go yuht ge jōu** 你要畀 ___ 今個月嘅租
  You have to pay this remaining month's rent.
4 **Faai dī sihk ___ dī hā kéuih lā** 快啲食 ___ 啲蝦佢啦
  Eat up the (remaining) shrimp.
5 **Ngóh chéng ___ ngóh go jái dī pàhngyáuh** 我請 ___ 我個仔啲朋友
  I'm inviting my son's friends (too).
6 **Léih yiu béi ___ gām go yuht ge jōu** 你要畀 ___ 今個月嘅租
  You have to pay (the whole of) this month's rent.
7 **Yám ___ dī tōng kéuih lā** 飲 ___ 啲湯佢啦
  Drink up (the rest of) the soup.
8 **Faai dī sihk ___ dī hā kéuih lā** 快啲食 ___ 啲蝦佢啦
  Eat up the (whole plate of) shrimp.

UNIT 16
Negative sentences

In this unit, we focus on aspects of negative sentences, in particular, words which have special meanings or functions in negative sentences. These are sentences including the main negative words coming before the verb (*Basic Cantonese*, Unit 14):

m̀h 唔	not	**Ngóh m̀h jaansìhng** 我唔贊成	I don't approve.
móuh 冇	haven't	**Kéuih móuh wán-gwo ngóh** 佢冇搵過我	He hasn't contacted me.
meih 未	not yet	**Meih yáuh sīusīk** 未有消息	There is no news yet.
mhóu 唔好	don't	**Mhóu gam sēungsām lā** 唔好咁傷心啦	Don't be so sad.

A number of words when used in negative sentences have meanings different from their usual meanings.

Negative word + joi 再 no longer

The adverb **joi** 再 'again' in conjunction with a negative word gives the meaning 'no longer':

Lī bouh gēi m̀h joi chēut ge la 呢部機唔再出嘅喇
This machine is no longer produced.
Ngóhdeih móuh joi dehng lī fahn boují 我哋冇再訂呢份報紙
We don't order this newspaper any more.
Mgōi léih mhóu joi tàih-héi kéuih 唔該你唔好再提起佢
Please don't mention him any more.
Ngóh m̀h hóyíh joi yán lohk-heui 我唔可以再忍落去
I can't stand it any longer.
Léih msái joi mùhn-jyuh ngóh la 你唔使再瞞住我啦
You don't need to hide it from me any more.

Jyuh 住 in negative sentences

The aspect marker **jyuh** 住 normally attaches to a verb to indicate continuous aspect (ongoing actions: see *Basic Cantonese*, Unit 19). In negative sentences, it comes at the end of the clause and means 'not . . . yet' or 'for the time being':

> **Ngóh m̀h fāan ūkkéi jyuh** 我唔返屋企住   I'm not going home yet.
> **Léih mhóu góng béi yàhn tēng jyuh**   Don't tell anyone yet.
> 你唔好講畀人聽住
> **Máih jáu jyuh!** 咪走住!   Don't go yet!
> **Ga chē meih jā dāk jyuh** 架車未揸得住   The car can't be driven yet.
> **Ngóhdeih jaahmsìh msái būn jyuh**   We don't need to move for the
> 我哋暫時唔使搬住   time being.

Although characteristic of negative sentences, this usage also appears in positive sentences together with the particle **sīn** 先:

> **Léihdeih sihk jyuh sīn; msái dáng ngóh** 你哋食住先；唔使等我
> You keep eating for the moment; no need to wait for me.
> **Léih tóuh-ngoh maih máaih dī yéh díng jyuh sīn lō** 你肚餓咪買啲嘢頂住先囉
> (overheard on the underground)
> If you're hungry, buy something to keep you going.
> **Doih jyuh sīn** 袋住先
> (government slogan promoting democratic reform package)
> Pocket it while you can.

Indefinite question words

The 'wh-words' as used in wh-questions (**bīngo** 邊個 'who', **mātyéh** 乜嘢 'what' etc.) also appear in negative sentences with special 'indefinite' meanings as follows:

	In questions	*In negative sentences*
bīngo 邊個	who?	anyone
mātyéh 乜嘢	what?	anything
bīndouh 邊度	where?	anywhere
dím (yéung) 點(樣)	how?	in any way
géi (dō) 幾(多)	how many?	many, much

In the negative sentences concerned, there is typically a negative word such as **m̀h** 唔 or **móuh** 冇 preceding the question word:

> **Móuh bīngo wúih gam chéun ge**   Hardly anyone would be so stupid.
> 冇邊個會咁蠢嘅

Léih gāmyaht móuh mātyéh jouh
你今日冇乜嘢做

You don't have anything much to do
today.

Ngóhdeih móuh bīndouh heui
我哋冇邊度去

We don't have anywhere much to go.

Ngóh móuh dím (yéung) lám-gwo
我冇點(樣)諗過

I hardly gave it any thought.

Móuh géi dō sìhgaan jihng
冇幾多時間淨

There's not much time left.

Note that the meaning is 'hardly at all' rather than 'not at all', which is
expressed using **dōu** 都 (see Unit 15):

Ngóhdeih m̀h wúih heui bīndouh
我哋唔會去邊度

We won't go anywhere much.

Ngóhdeih bīndouh dōu m̀h wúih heui
我哋邊度都唔會去

We won't go anywhere at all.

The difference is brought out in cases where it is spelt out that something,
however little, is done:

Léih gāmyaht móuh mātyéh jouh, jihnghaih yiu dá fūng seun jēk
你今日冇乜嘢做, 淨係要打封信唦
You don't have anything much to do today; just type up a letter.

**Ngóh m̀h wúih dím fáandeui, bātgwo ngóh wúih góng dī mahntàih béi
yàhn tēng**
我唔會點反對, 不過我會講啲問題畀人聽
I won't exactly object, but I'll tell people about the problems.

Gām-lín jauhsyun gā yàhn-gūng, dōu m̀h wúih gā gèi dō
今年就算加人工, 都唔會加幾多
This year, even if there's a pay raise, it won't be much.

The contexts in which these indefinite meanings apply are not limited to
negation itself but also include other 'negative polarity' contexts such as:

(a) Conditional sentences (see Unit 20):

Yùhgwó yáuh mātyéh mtóh, jīkhāak wah ngóh jī 如果有乜嘢唔妥, 即刻話
我知
If anything is wrong, let me know immediately.

Yùhgwó bīngo msyūfuhk, jeuhn faai chēut sēng 如果邊個唔舒服, 盡快出聲
If anyone is unwell, they should say so as soon as possible.

(b) 'Yes/no' questions:

Yáuh-móuh bīngo séung tái-háh lī go móhngyihp a? 有冇邊個想睇下呢個
網頁呀?

Is there anyone who wants to have a look at this web page?
Léih yáuh-móuh mātyéh sāangyaht yuhnmohng a? 你有冇乜嘢生日願望呀?
Do you have any birthday wish?

Conjunction in negative sentences: neither . . . nor

There are no words corresponding to 'neither . . . nor'. Instead, a conjunction of
two negative clauses is used, using **yauh . . . yauh** 又 . . . 又:

Kéuih yauh m̀h fūk ngóh ge seun yauh m̀h fūk ngóh ge dihnwá
佢又唔覆我嘅信又唔覆我嘅電話
He neither replies to my letters nor returns my calls.
Kéuihdeih yauh móuh chín yauh móuh mín 佢哋又冇錢又冇面
They have neither money nor face.

This corresponds to **yauh . . . yauh** 又 . . . 又 in positive sentences meaning
'both . . . and':

Kéuih yauh jūngyi duhk-syū yauh jūngyi wahnduhng 佢又鍾意讀書又鍾意
運動
She enjoys both studying and sports.

The auxiliaries yiu 要 and msái 唔使

Recall that the auxiliary **yiu** 要 'need', 'have to' has **msái** 唔使 as its negative
counterpart (*Basic Cantonese*, Unit 20).

Ngóh gāmyaht yiu fāan-hohk   I have to go to school today.
我今日要返學
Ngóh gāmyaht msái fāan-hohk   I don't have to go to school today.
我今日唔使返學

The form **sái** 使 without the negative prefix occurs only in rhetorical questions
(see Unit 17):

Sái léih gaau ngóh àh? As if I need you to teach me that!
使你教我呀?
Juhng sái góng mē? Needless to say!
仲使講咩?

Here the negation is implied by the rhetorical question.

Exercise 16.1

Express the following using **joi** 再 together with the appropriate negative word.

> Example: I'm no longer learning Thai. **(hohk Taai-mán** 學泰文**)** → **Ngóh móuh joi hohk Taai-mán** 我冇再學泰文

1 He no longer sees that doctor. **(gó go yīsāng** 嗰個醫生**)**
2 Don't go on deceiving yourself. **(ngāak jihgéi** 呃自己**)**
3 This matter cannot drag on any longer. **(tō lohk-heui** 拖落去**)**
4 Don't be so naughty **(yáih** 曳**)** any more.
5 His wound **(sēungháu** 傷口**)** does not hurt **(tung** 痛**)** any more.
6 She hasn't been throwing tantrums **(faat-pèihhei** 發脾氣**)** any more today.
7 You don't need to explain **(gáai-sīk** 解釋**)** any more.
8 We don't need to take care of them any more. **(jiugu kéuihdeih** 照顧佢哋**)**

Exercise 16.2

Negate the sentences using the appropriate negative word together with **jyuh** 住 to give the meaning specified.

> Example: **Màaih-dāan lā** 埋單啦   (Don't) pay the bill (yet).
> →   **Mhóu màaih-dāan jyuh (lā)**   (Don't) pay the bill (yet).
>   唔好埋單住(啦)

1 **Sāu-sin lā** 收線啦   (Don't) hang up (yet).
2 **Ngóh dásyun būn ūk**   I'm (not) planning to move house (yet).
     我打算搬屋
3 **Sāu-màaih fūng seun lā**   (Don't) put the letter away (yet).
     收埋封信啦
4 **Ngóhdeih heui dāk ge la**   We can(not) go (yet).
     我哋去得嘅喇
5 **Faht go hohksāang lā**   (Don't) punish the student (yet).
     罰個學生啦
6 **Dá hōi dī láihmaht lā**   (Don't) open the presents (yet).
     打開啲禮物啦
7 **Séuhng chòhng fan-gaau lā**   (Don't) go to bed (yet).
     上床瞓覺啦
8 **Kéuih wán dóu gūng**   She has (not) found a job (yet).
     佢搵到工
9 **Léih yīnggōi fonghei**   You should (not) give up (yet).
     你應該放棄
10 **Ngóh yiu hohk Póutūngwá**   I (don't) need to learn Putonghua (yet).
     我要學普通話

Exercise 16.3

Add a wh-word in its indefinite sense to give the meaning specified.

> Example: **Léih wúih-m̀h-wúih hauhfui a?** Do you regret it (in any way)?
> → **Léih wúih-m̀h-wúih (dím) hauhfui a?**
> 你會唔會後悔呀 → 你會唔會(點)後悔呀?

1 **Ngóh móuh gāp sih** I don't have (much) urgent business.
   我冇急事
2 **Léih gāmyaht yáuh-móuh heui máaih-sung a?** Did you go (anywhere)
   shopping today?
   你今日有冇去買餸呀?
3 **Hói-gwāan m̀h wúih chàh léih ge** 海關唔會查你嘅
   They won't inspect you (much) at the customs.
4 **Yùhgwó léih móuh mahntàih, ngóhdeih yìhgā hóyíh chīm yeuk**
   如果你冇問題, 我哋而家可以簽約
   If you don't have (any) questions, we can sign the contract now.
5 **Lóuhbáan m̀h wúih laauh léih ge** 老闆唔會鬧你嘅
   The boss won't scold you (in any way, much).
6 **Yùhgwó yáuh tàuhsou, hóyíh dá lī go lāmbá** 如果有投訴, 可以打呢個冧把
   If you have (any) complaints, you can dial this number.
7 **Kéuih yáuh-móuh chānchīk hóyíh jiugu kéuih ga?** 佢有冇親戚可以照顧
   佢㗎?
   Does he have (any) relatives who can take care of him?
8 **Yùhgwó léih heui léuih-hàhng, geidāk daai màaih ngóh heui**
   如果你去旅行, 記得帶埋我去
   If you go on holiday (anywhere), remember to take me along with you.
9 **Ngóhdeih móuh chín sái** 我哋冇錢洗
   We don't have (much) money to spend.
10 **Móuh yàhn làih taam ngóh** 冇人嚟探我
   Nobody (much) comes to visit me.

UNIT 17
Questions and answers

Disjunctive questions

Questions of the form 'A not A' are the usual way to ask 'yes/no' questions (see *Basic Cantonese*, Unit 23):

Tóuh-m̀h-tóuh-ngoh a? 肚唔肚餓呀?	Are you hungry?
Léih wán-m̀h-wán dóu kéuih a? 你搵唔搵到佢呀?	Did you find him?

Questions of the form 'A or B?' are formed with **dihng** 定 or **dihnghaih** 定係:

Léih béi yihn-gām dihng chīm-kāat a?
你畀現金定簽卡呀?
Will you pay with cash or credit card (*lit.* sign a card)?
Yáuh yàhn mahn gaugíng yāt go Jūnggwok dihng léuhng go Jūnggwok wóh
有人問究竟一個中國定兩個中國喎
People are asking if there is really one China or two Chinas.

This should not be confused with other conjunctions meaning 'or' which are used in statements but not in questions:

(a) **yāthaih ... yāthaih** 一係 ... 一係 'either ... or'

Ngóhdeih yāthaih làuh hái Hēunggóng yāthaih būn fāan Yīnggwok
我哋一係留喺香港一係搬返英國
Either we stay in Hong Kong, or we move back to England.
Léih yāthaih jihgéi jouh saai kéuih, yāthaih dáng ngóh jouh saai kéuih
你一係自己做晒佢, 一係等我做晒佢
Either you do it all yourself, or let me do it all myself.

(b) **waahkjé ... waahkjé** 或者 ... 或者 'maybe ... or maybe'

Ngóh waahkjé tīngyaht wán léih, waahkjé hauhyaht
我或者聽日搵你, 或者後日

Maybe I'll contact you tomorrow, or maybe the day after.
Ngóh waahkjé jyú-faahn waahkjé chēut heui sihk
我或者煮飯或者出去食
Maybe I'll cook, or maybe I'll go out to eat.

As the examples suggest, **yāthaih** 一係 represents a definitive choice (as in an ultimatum) while **waahkjé** 或者 is more tentative and implies indecision.

Particle questions: mē 咩 and àh 呀

The particles **mē** 咩 and **àh** 呀 turn a statement into a question of a particularly loaded kind; **mē** 咩 indicates surprise that something should be the case ('How can this be true?'):

Gám dōu lám m̀h dóu ge mē?
咁都諗唔到嘅咩?
Couldn't you even think of that?
Lī dī yéh dōu yiu ngóh léih màaih ge mē?
呢啲嘢都要我理埋嘅咩?
You mean I even have to deal with this stuff?

àh 呀 suggests surprise and often an element of disapproval ('If this is true I don't think much of it'):

Gam chín ge douhléih dōu m̀h mìhng àh?
咁淺嘅道理都唔明呀?
Can't you even understand such a simple principle?
Kéuih dou yìhgā dōu m̀h háng yùhnleuhng léih àh?
佢到而家都唔肯原諒你呀?
Is he still unwilling to forgive you even now?

Note that **àh** 呀 appears in 'disguised' forms such as **gàh** 㗎 and **làh** 嗱 as a result of contraction (see Unit 23).
The element of disbelief in such questions can be reinforced by beginning the question with **mtūng** 唔通 'can it be':

Mtūng yiu ngóh jouh saai mē? 唔通要我做晒咩?
Could it be that I have to do it all myself?
Mtūng yiu ngóh jouh saai àh? 唔通要我做晒呀?
Do you mean I have to do it all myself?

Here **mtūng** 唔通 suggests that the proposition is ridiculous. It can also mean 'could it be . . .' in a context of guesswork:

Kéuihdeih jeuigahn sèhngyaht yātchàih; mtūng kéuihdeih paak-gán-tō?
佢哋最近成日一齊, 唔通佢哋拍緊拖?
They're always together these days; could it be that they're dating?

Negative questions

A difficulty here is how to answer questions in the negative using **mē** 咩 and **àh** 呀. The word **haih** 係 literally means 'such is the case' and therefore has the effect of agreeing with the premise of the question:

A: **Léih gāmyaht msái fāan-gūng mē?**
你今日唔使返工咩?

Don't you have to go to work today?

B: **Haih a, msái** 係呀，唔使

No, I don't.

To disagree with the premise, **mhaih** 唔係 ('such is not the case') is used, corresponding to English 'yes' (much to the confusion of English speakers):

A: **Léih gāmyaht msái fāan-gūng mē?**
你今日唔使返工咩?

Don't you have to go to work today?

B: **Mhaih a, yiu** 唔係呀，要

Yes, I do.

The particle **ak** 呃 with its abrupt ending is often used to emphasise the disagreement:

A: **Léih móuh yéh jouh ge mē?**
你冇嘢做嘅咩?

Don't you have any work to do?

B: **Mhaih ak!** 唔係呃!

Yes I do! (Why would you think that?)

The **haih** 係 or **mhaih** 唔係 is often followed by an affirmation which includes the predicate of the original question or elaborates on it:

A: **Léih meih fa hóu jōng àh?**
你未化好妝呀?

Haven't you finished putting on your make-up?

B: **Haih a, juhng yáuh pàaih**
係呀，仲有排

No, I'll be a while yet.

A: **Ngóhdeih móuh saai jí làh?**
我哋冇晒紙嗱?

Haven't we got any paper?

B: **Mhaih ak, juhng yáuh daaih bá**
唔係呃，仲有大把

Yes, we do, we have plenty.

Multiple questions

It is possible to have two or more question words in the same sentence:

Bīngo máaih-jó mātyéh láihmaht a?
邊個買咗乜嘢禮物呀?

Who bought what present?

Confronted with a sick patient, a doctor might ask:

Léih géisìh hái bīndouh sihk-gwo dī mātyéh a? 你幾時喺邊度食過啲乜
嘢呀?
What did you eat where, and when?

The answer might be:

Kàhm-máahn hái jáudim sihk-gwo gāi-faahn; gām jīu hái ūkkéi sihk jūk
琴晚喺酒店食過雞飯; 今朝喺屋企食粥
Last night I had chicken rice at the hotel; this morning I had congee at home.

Such multiple questions are also likely to appear as indirect questions (see Unit 21):

Ngóh m̀h jī bīngo gwaai bīngo 我唔知邊個怪邊個
I don't know who's blaming whom.
Ngóh m̀h geidāk ngóhdeih hái bīndouh jouh-jó dī mātyéh
我唔記得我哋喺邊度做咗啲乜嘢
I don't remember what we did where.

Note the use of **dī** 啲 here to indicate that **mātyéh** 乜嘢 refers to more than one
thing (see Unit 8).

Rhetorical questions

A major function of questions is to make a point, without necessarily expecting
an answer. Each of the question words can be so used:

Bīngo wah ngóh m̀h sihk dāk yīn ga? 邊個話我唔食得煙㗎?
Who says I can't smoke?
Gam hāk, ngóh dím tái dóu a? 咁黑, 我點睇到呀?
How can I see when it's so dark?

bīndouh 邊度 'where' (or simply **bīn** 邊) is especially prone to such rhetorical
uses – even when no actual place is involved:

Ngóh bīndouh máaih dāk héi a? 我邊度買得起呀?
How can I afford (to buy) it?
Bīndouh yáuh yàhn wah léih m̀h leng a? 邊度有人話你唔靚呀?
When (*lit.* where) has anyone said you're not beautiful?
Ngóh bīndouh (or géisìh) yáuh góng-gwo gā yàhn-gūng a?
我邊度(幾時)有講過加人工呀?
When did I say anything about raising salaries?

mātyéh 乜嘢 'what', or its short form **māt** 乜, can be inserted into a word or phrase to make a rhetorical question:

Faat mātyéh pèihhei a?   What are you getting angry about?
發乜嘢脾氣呀?
Juhng góng mātyéh siu a?   What are you still joking about?
仲講乜嘢笑呀?

The form **sái māt** 使乜 'what's the use?' is a rare case of **sái** 使 'need' appearing without its negative prefix:

Sái māt tùhng kéuih gam haakhei a? 使乜同佢咁客氣呀?
What's the use of being so polite with him?

Colloquially, **gwái** 鬼 (see Unit 24) can appear in place of a wh-word in rhetorical questions:

Gwái giu léih gám m̀h síusām àh! 鬼叫你咁唔小心呀!
(*lit.* devil asked you to be so careless)
Serves you right for being so careless!
Gwái m̀h mohng kéuih móuh dāk sīng-jīk 鬼唔望佢冇得升職
Everyone hopes that she doesn't get promoted.
Ngóh chóh gam hauh, tái gwái dóu mē? 我坐咁後, 睇鬼到咩?
How can I see when I'm sitting so far back?

Exercise 17.1

Offer someone a choice of the form 'A or B?'

A: Using **dihng** 定

Example: congee (**jūk** 粥) or rice (**faahn** 飯)
         Léih séung sihk jūk dihng faahn a? 你想食粥定飯呀?
         Do you want to eat congee or rice?

1 working (**jouh** 做) a day shift (**yaht-gāang** 日更) or night shift (**yeh-gāang** 夜更)
2 taking leave (**fong-ga** 放假) this year (**gām-lín** 今年) or next (**chēut-lín** 出年)
3 classical music (**gúdín yāmngohk** 古典音樂) or pop music (**làuhhàhng yāmngohk** 流行音樂)
4 seeing a Chinese (**Jūng-yī** 中醫) or Western doctor (**Sāi-yī** 西醫)
5 staying in a private hospital (**sīga yīyún** 私家醫院) or a public hospital (**gūnglahp yīyún** 公立醫院)

B: Using **yāthaih ... yāthaih** 一係 ... 一係

Example: wearing a raincoat (**jeuk yúhlāu** 著雨褸) or carrying an umbrella
(**daai bá jē** 帶把遮)

→ **Léih yāthaih jeuk yúhlāu yāthaih daai bá jē** 你一係著雨褸一係帶
把遮

6 paying the rent immediately (**jīkhāak gāau-jōu** 即刻交租) or moving out
immediately (**jīkhāak būn jáu** 即刻搬走)
7 studying arts (**màhn-fō** 文科) or studying science (**léih-fō** 理科)
8 going with me (**tùhng ngóh yātchàih heui** 同我一齊去) or going by yourself
(**jihgéi heui** 自己去)
9 hiring a maid (**chéng gūngyàhn** 請工人) to look after the child (**chau-jái**
湊仔) or doing it by yourself (**jihgéi chau** 自己湊)
10 taking early retirement (**tàih jóu teuiyāu** 提早退休) or going part-time
(**jyun 轉 part-time**)

Exercise 17.2

Answer the following negative questions. Give both an affirmative answer
(agreeing with the premise of the question) and a negative one (disagreeing).

Example: **Léih meih wuhn sāam àh?**
你未換衫呀? Haven't you changed (clothes) yet?
Haih a, juhng meih wuhn 係呀, 仲未換 No, I haven't.
Mhaih ak, wuhn-jó ge la 唔係呃, 換咗嘅喇 Yes, I have.

1 **Māt kéuih móuh wah léih jī mē?**
乜佢冇話你知咩?

What, didn't he tell you?

2 **Léih yaht-yaht dōu msái chau-jái gàh?**
你日日都唔使湊仔㗎?

Don't you ever have to
look after your child?

3 **Māt léih móuh heui hōi-wúi mē?**
乜你冇去開會咩?

What, didn't you go to
the meeting?

4 **Chisó móuh saai chijí làh?**
廁所冇晒廁紙嘑?

Isn't there any paper left
in the lavatory?

5 **Léih móuh ngóh sáu-táih dihnwá houhmáh mē?**
你冇我手提電話號碼咩?

Don't you have my
mobile number?

6 **Léih msái dá-dihnwá fāan ūkkéi mē?**
你唔使打電話返屋企咩?

Don't you have to call
home?

7 **Kéuihdeih git-jó-fāan gam loih, juhng meih yáuh
bìhbī àh?**
佢哋結咗婚咁耐, 仲未有**BB**呀?

They have been married
for so long and still don't
have a baby?

8 **Kéuih jek geuk tung-jó gam loih juhng m̀h
háng heui tái yīsāng àh?**
佢隻腳痛咗咁耐仲唔肯去睇醫生呀?

His foot has been hurting
for so long and he still
won't go to see a doctor?

Exercise 17.3

Pose a rhetorical question to suggest the same idea as the negative sentence given. Use a wh-word such as **bīn(douh)** 邊(度), **dím** 點, **géisìh** 幾時, **māt** 乜 or the expletive **gwái** 鬼.

Example: **Yīnggwok móuh doihsyú** 英國冇袋鼠

There are no kangaroos in England.

→ **Yīnggwok bīn(douh) yáuh doihsyú a?** 英國邊(度)有袋鼠呀? or
Yīnggwok dím wúih yáuh doihsyú a? 英國點會有袋鼠呀?

Of course there aren't kangaroos in England.

1 **Ngóh tēng m̀h dóu** 我聽唔到   I cannot hear.
2 **Móuh yàhn bōng kéuih** 冇人幫佢   Nobody helps him.
3 **Ngóh móuh ngāak-gwo léih** 我冇呃過你 I've never cheated you.
4 **Ngóhdeih gāmyaht jouh m̀h saai**   We can't finish today.
   我哋今日做唔晒
5 **Msái kéuih gaau ngóh** 唔使佢教我   I don't need him to teach me.
6 **Léih msái gam hóu sām la** 你唔使咁好心啦 You don't need to be so kind.

UNIT 18
Relative clauses

Relative clauses are essentially a sentence modifying a noun, as in 'the things that you like to eat', where 'that you like to eat' modifies 'the things'. In Cantonese, the relative clause comes before the noun it modifies. There are two ways to form such a relative clause:

(a) With **ge** 嘅 linking the clause to the noun:
   ***Duhk Dākmán ge hohksāang** juhng meih dou*
   讀德文嘅學生仲未到
   The students who study German have not yet arrived.

   ***Léih jyú ge sung** béi ngóhdeih sihk saai la*
   你煮嘅餸畀我哋食晒喇
   The dishes you cooked have been eaten up by us.

These clauses refer to students and dishes in general, rather than to particular individual students or dishes. The use of **ge** 嘅 here is much like using an adjective to modify the noun (see *Basic Cantonese*, Unit 9), and it is useful to compare an attributive adjective with a simple relative clause:

   chūngmìhng ge hohksāang 聰明嘅學生
   intelligent students, students who are intelligent

   chāamgā ge hohksāang 參加嘅學生
   the students (who are) taking part

The constructions with **ge** 嘅 correspond closely to the Mandarin ones with **de** 的 and are especially appropriate in more formal contexts where the grammar of written Chinese is followed.

(b) Using **gó** 嗰 'that' and the appropriate classifier:
   ***Kàhmyaht dou gó fūng seun** hái bīndouh a?*
   琴日到嗰封信喺邊度呀? (classifier: **fūng** 封 for letters)
   Where's the letter that arrived yesterday?

   ***Ngóhdeih seuhng chi tái gó tou hei** ló-gwo jéung ga*
   我哋上次睇嗰套戲攞過獎㗎 (classifier: **tou** 套 for films)
   The film we saw last time had received an award.

Because it includes both **gó** 嗰 meaning 'that' and a classifier, a relative clause of this kind refers to a specific item: 'the ... which ...', not 'any ... which ...'. For more than one item, the plural classifier is used (**gó dī** 嗰啲; see Unit 8):

Yám-chàh gó dī yàhn 飲茶嗰啲人 The people who are having dim sum.

Kàhmyaht yíng gó dī séung　　　　The pictures we took yesterday.
琴日影嗰啲相

This type of relative clause with classifier is relatively colloquial.
Note how the noun itself can be dropped when its identity is clear from the context:

Ngóh haih *kàhmyaht dá-dihnwá làih gó go*
我係琴日打電話嚟嗰個
I'm the one who called yesterday.

***Ngóh séung wán gó dī* haih gám yéung ge**
我想搵嗰啲係咁樣嘅
The ones I'm looking for are like that.

This is a natural extension of the use of a classifier to stand for a noun, as in **lī dī** 呢啲 'these (ones)' (see Unit 8).

Relative clauses and topicalization

Sometimes a relative clause will come after the verb, especially when the relative clause modifies the object of the verb:

Ngóh m̀h sīk tēng *sīnsāang góng gó dī Yīngmán*
我唔識聽先生講嗰啲英文
I don't understand the English the teacher speaks.

Kéuih jūngyi tái *Gāmyùhng sé gó dī móuhhahp síusyut*
佢鍾意睇金庸寫嗰啲武俠小說
She likes to read the martial arts novels written by Jin Yong.

Such sentences tend to become clumsy especially when a further phrase is added after the object:

Léih báai-jó *ngóh gām-jīu máaih gó dī boují* hái bīndouh a?
你擺咗我今朝買嗰啲報紙喺邊度呀?
Where did you put the newspapers I bought this morning?

Ngóh ló-jó *gó yaht hái Gwóngchèuhng máaih gó gihn sāam* heui gōn-sái
我擺咗嗰日喺廣場買嗰件衫去乾洗
I took the blouse I bought the other day in the mall for dry cleaning.

The solution to this problem is to make the object the topic of the sentence and put it first, complete with the relative clause modifying it:

Ngóh gām-jīu máaih gó dī boují, **léih báai-jó hái bīndouh a?**
我今朝買嗰啲報紙, 你擺咗喺邊度呀?
The newspapers I bought this morning, where did you put (them)?

Gó yaht hái Gwóngchèuhng máaih gó gihn sāam, **ngóh ló-jó heui gōn-sái**
嗰日喺廣場買嗰件衫, 我擺咗去乾洗
I took the blouse I bought the other day at the shopping centre for dry cleaning.

As the comma suggests, one can (but need not) pause to catch breath between the topic and the rest of the sentence (on topicalization in general, see Unit 9 and *Basic Cantonese*, Unit 22).

Subject and object relatives

Within the relative clause, the noun being modified may have the role of subject or object:

Jīchìh ngóhdeih ge pàhngyáuh 支持我哋嘅朋友
friends that support us (**pàhngyáuh** 朋友 = subject of **jīchìh** 支持)

ngóhdeih jīchìh ge pàhngyáuh 我哋支持嘅朋友
friends that we support (**pàhngyáuh** 朋友 = object of **jīchìh** 支持)

In addition, one might wish to form relative clauses like 'the friends to whom we lend money' in which 'the friends' are the indirect object of the verb 'lend'. This can be done, but a 'resumptive' pronoun is needed, referring to the following noun:

A-Yīng je chín béi kéuihdeih gó dī tùhngsih **m̀h seun dāk gwo ga**
阿英借錢畀佢哋嗰啲同事唔信得過㗎
(*lit.* Ying lent money to them those colleagues not trustworthy)
The colleagues Ying lent money to are not trustworthy.

Ngóh sung láihmaht béi kéuih gó go gaausauh **haih go mahtléih-hohk-gā**
我送禮物畀佢嗰個教授係個物理學家
(*lit.* I gave gift to him that professor is a physicist)
The professor I gave a present to is a physicist.

Similarly when the noun is the object of a coverb such as **tùhng** 同 (Unit 7):

Ngóh tùhng kéuih yātchàih bātyihp gó go tùhnghohk **jouh-jó gōu-gwūn**
我同佢一齊畢業嗰個同學做咗高官
(*lit.* I with her graduated that classmate has become a senior official)
The classmate I graduated with has become a senior official.

The pronoun is also needed when the noun is an object followed by a complement clause:

Ngóh gin-gwo *kéuih* tiu-móuh gó go tùhngsih gām jīu dá-dihnwá làih
我見過佢跳舞嗰個同事今朝打電話嚟
(*lit.* I saw him dance that colleague this morning called)
The colleague whom I saw dancing called this morning.

Gūngsī gou *kéuih* kwāi hūng gūngfún gó go jīkyùhn chìh-jó-jīk
公司告佢虧空公款嗰個職員辭咗職
(*lit.* the company sued him embezzlement that employee has resigned)
The employee whom the company sued for embezzlement has resigned.

Relative clauses with indefinite words

As we saw in the case of negative sentences (Unit 16), the question words can have an 'indefinite' meaning. A distinct type of relative clause uses the same question words to mean 'whoever', 'whatever' and so on:

Bīngo m̀h ngāam jauh yiu douhhip 邊個唔啱就要道歉
Whoever is in the wrong should apologize.

Mātyéh gáam-ga jauh máaih mātyéh 乜嘢減價就買乜嘢
Whatever is on sale, we'll buy it.

Note the repetition of the question word and the use of **jauh** 就 as in conditional sentences (Unit 20). Similarly with other question words:

Bīn gāan gūngsī chéng ngóh, ngóh jauh heui bīn gāan jouh lō
邊間公司請我，我就去邊間做囉
I'll go to work for whichever company employs me.

Léih séung dím jauh dím lā 你想點就點啦
Do as you like.

Bīndouh yáuh hói-tāan, ngóhdeih jauh heui gódouh wáan
邊度有海灘，我哋就去嗰度玩
We'll go on holiday wherever there's a beach.

Exercise 18.1

Based on the sentence provided, construct a classifier relative clause to modify the italicized noun.

Example: **Gó dī *yàhn* páau-gán bouh**   Those people are jogging.
               嗰啲人跑緊步

→   **Páau-gán bouh gó dī yàhn**   The people who are jogging
               跑緊步嗰啲人

1 **Gó go** *deihcháan gīnggéi* **tàuhsīn dá-dihnwá làih** 嗰個地產經紀頭先打電話嚟
   That estate agent has just called.
2 **Go** *wuihgaisī* **chìh-jó-jīk** 個會計師辭咗職
   The accountant has resigned.
3 **Gó dī** *geijé* **yíng-gán-séung** 嗰啲記者影緊相
   Those reporters are taking pictures.
4 **Jek** *gáu* **sātjūng-jó sāam yaht** 隻狗失蹤咗三日
   The dog went missing for three days.
5 **Dī** *hohksāang* **jouh-gán sahtyihm** 啲學生做緊實驗
   The students are doing experiments.
6 **Go** *behngyàhn* **chēut-jó yún** 個病人出咗院
   The patient has gotten out of the hospital.
7 **Dī** *jyūn-gā* **yātchàih yìhn-gau lī go mahntàih** 啲專家一齊研究呢個問題
   The specialists are studying this problem together.
8 **Go** *pàhngyáuh* **taam-gwo ngóh géi chi** 個朋友探過我幾次
   The friend has visited me a few times.
9 **Ga** *chē* **johng chān jek māau** 架車撞親隻貓
   The car has bumped into a cat.
10 **Go** *yīsāng* **bōng kéuih hōi-dōu** 個醫生幫佢開刀
   The surgeon has performed the operation for him.

Exercise 18.2

Translate these sentences into Cantonese.

1 The company that had lost **(siht-jó** 蝕咗**)** a lot of money went bankrupt.
   (jāp-jó-lāp 執咗笠**)**
2 The man I bumped into **(johng dóu** 撞到**)** yesterday was my boss.
3 The watch **(jek bīu** 隻錶**)** that he wears **(daai-jyuh** 戴住**)** all the time is
   beautiful.
4 The professors that we visited **(taam-gwo** 探過**)** once are Americans.
5 The computer that I'm using is too old. **(gauh** 舊**)**
6 Those few letters that I've written have disappeared. **(mgin-jó** 唔見咗**)**
7 Those Cantonese books that we've bought are expensive. **(gwai** 貴**)**
8 The films that you like to see are too slow. **(maahn** 慢**)**
9 The wine that they've drunk smells nice. **(hóu hēung** 好香**)**
10 The medicine that she takes is effective. **(hóu yáuh-haauh** 好有效**)**

Exercise 18.3

Construct a colloquial relative clause using **gó** 嗰 to replace those given using
ge 嘅:

Example: **Ngóh jā ge chē móuh láahnghei** 我揸嘅車冇冷氣
          The car I drive has no air conditioning.
→   **Ngóh jā gó ga chē móuh láahnghei** 我揸嗰架車冇冷氣

1 **Ngóh tái-hōi ge yīsāng haih Gimkùuh bātyihp ge** 我睇開嘅醫生係劍橋畢業嘅
   The doctor I've been consulting graduated from Cambridge.

2 **Kéuih dī jáiléui duhk ge hohkhaauh sāu hóu gwai hohkfai** 佢啲仔女讀嘅
   學校收好貴學費
   The school his children go to charges expensive fees.

3 **Kéuih jyú ge sung móuh lohk yìhm** 佢煮嘅餸冇落鹽
   The dishes she cooked did not have salt.

4 **Ngóh chéng ge yàhn-haak chyùhnbouh lèih chàih saai** 我請嘅人客全部嚟齊晒
   The guests I invited have all arrived.

5 **Chìh dou ge hohksāang hóyíh chóh hái hauhbihn** 遲到嘅學生可以坐喺後便
   The students who arrived late can sit in the back.

6 **Syūnbou hóu yihpjīk ge gūngsī jeuigahn kòhng sīng** 宣布好業績嘅公司最
   近狂升
   The companies which announced good results have risen in value lately.

7 **Ngāam-ngāam máaih ge gongkàhm yàuh Dākgwok wahn dou** 啱啱買嘅
   鋼琴由德國運到
   The piano we have just bought arrived from Germany.

8 **Go jái waahk ge wá hóyíh sung béi yàhn** 個仔畫嘅畫可以送畀人
   The pictures that my son drew can be given (as gifts) to people.

9 **Lóuhbáan chéng ge beisyū meih chìh dou gwo** 老闆請嘅秘書未遲到過
   The secretary the boss employed has never been late.

10 **Ngóh jūngyi ge síusyut dōsou móuh bouhlihk ge** 我鍾意嘅小說多數冇暴力嘅
   The novels I like usually don't have violence.

†Exercise 18.4

Use a relative clause to combine the sentences provided.

Example: **Léih bōng ngóh máaih gihn sāam; gihn sāam mgin-jó**
   你幫我買件衫; 件衫唔見咗
   You bought a dress for me; the dress has disappeared.

→ **Léih bōng ngóh máaih gó gihn sāam mgin-jó** 你幫我買嗰件衫唔見咗
   The dress you bought for me has disappeared.

1 **Kéuih gei go bāau-gwó béi ngóh; go bāau-gwó chúhng dou līng m̀h héi** 佢
   寄個包裹畀我；個包裹重到拎唔起
   He sent me a parcel; the parcel is so heavy that I can't lift it.

2 **Léih tēuijin go hohksāang; go hohksāang háau-síh chēut-māau** 你推薦個
   學生; 個學生考試出貓
   You recommended the student; the student cheated in the exam.

3 **Léih gaaisiuh go tùhngsih làih gūngsī jouh-yé; go tùhngsih haih ngóh**
   gauh tùhnghohk 你介紹個同事嚟公司做嘢; 個同事係我舊同學
   You introduced a colleague to work in our company; the colleague is an
   old classmate of mine.

4 **Chàhmyaht tái-jó tou hei; tou hei ge jyúgok haih ngóh ge muhng jūng chìhngyàhn** 琴日睇咗套戲; 套戲嘅主角係我嘅夢中情人
I saw a film yesterday; the star of that film is my dream lover.

5 **Go-go jaan go sailouh dākyi; go sailouh haih wahnhyut-yìh** 個個讚個細路得意; 個細路係混血兒
Everyone praises the child as cute; the child is a mixed-race child.

6 **Ngóhdeih syún-jó go leuhtsī jouh yíhyùhn; go leuhtsī m̀h jéun heui Bākgīng** 我哋選咗個律師做議員; 個律師唔准去北京
We elected a lawyer to be a legislator; the lawyer is not allowed to go to Beijing.

7 **Ngóh dehng-jó bún sān syū; bún sān syū yuhng làih jouh chāamháau** 我訂咗本新書; 本新書用嚟做參考
I ordered a new book; the new book is used for reference.

8 **Kéuih wán dóu dī yeuhk; dī yeuhk yiu hūng-tóuh sihk ge** 佢搵到啲藥; 啲藥要空肚食嘅
He found the medicine; the medicine needs to be taken on an empty stomach.

9 **Ngóh sung jek gaaijí béi go léuihjái; go léuihjái haih ngóh meih-fānchāi** 我送隻戒指畀個女仔; 個女仔係我未婚妻
I gave the girl a ring; the girl is my fiancée.

10 **Ngóh mùihmúi tùhng go yīsāng paak-tō; go yīsāng làih sihk-faahn** 我妹妹同個醫生拍拖; 個醫生嚟食飯
My sister is dating a doctor; the doctor is coming to dinner.

UNIT 19
Subordinate clauses

Subordinate clauses as a whole are used less than in English and European languages because other means such as serial verb constructions are used instead, especially in colloquial speech (see below on 'before'/'after', and Unit 11). It is often possible to combine two clauses without the use of conjunctions.

Double conjunctions

A characteristic feature of Chinese syntax is the use of two conjunctions in concert to express the relationship between a main clause and a subordinate one. Such patterns often appear in Chinese speakers' English (as in 'although I haven't met him, *but still I like him'). The main pairs of this kind are:

yānwaih ... sóyíh 因為 ... 所以	because ... therefore
dōng ... gójahnsìh 當 ... 嗰陣時	when ... then
yùhgwó ... jauh 如果 ... 就	if ... then
sēuiyìhn ... daahnhaih 雖然 ... 但係	although ... but
mòuhleuhn ... dōu 無論 ... 都	however ... still

The first conjunction may come either:

(a) Before the subject of the subordinate clause, much as in English:
Yānwaih kéuih behng-jó sóyíh yiu wán yàhn doih kéuih séuhng-tòhng
因為佢病咗所以要搵人代佢上堂
Because he got ill, he has to look for somebody to do substitute teaching.

Sēuiyìhn Luhk Síujé móuh gīngyihm, daahnhaih bíuyihn chēutsīk
雖然陸小姐冇經驗, 但係表現出色
Although Ms Luk had no experience, her performance was outstanding.

(b) After the subject of the clause (or the topic of the sentence):
Kéuih yānwaih behng-jó sóyíh yiu wán yàhn doih kéuih séuhng-tòhng
佢因為病咗所以要搵人代佢上堂
(*lit.* he because got ill, so has to look for someone to do substitute teaching)
Because he got ill, he has to look for somebody to do substitute teaching.

Luhk Síujé sēuiyìhn móuh gīngyihm daahnhaih bíuyihn chēutsīk
陸小姐雖然冇經驗但係表現出色
Although Ms Luk had no experience, her performance was outstanding.

An exceptional pair is **chèuihjó ... jī-ngoih** 除咗 ... 之外, coming at either end of the subordinate clause:

Chèuihjó cheung-gō jī-ngoih, Wòhng Fēi juhng líhng douh chìuh-làuh
除咗唱歌之外，王菲仲領導潮流
Apart from singing, Faye Wong is also a trendsetter.

An alternative word order is to have the subject of the main clause appearing before **chèuihjó** 除咗:

Ngóh chèuihjó léih jī-ngoih, m̀h wúih oi-séuhng kèihtā yàhn
我除咗你之外，唔會愛上其他人
Apart from you, I won't fall in love with any other person.

Reasons

yānwaih ... sóyíh 因為 ... 所以 is the usual pair of conjunctions for stating cause and effect, reasons and consequences:

Yānwaih kéuih gánjēung léih sóyíh gam lāu léih
因為佢緊張你所以咁嬲你
Because he cares about you, (that's why) he's so angry with you.

The point to remember is that the second conjunction **sóyíh** 所以 must be included, otherwise the sentence will sound incomplete (as in **Yānwaih kéuih gánjēung léih, gam lāu léih** 因為佢緊張你，咁嬲你).

The conjunction **wàahngdihm** 橫掂 'since' includes a causal element ('since this happens to be the case anyway ...'). It is typically matched by **bātyùh** 不如 in the following main clause:

Ngòh wàahngdihm yiu jā-chē fāan heui, bātyùh chē màaih léih ā
我橫掂要揸車返去，不如車埋你吖
Since I'm driving back anyway, I might as well give you a lift.

Léih wàahngdihm hái gódouh jouh dāk m̀hōisām, bātyùh làih ngóh douh jouh lā
你橫掂喺嗰度做得唔開心，不如嚟我度做啦？
Since you're not happy working there anyway, why not come to work with me?

geiyìhn 既然 is a more formal conjunction meaning 'since' in a causal sense:

Geiyìhn léih háau m̀h dóu yahp daaih-hohk, bātyùh wán yéh jouh lā
既然你考唔到入大學，不如搵嘢做啦？
Since you didn't get into university, why not look for a job?

Geiyìhn léih m̀h joi oi ngóh, bātyùh fān-sáu lā 既然你唔再愛我, 不如分手啦
Since you don't love me any more, let's split up.

Note that neither **wàahngdihm** 橫掂 nor **geiyìhn** 既然 is used for 'since' in the
sense of time ('ever since . . . happened'), for which see **jihchùhng** 自從 below.

Time clauses

The main conjunctions used to express time relations come at the end of the clause:

. . . **gójahnsìh** 嗰陣時	when, while
. . . **jīchìhn** 之從	before
. . . **jīhauh** 之後	after

gójahnsìh 嗰陣時 (or **gójahnsí** with changed tone), literally '(at) that time',
serves as a conjunction meaning 'when', 'while':

Kéuih behng gójahnsí sau-jó géi bohng 佢病嗰陣時瘦咗幾磅
While she was ill, she lost a few pounds of weight.

Ngóh git-fān gójahnsìh dāk sahpbaat seui 我結婚嗰陣時得十八歲
I was just eighteen when I got married.

This can be shortened to **gójahn** 嗰陣 **(or góján** with changed tone):

Ngóh duhk-syū góján m̀h sīk lám ngóh ge chìhntòuh 我讀書嗰陣唔識諗我嘅前途
While I was studying, I didn't think about my future.

In more formal language, there is also a pair **dōng . . . gójahnsìh** 當 . . . 嗰陣時:

Dōng ngóh jihkmohk gójahnsìh, (jauh) wúih lám héi léih
當我寂寞嗰陣時, (就)會諗起你
When I'm lonely, I think of you.

Another formal alternative, with or without **dōng** 當, is **. . . ge sìh-hauh** 嘅時候
(corresponding to Mandarin **de shíhou** 的時候):

(Dōng) léih hái ngóh sānbīn ge sìh-hauh, ngóh jauh hōisām ge la
(當)你喺我身邊嘅時候, 我就開心嘅喇 (from a film)
When you're at my side, I'm happy.

. . . jīhauh 之後 'after ' and **. . . jīchìhn** 之前 'before' come at the end of the
subordinate clause:

Léih fāan dou ūkkéi jīhauh dá go dihnwá béi ngóh ā
你返到屋企之後打個電話畀我吖
Give me a call after you get home.

Ngóh fāan-gūng jīchìhn yiu fa bun go jūngtàuh jōng
我返工之前要化半個鐘頭妝
Before I get to work, I have to spend half an hour putting on make-up.

Fan-gaau jīchìhn yiu góng gújái 瞓覺之前要講故仔
We have to tell stories before going to sleep.

Here it is common to add an expletive **meih** 未 to emphasize that the event has not yet happened:

Ngóh meih bātyihp jīchìhn yíhgīng yáuh yāt fahn gūng
我未畢業之前已經有一份工
Before graduating, I already had a job.

Notice that the meanings 'before' and 'after' are commonly expressed or implied by a series of verbs (Unit 11), especially in colloquial language. For example, 'after' can be expressed by using **yùhn** 完 'finish' and **hóu** 好 'done' after the first verb:

Léih tái yùhn yīsāng jauh jī haih-mhaih yáuh-jó
你睇完醫生就知係唔係有咗
After seeing the doctor, you'll know if you're pregnant.

Dī sung jyú hóu la; sái sáu sihk-faahn lā
啲餸煮好喇; 洗手食飯啦
The food's ready; wash your hands before eating.

jihchùhng . . . jīhauh 自從 . . . 之後 expresses 'since' in a temporal sense (as opposed to the causal 'since' discussed above)

Jihchùhng kéuih sātyihp jīhauh, sèhng go móuh saai sām-gēi
自從佢失業之後, 成個冇晒心機
Ever since she lost her job, she's been all listless.

Ngóh jihchùhng būn-jó ūk jīhauh, hóu loih móuh fāan làih lī tàuh
我自從搬咗屋之後, 好耐冇返嚟呢頭
Ever since I moved, I haven't come back to this area for a long time.

Purpose clauses

Like sequences of actions, purpose is commonly expressed by serial verbs (Unit 11):

Ngóh yiu wán dī yéhsihk wai māau
我要搵啲嘢食餵貓
I need to find some food to feed the cat.

Alternatively, in more formal language, the coverb **waih-jó** 為咗 'for the sake of' (Unit 11) can introduce a clause:

Waih-jó gáam síu hūnghei wūyíhm, ngóhdeih jeuhn-leuhng m̀h jā-chē
為咗減少空氣污染，我哋盡量唔揸車
In order to reduce air pollution, we avoid driving as much as possible.

Concessive clauses: although

The concessive meaning 'although' is typically expressed by the pair of conjunctions **sēuiyìhn** ... **daahnhaih** 雖然 ... 但係 'although ... but':

Kéuih sēuiyìhn haih go hóu yīsāng, daahnhaih meih bīt bōng dóu léih
佢雖然係個好醫生，但係未必幫到你
Although he's a good doctor, he won't necessarily be able to help you.

The concessive sense can also be conveyed using **juhng** 仲 'still' in the second clause:

Kéuihdeih gam yáuh-chín juhng jyuh fāan gāan gauh ūk
佢哋咁有錢仲住返間舊屋
Although they're so well off, they still live in the old house.

The pair **mòuhleuhn** ... **dōu** 無論 ... 都 'no matter how ...' is used together with an indirect question:

Mòuhleuhn bīngo m̀h ngāam dōu yiu douhhip
無論邊個唔啱都要道歉
Whoever was in the wrong, it's still necessary to apologize.

Mòuhleuhn géi dō chín ngóh dōu háng béi
無論幾多錢我都肯畀
However much money, I'm still willing to pay.

Ngóhdeih mòuhleuhn géi làahn dōu m̀h wúih fonghei
我哋無論幾難都唔會放棄
We won't give up however difficult it is.

Mòuhleuhn yáuh-móuh yàhn fáandeui, jingfú dōu m̀h wúih léih ge la
無論有冇人反對，政府都唔會理嘅喇
The government will not care, whether or not anyone objects.

Notice once again how the English departs from the Cantonese order in which the circumstance comes first and the result second.

Exercise 19.1

Add the missing conjunction:

1 **Sēuiyìhn ngóh hóu jyūnjuhng kéuih, _____ ngóh m̀h tùhngyi kéuih ge táifaat**

雖然我好尊重佢, _____ 我唔同意佢嘅睇法
Although I respect him, I don't agree with his views.

2 **Léih jauhsyun m̀h jūngyi, _____ yiu jaansìhng ge la**
你就算唔鍾意, _____ 要贊成嘅喇
Even though you don't like it, you've got to approve it.

3 **Lohk-tòhng _____, léihdeih yiu gāau gūngfo béi ngóh**
落堂 _____, 你哋要交功課畀我
Before the lesson finishes, you have to turn in the homework to me.

4 **Yàuh yùhn séui _____, dī pèihfū saai dou hùhng saai**
游完水 _____, 啲皮膚曬到紅晒
After swimming, the skin was all burnt red by the sun.

5 **Hah go hohkkèih hōichí _____, ngóh yiu sé yùhn lī bún syū**
下個學期開始 _____, 我要寫完呢本書
Before the beginning of next term, I have to finish writing this book.

6 _____ **géi ngàih-hím, kéuih dōu wúih bōng ngóhdeih ge**
_____ 幾危險, 佢都會幫我哋嘅
However dangerous it is, he'll help us.

7 **Jihchùhng kéuih sīng-jó-jīk _____, hóu síu gin ngóhdeih**
自從佢升咗職 _____, 好少見我哋
Ever since he got promoted, he seldom sees us.

8 _____ **géi sānfú ngóh dōu yiu jouh lohk-heui**
_____ 幾辛苦我都要做落去
However difficult it is, I'll continue to work.

9 _____ **léih fan m̀h jeuhk ge sìh-hauh, jeui hóu tēng-háh yāmngohk**
_____ 你瞓唔著嘅時候, 最好聽下音樂
When you can't fall asleep, it's best to listen to music.

10 _____ **kéuih msíusām, sóyíh dit chān jek jó geuk**
_____ 佢唔小心, 所以跌親隻左腳
Because he's careless, he broke his left foot.

11 **Kéuih git-fān _____, ngóh jouh buhnléung**
佢結婚 _____, 我做伴娘
When she got married, I was the bridesmaid.

12 _____ **léih góng mātyéh, ngóh dōu m̀h seun léih ge la**
_____ 你講乜嘢, 我都唔信你嘅喇
No matter what you say, I won't trust you.

Exercise 19.2

Add suitable conjunctions to connect the two clauses provided:

Example: ***Mòuhleuhn* léih géi lāu *dōu* m̀h yīnggōi lyún faat-pèihhei**
無論你幾嬲都唔應該亂發脾氣
However angry you are, you should not throw tantrums.

1 _____ **kéuihdeih paak-tō** 佢哋拍拖 _____, **sèhngyaht chēut sēung yahp deui** 成日出雙入對
Since they've been dating, they're always going around together.

2 _____ **léih gokdāk jihkmohk** 你覺得寂寞 _____ **léih hóyíh dá-dihnwá béi ngóh** 你可以打電話畀我

When you feel lonely, you can call me.

3 _____ **kéuih m̀h syūfuhk** 佢唔舒服 _____ **yiu chéng ga** 要請假

He had to take leave because he was unwell.

4 **Kéuih hái yīyún** 佢喺醫院 _____ **sau dāk hóu gányiu** 瘦得好緊要

While she was in hospital, she lost a lot of weight.

5 **Kéuih gāan ūk** 佢間屋 _____ **yáuh wihng-chìh** 有泳池 _____,
_____ **yáuh go daaih fāyún** 有個大花園

Apart from having a swimming pool, her house has a big garden.

6 **Ngóhdeih** 我哋 _____ **būn làih līdouh** 搬嚟呢度 _____, **jauh yíh-gīng hóu jūngyi līdouh** 就已經好鍾意呢度

Before we moved here, we already liked this area very much.

7 **Gāan ūk** 間屋 _____ **hóu daaih** 好大 _____ **hóu lyuhn** 好亂

Although the house is big, it's messy.

8 _____ **léih dím deui ngóh, ngóh** 你點對佢, 我 _____ **m̀h wúih gwaai léih** 唔會怪你

No matter how you treat me, I won't blame you.

9 _____ **kéuih teuiyāu** 佢退休 _____, **sèhngyaht chēut heui léuih-hàhng** 成日出去旅行

Since he retired, he has been taking holidays all the time.

10 **Kéuih** 佢 _____ **sei jī faatdaaht** 四肢發達, _____ **tàuhlóuh gáandāan** 頭腦簡單

Although he's well-built, his mind is overly simple.

Exercise 19.3

Match the first and second clauses.

1 **Ngóhdeih sēuiyìhn hóu kùhng**
我哋雖然好窮

2 **Ngóh yānwàih gam oi léih**
我因為咁愛你

3 **Kéuih chèuihjó háu-chòih hóu jī-ngoih**
佢除咗口才好之外

4 **Ngóh gin dóu lī jēung séung góján**
我見到呢張相嗰陣

5 **Léih mòuhleuhn béi géi dō chín**
你無論畀幾多錢

6 **Ngóhdeih wàahngdihm jóu dou**
我哋橫掂早到

7 **Kéuih geiyìhn heung léih douhhip**
佢既然向你道歉

8 **Waih-jó daaihgā ge ōnchyùhn**
為咗大家嘅安全

a **sóyíh sīn gam hahn léih**
所以先咁恨你

b **jauh wúih lám héi léih**
就會諗起你

c **bātyùh jāuwàih hàahng-háh**
不如周圍行下

d **ngóhdeih jeuhn faai lèih-hōi**
我哋盡快離開

e **juhng hóu lengjái**
仲好靚仔

f **ngóh dōu m̀h maaih**
我都唔賣

g **daahnhaih hóu hōisām**
但係好開心

h **léih jauh yīnggōi yùhnleuhng kéuih** 你就應該原諒佢

UNIT 20
Conditional sentences

The key words in Cantonese conditional sentences are **yùhgwó** 如果 'if' and **jauh** 就 'then'. A fully explicit conditional sentence uses both these conjunctions together – just like the clauses we have seen using pairs such as **yānwaih . . . sóyíh** 因為 . . . 所以 'because . . . therefore' (Unit 19):

> **Yùhgwó tīngyaht lohk yúh, yāmngohk-wúi jauh yiu chéuisīu**
> 如果聽日落雨, 音樂會就要取消
> If it rains tomorrow, (then) the concert will have to be cancelled.

However, in colloquial speech, either **yùhgwó** 如果 or **jauh** 就 is often left out:

> **Tīngyaht lohk yúh yāmngohk-wúi jauh yiu chéuisīu** 聽日落雨音樂會就要取消
> (If) it rains tomorrow, then the concert will have to be cancelled.

> **Léih chìh dou ngóhdeih (jauh) m̀h dáng léih ge la** 你遲到我哋(就)唔等你嘅喇
> (If) you're late, we won't wait for you.

> **Yùhgwó yáuh dāk gáan, ngóh m̀h wúih yiu lī go lóuhdauh**
> 如果有得揀, 我唔會要呢個老竇 (from a film)
> If it were up to me, I wouldn't want this father.

> **Ngóh yùhgwó m̀h léih kéuih, móuh yàhn léih kéuih ge la**
> 我如果唔理佢, 冇人理佢嘅喇
> If I don't care about him, nobody will.

Conditional statements can even be made without either conjunction, especially when one or both clauses is in the negative:

> **Léih m̀h tùhng ngóh heui, ngóh m̀h fong-sām** 你唔同我去, 我唔放心
> (If) you don't go with me, I won't be at ease.

> **Léih tóuh-ngoh, sihk-faahn sīn lā** 你肚餓, 食飯先啦
> (If) you're hungry, have your dinner first.

> **Léih m̀h tēng ngóh góng, léih séi ngaahng la** 你唔聽我講, 你死硬喇 (triad film)
> Disobey me, and you've had it.

A conditional sentence can be made more explicit by the addition of **ge wah/ge wá** 嘅話 at the end of the 'if clause (corresponding to **de huà** 的話 in Mandarin):

> **Yùhgwó háau m̀h dóu daaih-hohk ge wah, jauh yiu heui wán gūng**
> 如果考唔到大學嘅話，就要去搵工
> If I don't get into university, I'll go and look for a job.

> **Léih dākhàahn ge wá, hóyíh heui hàahng-háh** 你得閒嘅話，可以去行下
> If you have some free time, you can go and have a walk.

Syntax of conditional sentences

Some general rules of syntax apply to all the conditional constructions described in this unit:

(a) The 'if' clause should normally be placed before the 'then' clause:
> **Yùhgwó tīnhei hóu, ngóhdeih heui Sāandéng tái fūnggíng lo**
> 如果天氣好，我哋去山頂睇風景囉
> If the weather's fine, we'll go to the Peak to see the view.

The main exception is when the 'if' clause is added as an afterthought (see Unit 24):

> **Ngóhdeih heui Sāandéng tái fūnggíng lo, yùhgwó tīnhei hóu (ge wá)**
> 我哋去山頂睇風景囉，如果天氣好(嘅話)
> We'll go to the Peak to see the view, if the weather's fine, that is.

(b) The first conjunction may come either before or after the subject of the 'if' clause:
> **Yùhgwó léih m̀h sīk jouh, dáng ngóh gaau léih ā**
> 如果你唔識做，等我教你吖
> If you don't know how to do it, let me show you.

> or **Léih yùhgwó m̀h sīk jouh, dáng ngóh gaau léih ā** 你如果唔識做，等我教你吖
> If you don't know how to do it, let me show you.

(c) The second conjunction comes after the subject of the clause:
> **Yīgā béi go gēiwuih léih, léih jauh yiu chùhngsān jouh yàhn**
> 而家畀個機會你，就要重新做人
> Now you are given another chance, you should turn over a new leaf.

Conditional meanings

The basic structures introduced above can express a range of conditional meanings, including hypothetical and even counterfactual situations:

> **Yùhgwó ngóh haih léih, ngóh yātdihng m̀h wúih dáng kéuih**
> 如果我係你，我一定唔會等佢
> If I were you, I would definitely not wait for him.

Yùhgwó móuh léih ge jīchìh, ngóh dím wúih yáuh gāmyaht ge sìhngjauh a?
如果冇你嘅支持，我點會有今日嘅成就呀**?**
If it had not been for your support, how would I have been where I am today?

Yùhgwó mhaih go yīsāng hōi-dōu, léih yātjóu jauh wáan yùhn la
如果唔係個醫生開刀，你一早就玩完喇 (from a film)
Had the surgeon not operated, it would have been over for you.

Alternative conditional markers

gáyùh 假如 and **gáchit** 假設 'supposing' contain the word **gá** 假 'false' and are used for hypothetical reasoning:

Gáyùh kéuih góng ge yéh haih jān ge, léih jauh baih la
假如佢講嘅嘢係真嘅，你就弊喇
If what he said is true, you're in trouble.

yeuhkgwó 若果 'if' is a formal conjunction:

Yeuhkgwó léih m̀h jipsauh lī go gin-yíh, hóyíh sèuhngsi kèihtā baahnfaat
若果你唔接受呢個建議，可以嘗試其他辦法
If you don't accept this proposal, you can try other solutions.

There are also particular conjunctions for special types of condition.

Necessary conditions: sīn(ji) 先(至)

The adverb **sīn** 先 expresses conditions meaning 'only ... if', that is necessary conditions, or in mathematical terms, 'iff'. It comes after the subject in the main clause:

Léih gau chín ngóh sīn yáuh hingcheui 你夠錢我先有興趣
I'm only interested if you have enough money.

There are variant forms **sīn** 先, **sīnji** 先至 and **ji** 至, which are to a large extent interchangeable:

Yùhgwó tīnhei hóu sīnji hóyíh heui sīu yéhsihk
如果天氣好先至可以去燒嘢食
We can only go for a barbecue if the weather is fine.

Yuhng ngóhdeih ge wuhháu ji syun haih jīngmìhng ge syúnjaahk
用我哋嘅戶口至算係精明嘅選擇 (from television advertisement)
It only counts as the best choice if you use our accounts.

Notice how the same structure can also mean 'only ... when':

Ngóhdeih gaau-yùhn-syū sīn heui dāk 我哋教完書先去得
We can only go when we've finished teaching.

In all these constructions, the consequent clause, which often comes first in English, comes last in Cantonese. As in the case of serial verbs (Unit 11), it can be observed that the Cantonese syntax reflects the logical order of cause/condition and effect/consequence.

Sufficient conditions: jíyiu 只要

Contrasting with necessary conditions are sufficient conditions, expressed by **jíyiu** 只要 'as long as':

Jíyiu léih yáuh sáu yáuh geuk, msái gēng ngoh séi ge
只要有手有腳，唔使驚餓死嘅 (common saying)
As long as you have hands and feet (to work with), you don't need to worry about starving.

Jíyiu kéuih háng góng geui deui-mjyuh, ngóh jauh wúih yùhnleuhng kéuih
只要肯講句對唔住，我就會原諒佢
As long as he's willing to say he's sorry, I'll forgive him.

Note the use of **jauh** 就 in the main clause, as with **yùhgwó** 如果.

Concessive conditions: jauhsyun 就算

Concessive conditions combine the concessive meaning 'although' and the conditional meaning 'if'. The conjunction **jauhsyun** 就算 'even if' is matched by **dōu** 都 'still' in the main clause (compare other concessive clauses as illustrated in Unit 19):

Léih jauhsyun móuh sìhgaan dōu hóyíh tái-háh
你就算冇時間都可以睇下
You can have a look even if you don't have time.

Jauhsyun léih dím mòhng dōu yīnggōi pùih-háh ūkkéi yàhn
就算你點忙都應該陪下屋企人
However busy you are, you should still spend time with your family.

Léih jauhsyun m̀h waih jihgéi jeuhkséung, dōu waih-háh dī jáiléui jeuhkséung ā
你就算唔為自己著想，都為下啲仔女著想吖
Even if you don't show consideration for yourself, show it to your children.

Note again how the 'if' clause comes first, while in English it often comes last.

Negative conditions: chèuihfēi 除非....

chèuihfēi 除非 'unless' can be used on its own as a conjunction:

Chèuihfēi ngóh hóu kùhng, ngóh m̀h wúih heui gódouh sihk ge
除非我好窮，我唔會去嗰度食嘅
I wouldn't go there to eat unless I was really hard up.

Chèuihfēi léih ga béi ngóh, ngóh m̀h héi-sān ga
除非你嫁畀我，我唔起身㗎 (from a romantic comedy)
I won't get up (off my knees) unless you marry me.

To make the meaning more explicit, **chèuihfēi** 除非 in the subordinate clause is matched in the main clause by **yùhgwó mhaih** 如果唔係 'if not':

Chèuihfēi ngóh hóu kùhng, yùhgwó mhaih ngóh m̀h wúih heui gódouh sihk ge
除非我好窮，如果唔係我唔會去嗰度食嘅
(*lit.* unless I were very poor, if not I would not go there to eat)
I wouldn't go there to eat unless I was really hard up.

Chèuihfēi léih góibin jyúyi, yùhgwó mhaih móuh hēimohng ge la
除非你改變主意，如果唔係冇希望嘅喇
Unless you change your mind, there's no hope.

Chèuihfēi yáuh dahkbiht sih, yùhgwó mhaih ngóhdeih sīngkèih-yāt gin
除非有特別事，如果唔係我哋星期一見
Unless something special happens, we'll see each other on Monday.

yuht ... yuht 愈 ... 愈 the more ... the more

An implicitly conditional construction is formed with **yuht** 愈 in each clause:

Yuht chigīk kéuih yuht jūngyi 愈刺激佢愈鍾意
The more thrilling, the more he likes it.

Yuht yeh yuht méihlaih 愈夜愈美麗 (title of a song)
The darker the night, the more beautiful. ...

Yuht faailohk yuht dohlohk 愈快樂愈墮落 (title of a film)
The happier ... the more decadent.

Jáu yuht yám dāk dō, chìhng-séuih yuht dāi-lohk
酒愈飲得多，情緒愈低落
The more wine you drink, the more depressed you feel.

A related expression, **yuht làih yuht** 愈嚟愈 'more and more' can be used with any adjective:

Yuht làih yuht dō yàhn séuhng-móhng 愈嚟愈多人上網
More and more people get on the Internet.

Síhkēui ge hūnghei yuht làih yuht chā 市區嘅空氣愈嚟愈差
The air quality in urban areas is getting worse and worse.

Exercise 20.1

As they stand, the following sentences can already be understood as implicit conditionals. Add the appropriate conjunctions to make the first clause explicitly a condition for the second.

Example: **Gúsíh daaih dit, ngóh m̀h gau chín máaih ūk**
股市大跌, 我唔夠錢買屋

(If) the stock market crashes, I won't have enough money to buy a house.

→   **Yùhgwó gúsíh daaih dit, ngóh jauh m̀h gau chín máaih ūk**
如果股市大跌, 我就唔夠錢買屋

1   **Léih m̀h hahpgaak, ngóh wúih hóu sātmohng**
你唔合格, 我會好失望
(If) you don't pass, I'll be disappointed.
2   **Léih chóh háidouh, léih wúih syūfuhk dī**
你坐喺度, 你會舒服啲
(If) you sit here, you'll be more comfortable.
3   **Yáuh mātyéh sān líu, gei-jyuh wán ngóh gòhgō**
有乜嘢新料, 記住搵我哥哥
(If) there's some/any new information, remember to get hold of my brother.
4   **Kéuih haih jān pàhngyáuh, kéuih wúih mòuh tiuhgín bōng léih**
佢係真朋友, 佢會無條件幫你
(If) he's a true friend, he'll help you unconditionally.
5   **Léih juhng m̀h sāu-sin, ngóh sāu-sin** 你仲唔收線, 我收線
(If) you still won't hang up, I'll hang up.
6   **Léih bou-gíng, ngóhdeih séi ngaahng** 你報警, 我哋死硬
(If) you call the police, we've had it.
7   **Ngóh m̀h daai ngáahn-géng, yehmáahn tái m̀h dóu louh páai**
我唔帶眼鏡, 夜晚睇唔到路牌
(If) I don't wear glasses, I can't see the road signs in the night.
8   **Léih kàhnlihk dī, yātdihng hóyíh háau dóu hóu hohkhaauh**
你勤力啲, 一定可以考到好學校
(If) you work a bit harder, surely you can get into a good school.

Exercise 20.2

Add the appropriate conjunctions to give the two meanings for the following sentences.

Example:
a   *Yùhgwó* **léih mahn kéuih kéuih** *jauh* **wúih bōng léih** 如果你問佢佢就會幫你
She can help you if you ask her.
b   *Yùhgwó* **léih mahn kéuih kéuih** *sīn* **wúih bōng léih** 如果你問佢佢先會幫你
She can only help you if you ask her.

1a **Go jái _____ faat-pèihhei, _____ m̀h yīnggōi laauh kéuih**

個仔_____發脾氣，_____唔應該鬧佢

Even if your son throws a tantrum, you shouldn't scold him.

b **Go jái _____ faat-pèihhei, _____ m̀h yīnggōi laauh kéuih**

個仔_____發脾氣，_____唔應該鬧佢

Unless your son throws a tantrum, you shouldn't scold him.

2a **_____ yáuh yàhn háng gyūn chín, ngóhdeih _____ yáuh hēimohng**

_____有人肯捐錢，我哋_____有希望

If people are willing to donate funds, we have a chance.

b **_____ yáuh yàhn háng gyūn chín, ngóhdeih _____ yáuh hēimohng**

_____有人肯捐錢，我哋_____有希望

Only if people are willing to donate funds do we have a chance.

3a **Léih _____ m̀h góng-yéh, _____ móuh yàhn wah léih ngá ge**

你_____唔講嘢，_____冇人話你啞嘅

Even if you keep your mouth shut, nobody will say you are dumb.

b **Léih _____ m̀h góng-yéh, _____ móuh yàhn wah léih ngá ge**

你_____唔講嘢，_____冇人話你啞嘅

Unless you keep your mouth shut, nobody will say you are dumb.

4a **_____ dī làuhga bóuchìh pìhngwán, sān láu _____ máaih dāk gwo laak**

_____啲樓價保持平穩，新樓_____買得過嘞

As long as house prices keep stable, it's safe to buy new houses.

b **_____ dī làuhga bóuchìh pìhngwán, sān láu _____ máaih dāk gwo gé**

_____啲樓價保持平穩，新樓_____買得過嘅

If house prices keep stable, it'll be safe to buy new flats.

5a **Léih _____ heung ngóh douhhip, _____ ngóh yíhhauh m̀h chói léih**

你_____向我道歉，_____我以後唔睬你

Unless you apologize to me, I won't have anything more to do with you.

b **Léih _____ heung ngóh douhhip, ngóh yíhhauh _____ m̀h chói léih**

你_____向我道歉，_____我以後唔睬你

Even if you apologize to me, I won't have anything more to do with you.

6a **Léih 你 _____ yāusīk gau 休息夠 _____ wúih hóu fāan 會好返**

As long as you take more rest, you'll get better.

b **Léih 你 _____ yāusīk gau 休息夠_____ wúih hóu fāan 會好返**

You'll only get better if you take more rest.

7a **_____ yáuh sàhnjīk 有神蹟, _____ móuh dāk gau ge la 冇得救嘅喇**

Unless there's a miracle, there's no way out.

b **_____ yáuh sàhnjīk 有神蹟, _____ móuh dāk gau ge la 冇得救嘅喇**

Even if there's a miracle, there's still no way out.

8a **_____ léih tàuh ngóh yāt piu, ngóh _____ hóyíh waih léih fuhkmouh**

_____你投我一票，我_____可以為你服務

I can only serve you if you vote for me.

b **_____ léih tàuh ngóh yāt piu, ngóh _____ hóyíh waih léih fuhkmouh**

_____你投我一票，我_____可以為你服務

I can serve you as long as you vote for me.

Exercise 20.3

Express the following pairs using **yuht làih yuht** 愈嚟愈 and **yuht ... yuht** 愈 ... 愈:

Example: a You're getting more and more forgetful.
　　　　　 b The older you get the more forgetful you become.
　　　　　 a **Léih yuht làih yuht móuh-geisīng** 你愈嚟愈冇記性
　　　　　 b **Léih yuht lóuh yuht móuh-geisīng** 你愈老愈冇記性

1a I get more and more scared. **(gēng 驚)**
　b The more I think about it **(lám 諗)**, the more scared I get.
2a I miss him **(gwa-jyuh kéuih 掛住佢)** more and more.
　b The more I miss him, the more I want to see him.
3a Her daughter gets better and better looking. **(leng 靚)**
　b Her daughter gets better looking the older **(daaih 大)** she gets.
4a I like this song **(jūngyi lī sáu gō 鍾意呢首歌)** more and more.
　b The more I listen to **(tēng 聽)** this song, the more I like it.
5a The matter **(gihn sih 件事)** becomes harder and harder **(làahn 難)** to solve.
　　(gáaikyut 解決)
　b The longer the matter drags on **(tō 拖)**, the harder it is to solve.

UNIT 21
Reported speech

Reported (or indirect) speech is used to relate what another person has said. It is expressed quite straightforwardly, without particular distinctions of tense or mood, but attention should be paid to the use of sentence particles.

Verbs of saying

In reporting speech, **wah** 話 'say' is followed directly by the reported statement: there is no counterpart to 'that'.

> **Ngóh a-gō wah Sīng Hòhng jeui dái** 我阿哥話星航最抵
> My brother says Singapore Airlines is the best value.

Note how the subject of the reported statement can be omitted if the person referred to is already present as the subject of the verb of saying, like 'May' in the following:

> **A-May wah (kéuih) móuh hingcheui** 阿May話(佢)冇興趣
> May said she wasn't interested.

wah 話 is also used following other verbs of saying such as **góng** 講 'speak' and **tàuhsou** 投訴 'complain':

> **Kéuih tùhng ngóh góng wah taai guih** 佢同我講話太劫
> He told me that he was too tired.

> **Kéuih tùhng ngóh tàuhsou wah dī tùhngsih móuh láihmaauh**
> 佢同我投訴話啲同事冇禮貌
> He complained to me (saying) that his colleagues were not polite.

Particles: wo 喎 and wóh 喎

These two sentence particles (see *Basic Cantonese*, Unit 25) play an important role in reported speech. Adding the particle **wo** 喎 flags the item as 'news'.

Boují wah gó tou hei hóu-tái wo 報紙話嗰套戲好睇喎
The paper says that film is good.

Adding the variant **wóh** 喎 shows that what is reported is second-hand information:

A-Sīn wah gó tou hei hóu-tái wóh 阿先話嗰套戲好睇喎
Sin says that film is good.

These particles can also be used without indirect speech. Use of **wo** 喎 then marks the content of the sentence as news, while **wóh** 喎 implies indirect speech:

Kéuih sāang-jó go léui wo! 佢生咗個女喎!	She's had a daughter! (surprisingly)
Kéuih sāang-jó go léui wóh 佢生咗個女喎	She's had a daughter. (reportedly)
Jáu dāk la wo 走得喇喎	We can leave now. (you know)
Jáu dāk la wóh 走得喇喎	We can leave. (according to what someone has said)

There are also explicit phrases to introduce hearsay information, such as **tēng-góng (wah)** 聽講(話), which are typically used together with **wo** or **wóh** 喎:

Tēng-góng (wah) léih sīng-jó jīk wo! 聽講(話)你升咗職喎**!**
I hear you've been promoted!
Tēng-góng (wah) kéuih git-jó-fān wóh 聽講(話)佢結咗婚喎
I hear she's gotten married.

Verbs of thinking

Verbs of thinking, belief etc., work like verbs of speaking, with the content of a person's thoughts being reported like that of speech.

lám 諗	think
sēungseun 相信	believe
yíhwàih 以為	think, believe (mistakenly/falsely or dubiously)

Ngóh lám jeui hóu wán go sīfú 我諗住最好搵個師傅
I think it's best to contact a professional.

Ngóh sēungseun ngóhdeih jouh dāk dóu 我相信我哋做得到
I believe we can manage it.

Léih yíhwàih hóyíh ngāak kéuih mē? 你以為可以呃佢咩?
Did you really think you could cheat him?

Note the distinction between **lám** 諗 and **sēungseun** 相信, on the one hand, and **yíhwàih** 以為, which suggests that the belief is false.

Indirect questions

Reported questions are based straightforwardly on direct questions (see *Basic Cantonese*, Units 23–24), introduced by the verb **mahn** 問 'ask':

Direct question	Indirect question
Léih heui-m̀h-heui ngoihgwok a? 你去唔去外國呀?	**Sailóu mahn léih heui-m̀h-heui ngoihgwok** 細佬問你去唔去外國
Are you going abroad?	Brother asked if you were going abroad.
Léih yáuh-móuh hingcheui a? 你有冇興趣呀?	**Ngóh mahn léih yáuh-móuh hingcheui jē** 我問你有冇興趣啫
Are you interested?	I'm just asking if you're interested.
Ngóhdeih heui bīndouh a? 我哋去邊度呀?	**A-mēi mahn ngóhdeih heui bīndouh** 阿**May**問我哋去邊度
Where are we going?	May asked where we were going.

The particle **a** 呀, which usually accompanies direct questions, can be omitted since the indirect question no longer has the force of a question. Again **wóh** 喎 can be added in its place to stress that the question is a quoted one:

Kéuih mahn léih tùhng bīngo heui gāai wóh 佢問你同邊個去街喎
She asked who you went out with.

Indirect commands

In reporting commands, the verb **giu** 叫 'tell' is the main reporting verb. The pattern used is based on that for imperative sentences (see *Basic Cantonese*, Unit 26):

Imperative	Indirect command
Léihdeih jóu dī làih lā 你哋早啲嚟啦	**Ngóh giu kéuihdeih jóu dī làih** 我叫佢哋早啲嚟
Come a bit earlier.	I told them (to) come earlier.

The particles **ā** 吖 and **lā** 啦, which are characteristic of imperatives, are omitted (since the sentence no longer has the force of an imperative), unless the report is itself a command:

Léih giu kéuihdeih jóu dī làih lā Tell them (to) come earlier.
你叫佢哋早啲嚟啦

Other verbs used are **hyun** 勸 'urge', **mihnglihng** 命令 'order', **gínggou** 警告 'warn' and **gin-yíh** 建議 'suggest':

Ngóh māmìh sèhngyaht hyun ngóh git-fān 我媽味成日勸我結婚
My mother is always urging me to get married.

Yīsāng gin-yíh ngóh jouh dō dī wahnduhng 醫生建議我做多啲運動
The doctor suggests that I take more exercise.

In the case of a negative command, **mhóu** 唔好 'don't' is retained in the reported form:

Imperative	Indirect command
Léih mhóu gam gāp lā! 你唔好咁急啦!	**Yīsāng giu ngóh mhóu gam gāp** 醫生叫我唔好咁急
Don't be in such a hurry!	The doctor told me not to be in such a hurry.
Mhóu tàuhjī taai dō wo! 唔好投資太多喎!	**Kéuih gínggou ngóh mhóu tàuhjī taai dō wóh** 佢警告我唔好投資太多喎
Don't invest too much!	She warned me not to invest too much.
Mhóu gam jóu teuiyāu lā! 唔好咁早退休啦!	**Kéuih hyun ngóh mhóu gam jóu teuiyāu** 佢勸我唔好咁早退休
Don't retire too early!	He urged me not to retire too early.
Mhóu sihk-yīn wo! 唔好食煙喎!	**Lóuhbáan mihnglihng ngóh mhóu sihk-yīn** 老闆命令我唔好食煙
Don't smoke, OK!	The boss ordered me not to smoke.

Exercise 21.1

Report the following statements:

Example: **Lóuhbáan** 老闆 (boss): **tīngyaht yiu hōi-wúi** 聽日要開會
We need to have a meeting tomorrow.
→   **Lóuhbáan wah tīngyaht yiu hōi-wúi (wóh)** 老闆話聽日要開會(喎)
The boss says we need to have a meeting tomorrow.

1 **Mùihmúi** (sister): **ngóh móuh chín la** 妹妹: 我冇錢喇   I'm out of money.

2 **Sīnsāang** (teacher): **léihdeih jáu dāk ga la** 先生: 你哋走得嘅喇   It's all right for you to leave.

3 **Gíngchaat** (police): **ngóhdeih wán-gán
jing-yàhn**
警察: 我哋搵緊證人

We're looking for witnesses.

4 **Leuhtsī** (solicitor): **léih yiu faai dī
chīm-méng**
律師: 你要快啲簽名

You have to sign quickly.

5 **Yīsāng** (doctor): **léih m̀h yīnggōi sihk
tìhm yéh**
醫生: 你唔應該食甜嘢

Don't eat sweet things.

6 **Pòhpó** (grandmother): **kéuihdeih m̀h
sīk louh fāan ūkkéi**
婆婆: 佢哋唔識路返屋企

They can't find their way home.

7 **A-Yī** (aunt): **ngóh máaih-jó láihmaht
béi léih dī jáiléui**
阿姨: 我買咗禮物畀你啲仔女

I bought some gifts for your
children.

8 **Go léui** (my daughter): **ngóh yiu heui
sāangyaht-wúi**
個女: 我要去生日會

I have to go to a birthday party.

9 **Bōsí** (boss): **gūngsī gām-lín m̀h gā
yàhn-gūng**
波士: 公司今年唔加人工

The company is not raising
salaries this year.

10 **Ngóh taai-táai** (my wife): **gām jīu
yáuh geijé wán léih**
我太太: 今朝有記者搵你

This morning the reporters
were looking for you.

Exercise 21.2

Use an indirect question to report the direct question provided:

Example: **Go sīgēi** 個司機: **Léih jyuh hái bīndouh a?** 你住喺邊度呀?
→ **Go sīgēi mahn ngóh jyuh hái bīndouh wóh** 個司機問我住喺邊度喎

1 **A-mā: Kéuihdeih géisìh bātyihp a?**
阿媽: 佢哋幾時畢業呀?

When do they graduate?

2 **Mìhng-jái: Léih jūng-m̀h-jūngyi tái hei a?**
明仔: 你鍾唔鍾意睇戲呀?

Do you like watching films?

3 **Dī hohksāang: Léih lóuhgūng haih-m̀h-
haih Yīnggwok-yàhn a?**
啲學生: 你老公唔係英國人呀?

Is your husband English?

4 **A-Sīn: Léih séung-m̀h-séung làuh hái
Hēunggóng a?**
阿先: 你想唔想留喺香港呀?

Do you want to stay in Hong
Kong?

5 **A-Dāk: Mātyéh haih léihdeih sìhnggūng ge beikyut a?** What's the secret of your success?
阿德: 乜嘢係你哋成功嘅秘訣呀?

6 **Yīsāng: Dímgáai léih gam gihnhōng gé?** How come you're so healthy?
醫生: 點解你咁健康嘅?

7 **Go beisyū: Léih jouh māt gam hīngfáhn a?** What are you excited about?
個秘書: 你做乜咁興奮呀?

8 **Sī gaausauh: Léih gokdāk bīngo jeui yáuh chìhmjāt a?** Who do you think has the most potential?
施教授: 你覺得邊個最有潛質呀?

9 **Dī chānchīk: Léihdeih dī jáiléui góng Jūngmán dihng Yīngmán a?** Do your children speak Chinese or English?
啲親戚: 你哋啲仔女講中文定英文呀?

10 **Go tùhngsih: Dím sīn hóyíh máaih dóu lī go yúhn-gín a?** How can one buy this software?
個同事: 點先可以買到呢個軟件呀?

Exercise 21.3

Report the imperatives as indirect commands using appropriate verbs such as **giu** 叫 'ask', **hyun** 勸 'urge', **mihnglihng** 命令 'order', and **gin-yíh** 建議 'suggest':

Example: **Lóuhbáan** 老闆 (your boss): **Léih faai dī fāan làih lā** 你快啲返嚟啦
You come back quickly.
→ **Lóuhbáan giu ngóh faai dī fāan làih** 老闆叫我快啲返嚟
My boss asked me to come back quickly.

1 **Ngóh pàhngyáuh** 我朋友 (friend):
Mhóu gam sēungsām lā 唔好咁傷心啦 Don't be so sad.

2 **Sīnsāang** 先生 (teacher):
Léihdeih jīkhāak tìhng bāt lā 你哋即刻停筆啦 Stop writing straight away.

3 **Go tùhngsih** 個同事 (colleague):
Mgōi bōng-sáu ā 唔該幫手吖 Give me a hand, please.

4 **Gíngchaat** 警察 (police):
Léih jīkhāak fong dāi bá chēung 你即刻放低把槍 Put down the gun immediately.

5 **Jyūn-gā** 專家 (experts):
Maahn-máan dáng-háh sīn lā 慢慢等下先啦 Wait patiently.

6 **Yīsāng** 醫生 (doctor):

   Faai dī gaai yīn lā 快啲戒煙啦   Hurry up and give up smoking.

7 **Lóuhpòh** 老婆 (wife):

   Mhóu gam yeh fāan ūkkéi a   Don't come home too late.
   唔好咁夜返屋企呀

8 **Go tùhnghohk** 個同學 (classmate):

   Yiu hóu hóu bóujuhng sāntái a   Look after your health.
   要好好保重身體呀

9 **Go leuhtsī** 個律師 (lawyer):

   Jīkhāak faat fūng leuhtsī seun béi go Serve notice on the tenant
   jōuhaak   immediately.
   即刻發封律師信畀個租客

10 **Ngoh lóuhgūng** 我老公 (my husband):

   Pùih ngóh chēut heui sihk-faahn lā   Come out to dinner with me.
   陪我出去食飯啦

UNIT 22
Cantonese speech conventions

Everyday greetings

One of the first items taught to learners of Cantonese is often **léih hóu ma?** 你好嗎? Unfortunately, this greeting is rarely used and seems to have developed as an awkward equivalent to the English 'How do you do?' A set of conventional greetings is more widely used:

Hóu loih móuh gin wo 好耐冇見喎	Long time no see.
Sihk-jó faahn meih a? 食咗飯未呀?	How's it going? (*lit.* have you eaten yet?)

These are probably used more than the equivalents of Western greetings, such as:

léih hóu 你好	How do you do?	**jóu sàhn** 早晨	good morning
joi gin 再見	goodbye	**jóu táu** 早抖	good night

Especially in Hong Kong Cantonese, the English-derived **hā-lóu** 哈囉 and **bāai-baai** 拜拜 are widely used – the latter much more often than the formal **joi gin** 再見.

Another set of greetings consists of mundane observations about the situation:

(Māt) gam āam a! (乜)咁啱呀!	What a coincidence! (to bump into you)
(Léih) fāan làih làh! (你)返嚟嘑!	You're back!
Fāan-gūng àh? 返工呀?	On your way to work?
Hàahng-gūngsī àh? 行公司呀?	Out shopping, are you?
Máaih-yéh àh? 買嘢呀?	Doing your shopping, are you?

These greetings, which appear redundant to the English speaker, are the social equivalent of observations about the weather (which seem similarly redundant to Chinese speakers).

Greetings for special occasions

Gūnghéi (saai) 恭喜(晒) 'congratulations' is an all-purpose greeting for happy occasions such as births, weddings, graduations and promotions:

Gūnghéi léih, sāang-jó go léui! Jūk kéuih faai gōu jéung daaih, yuht daaih yuht leng 恭喜你，生咗個女! 祝佢快高長大，愈嚟愈靚
Congratulations on having a baby daughter! May she grow up quickly, more and more beautiful.

Gūnghéi saai wo, gam faai jauh sīng-jīk 恭喜晒喎, 咁快就升職
Congratulations on getting your promotion so soon.

Gūnghéi faat chòih 恭喜發財 (*lit.* congratulations, make money)
Happy (Chinese) New Year

Other useful phrases for different occasions include:

Sānlìhn faailohk 新年快樂	Happy New Year
Singdaan faailohk 聖誕快樂	Happy Christmas
Sāangyaht faailohk 生日快樂	Happy birthday
Sānfān faailohk 新婚快樂	Congratulations (to newly-weds)

Note the use of **jūk** 祝 'wish' in the following conventional expressions:

Jūk léih léuihtòuh yuhfaai 祝你旅途愉快	(Wish you) have a pleasant journey.
Jūk léih yāt louh seuhn fūng 祝你一路順風	(Wish you) have a smooth journey (by air or sea).
Jūk léih jóu yaht hōngfuhk 祝你早日康復	(Wish you) get well soon.

Introductions

While the usual classifier to refer to people is **go** 個, as in **lī go yàhn** 呢個人 'this person', the polite classifier **wái** 位 is used to confer respect, as when a person is being introduced:

Lī wái haih Máh gīngléih 呢位係馬經理	This is the manager, Mr Ma.
Chéng gó wái léuihsih séuhng tòih 請嗰位女士上台	May I invite that lady onto the stage.
Yáuh géi wái tùhngsih tàih-yíh gói kèih 有幾位同事提議改期	A few colleagues have suggested changing the date.

gok wái 各位 'everyone' is a polite form of address:

Gok wái gābān, fūnyìhng léihdeih chāamgā gām chi ge yìhntóuwúi
各位嘉賓，歡迎你哋參加今次嘅研討會
Honoured guests, you are all welcome to participate in this seminar.

wái 位 is also used by waiters:

Géi dō wái a? 幾多位呀?	How many are you?
Yám mātyéh chàh a, léuhng wái?	What tea would (the two of) you like?
飲乜嘢酒呀，兩位?	
Mgōi lìbihn ā, gam dō wái	Please come this way (all of you).
唔該呢便吖，咁多位	

Concerning names (**sing** 姓, surname) and professions:

A: **Léih gwai sing a?** 你貴姓呀?　What is your name?
B: **Ngóh sing Máh ge** 我姓馬嘅　My name is Ma.
A: **(Léih) jouh sihng hòhng a?** (你)做盛行呀?
　　(formal)　What is your profession?
　　Léih jouh bīn hòhng a? 你做邊行呀? or
　　Léih jouh mātyéh jīkyihp a? 你做乜嘢職業呀?
B: **Ngóh jouh bóuhím ge** 我做保險嘅　I'm in insurance.

Kinship terms

Kinship terms are widely used within the family as terms of address, in preference to personal names. Use of the appropriate kinship term is a sign of due respect, especially for senior relatives: to call an uncle or grandparent by their first name as in contemporary Western culture is unheard of.

	Elder	*Younger*
sister	**gājē** 家姐	**mùihmúi** 妹妹
brother	**gòhgō** 哥哥	**sailóu** 細佬

Modifiers or numbers are added to distinguish multiple brothers and sisters:

daaih gō 大哥	big brother
sai múi 細妹	little sister
yih gājē 二家姐	second (eldest) sister

For grandparents, aunts, and uncles, the kinship terms distinguish between paternal and maternal relatives. There are also different terms for aunts and uncles based on whether they are older or younger than one's father/mother.

	Paternal	*Maternal*
aunt: older	**gū-mā** 姑媽	**yìh-mā** 姨媽
aunt: younger	**gū-jē** 姑姐	**a-yī** 阿姨
uncle: older	**a-baak** 阿伯	**kau-fú** 舅父
uncle: younger	**a-sūk** 阿叔	**kau-fú** 舅父
grandmother	**a-màh** 阿嬤, **màh-màh** 嫲嫲	**a-pòh** 阿婆, **pòh-pó** 婆婆
grandfather	**a-yèh** 阿爺, **yèh-yé** 爺爺	**a-gūng** 阿公, **gūng-gūng** 公公

Divorcees and exes are referred to as follows:

chìhn-douh làahmyáuh ex-boyfriend **chìhn-chāi** ex-wife
前度男友   前妻

chìhn-douh léuih-yáuh ex-girlfriend **chìhn-fū** ex-husband
前度女友   前夫

Many of these terms can also be used in an extended way to address strangers of an appropriate age.

a-baak 阿伯   sir (for older men)
a-pòh 阿婆   madam (for older women)
sīnsāang 先生   sir
síujé 小姐   miss, madam (for younger women)

Names

The usual format is surname – given name:

Jāu Yeuhn Faat 周潤發   Chow Yun Fat (actor)
Wòhng Fēi 王菲   Faye Wong (pop diva)

The given name usually has two syllables in Hong Kong, but often just one in mainland China.
A few surnames have two syllables:

Sī-tòuh Wàh 司徒華   Szeto Wah (democratic politician)
Āu Yèuhng Wáih Hòuh 歐陽偉豪 Ben Au Yeung (language commentator)

Maiden names are commonly used, as seen in some of the celebrities and distinguished women in Hong Kong. The husband's surname comes first, followed by the woman's maiden name and first name:

Chàhn Fōng Ōn-Sāng   Mrs Anson Chan (née Fong) – The first
陳方安生   Chief Secretary of the Hong Kong Special
             Administrative Region
Fok Jyū Lìhng Líng   Ms Loretta Fok (née Chu) – a former Miss
霍朱玲玲   Hong Kong

These women would be addressed as **Chàhn Táai** 陳太 and **Fok Táai** 霍太. On the other hand, many married women do not go by their husband's surname but are addressed as **síujé** 小姐 or **léuihsih** 女士 as in **Fōng síujé** 方小姐 or **Fōng léuihsih** 方女士 'Ms Fong'. When single syllables, either given names or surnames are used, one of the following is normally added:

(a) The prefix **a-** 阿, together with a change of tone (see Unit 3):

> **Tàahm Wihng Lèuhn** 譚詠麟   → **A-Léun** 阿麟 Alan Tam (singer)
> **Mùih Yihm Fōng** 梅艷芳   → **A-Mūi** 阿梅 Anita Mui (Canto-pop diva)
> **Làhm Jí Chèuhng** 林子祥   → **A-Lēm** 阿林 Alex Lam (singer)

(b) Colloquially, epithets are added to names:

> **Lóuh-Léi** 老李   Old Mr Lee
> **Fèih-Páang** 肥彭   fatty Pang (nickname of **Pàahng Dihng Hōng** 彭定康, Christopher Patten, the last British governor of Hong Kong)

(c) The suffix **jái** 仔 for males and **léui** 女 for females are attached to given names to show familiarity:

> **Wàh-jái** 華仔   Lau Dak Wah (Andy Lau, actor and singer)
> **Ōn-jái** 安仔   Hui Chi On (singer)
> **Màhn-léui** 敏女   Wu Si Man (girl's name)
> **Hàh-léui** 霞女   Lau Lai Ha (girl's name)

Older people may be addressed using **gō** 哥 'elder brother' and **jē** 姐 'elder sister':

> **Faat-gō** 發哥   Chow Yun Faat (actor)
> **Dōu-jē** 嘟姐   Cheng Yu Ling (commonly referred to as Dodo) (actress)

Occupational terms

It is often appropriate to address people by their occupation:

sīgēi 司機	driver (taxi or bus drivers)
sīfú 師傅	craftsmen (implies a certain expertise, such as decorators, electricians, tailors)
lóuhbáan 老闆, **lóuhsai** 老細 or **bōsí** 波士	boss
daaihlóu 大佬	(boss) – also used as an interjection

Some of the more professional terms are used together with surnames, as in
Màh sìfú 馬師傅 for a craftsman named Ma, **Chàhn leuhtsī** 陳律師 for a lawyer
named Chan, **Jēung lóuhsī** 張老師 for a teacher named Cheung etc.

Taboo words

Superstitions live on in China, sometimes branding as taboo certain words
which sound too much like an inauspicious term. The most commonly encountered examples are with numbers, notably **sei** 四 (4), which rhymes with **séi**
死 'to die' (see *Basic Cantonese*, Unit 28). In addition, a number of words are
subject to taboo because they resemble unlucky words:

Taboo word	Substitute auspicious word
hūng láu 空樓 empty flat (as in **hung** 凶 an ominous word associated with hazard and havoc)	**gāt láu** 吉樓
hūng-sām choi 空心菜 water spinach (same reason as above)	**tūng choi** 通菜
fú-gwā 苦瓜 bitter gourd (**fú** 苦 'bitter', as in **sauh-fú** 辛苦 'to suffer')	**lèuhng gwā** 涼瓜
sit 舌 tongue (too close to **siht** 蝕 'to lose money')	**leih** 脷 as in **ngàuh leih** 牛脷 ox tongue
yám gōn 飲乾 drink up	**yám sing** 飲勝 cheers
gōn 乾 'dry' is unwelcome as 'Money is water' (**Séui wàih chòih** 水為財)	

The use of **gāt** 吉 to avoid **hung** 凶 can be extended to **gāt chē** 吉車 (empty
vehicle), **gāt gēi** 吉機 (empty plane) and so on. Estate agents, in particular, are
careful:

gāan ūk gāt-jó géi go yuht The house has been empty for a few months.
間屋吉咗幾個月

Exercise 22.1

Choose a suitable term to address:

1 your boss
2 a plumber to whom you wish to be polite
3 a taxi driver
4 Mrs Wong
5 Chow Yun Faat (a famous actor), you are a fan of his
6 an old woman selling vegetables

Exercise 22.2

Provide a suitable greeting for the following occasions.

> Example: You have just come home from work: **Ngóh fāan làih la!** 我返嚟喇!
> (I'm back!)

1   You bumped into a friend on the aeroplane.
2   a friend's wedding
3   Your friend has given birth to a new baby.
4   a friend's birthday
5   at Christmas
6   A friend is going on holiday.
7   A friend is ill.
8   when somebody proposes a toast
9   Chinese New Year
10   A friend is moving to a new country.

Exercise 22.3

Introduce the following people, starting with **Lī go/wái (haih)** 呢個/位(係) 'This is. . . .':

1   a colleague
2   your doctor
3   your professor
4   a classmate
5   your wife
6   your ex-husband
7   your first son
8   your ex-girlfriend
9   your former student
10   your husband

UNIT 23
Particles and interjections

As a tonal language, Cantonese does not make use of intonation to the extent that English and other European languages do. Some of the typical functions of intonation, such as providing assurance or suggesting scepticism, are taken on by sentence particles. They range from purely grammatical ones to highly meaning-ful ones and from optional to virtually obligatory (like **a** 呀 in some questions).

Using particles appropriately is best learnt from practice and experience. Many are untranslatable, the ideas being expressed in English by intonation patterns and tone of voice rather than words. A coy tone of voice, for example, would be rendered by **jēk** 唧:

Léih máaih-m̀h-máaih béi ngóh jēk? 你買唔買畀我唧?
Will you buy it for me?

Some particles are characteristic of particular types of sentence:

a 呀, which goes with neutral questions (*Basic Cantonese*, Units 23–24)
lā/ā 啦/吖, which accompany imperatives (*Basic Cantonese*, Unit 26)
mē 咩 and **àh** 呀, which form questions (Unit 17)
wo 喎 and **wóh** 喎, which appear in indirect speech (Unit 21)

Evidence and uncertainty

A group of particles suggests something about the status of the information in the sentence – such as how widely known or established it is or where the infor-mation comes from. **lō** 囉 gives a suggestion that what is said should be obvious:

Q: **Léih daaih-hohk duhk géi dō lìhn sīn bātyihp a?** 你大學讀幾多年先畢業呀?
How long does it take to graduate from university?
A: **Sāam lìhn lō** 三年囉
Three years. (of course, everyone knows that)
Q: **Kéuih gám jouh jānhaih móuh léihyàuh ge** 佢咁做真係冇理由嘅
It's unreasonable for him to do this.
A: **Jauh haih lō!** 就係囉!
Yes, of course!

Māmìh 媽咪: **Léih háidouh jouh māt a?** Mum: What are you doing?
你喺度做乜呀?

Go jái 個仔: **Jouh gūngfo lō** 做功課囉　Son: Doing homework, obviously.

lō 囉 is often used together with **maih** 咪 'then', which suggests that what follows is an obvious conclusion:

Léih jouh dāk mhōisām maih wán daih yih fahn gūng lō
你做得唔開心咪搵第二份工囉
If you're not happy in your work, then find another job.

Chèuhng tàuhfaat daai ngáahn-géng gó go maih haih kéuih chìhnchāi lō
長頭髮戴眼鏡嗰個咪係佢前妻囉
The one with long hair and glasses is his ex-wife.

āma 吖嘛 draws attention to something which should be known, typically in response to a question:

A: **Dímgáai gam chìh juhng meih fāan làih a?** 點解咁遲仲未返嚟呀?
How come she's still not back?
B: **Juhng hōi-gán-wúi āma** 仲開緊會吖嘛
Because she's still in the meeting (of course)

Contrast the same response with **gwa** 啩:

B: **Juhng hōi-gán-wúi gwa** 仲開緊會啩　She's still in the meeting, I guess.

gwa 啩 here indicates uncertainty – the sentence contains an element of guesswork:

A: **Léih gú kéuih wúih-m̀h-wúih làih lē** 你估佢會唔會嚟呢
Guess whether she'll come or not.
B: **Wúih gwa** 會啩
I guess she will.

Similarly, a common response is **haih gwa** 係啩 'I guess so', 'I suppose so' or **mhaih gwa** 唔係啩 'I guess not'.
Other common uses of **āma** 吖嘛 include:

• Teaching or reminding people of rules and facts which may or may not be obvious, as when a parent is teaching her child the social expectation that one greets (**giu** 叫) a person by their name:

Léih yiu giu yàhn āma
你要叫人吖嘛
You should greet people, you know.

- To make an excuse, as when a parent tries to explain why the children are so naughty:

Kéuih juhng sai āma. Dím sīk gam dō yéh a?
佢仲細吖嘛。點識咁多嘢呀?
He's still young. How could he know so much?

- To correct a mistake or faulty information, as when one gets on the wrong bus and the bus driver says:

Mhaih sahp houh a, yīnggōi daap yāt houh āma
唔係十號呀, 應該搭一號吖嘛
You should take number 1, not number 10.

Particles and questions

In addition to **a** 呀 in neutral questions, a variety of particles can be added to achieve particular rhetorical effects:

há 吓 and **hó** 呵 invite agreement, much like a question 'tag' in English. **há** 吓 is typically added to instructions ('OK?'):
Léih gei-jyuh daai fūng seun fāan làih a há? 你記住帶封信返嚟呀吓?
Remember to bring the letter back, OK?

Léih yiu síusām jiugu jihgéi a há? 你要小心照顧自己呀吓?
You've got to take care of yourself, OK?

hó 呵 is used to check facts ('isn't that right?')

Gāan ūk gau saai daaih a, hó? 間屋夠晒大呀, 呵?
The big is big enough, huh?

Gaau daaih-hohk géi sānfú ge, hó? 教大學幾辛苦嘅, 呵?
Quite a task to teach at the university, isn't it?

Contractions

The particles beginning with the vowel **a** 呀 combine with preceding particles to form contracted syllables:

	+ *a* 呀	+ *āma* 吖嘛	+ *àh* 呀
ge 嘅	**ga** 㗎	**gāma** 㗎嘛	**gàh** 㗎
je/jē 啫	**ja** 咋	**jāma** 喳嘛	**jàh** 咋
la 喇		**lāma** 啦嘛	**làh** 嗱

The effect of the contraction combines that of the two individual particles involved. We can see this clearly by companying the contracted forms with **je** 啫 'only':

(a) **Dāk ńgh go yàhn làih-jó ja, kèihtā yàhn lē?** 得五個人嚟咗咋，其他人呢？
Only five people have come; what about the others?

(b) **Dāk ǹgh go yàhn làih-jó jāma; msái gēng m̀h gau yéhsihk**
得五個人嚟咗喳嘛；唔使驚唔夠嘢食
Only five people have come; there's no need to worry that there won't be enough to eat.

(c) **Dāk ǹgh go yàhn làih-jó jàh! Bīngo bōng ngóh sihk saai dī yéh a?**
得五個人嚟咗咋！邊個幫我食晒啲嘢呀？
(*lit.* fewer than expected, constituting a disappointment)
What, only five people have come! Who'll help me eat all this food?

Version (a) with **je** 啫 and **a** 呀 is neutral, while in version (b), **jāma** 喳嘛 combines the downplaying sense of **je** 啫 and the obvious consequence (suggested by **āma** 吖嘛) that there is nothing to worry about. In version (c), **jàh** 咋 combines the downplaying sense of **je** 啫 and the disapproval or disappointment suggested by **àh** 呀.

Variants of ge 嘅

In addition to the contracted forms **ga** 㗎, **gāma** 㗎嘛 and **gàh** 㗎 as shown above (on **ga** 㗎 see *Basic Cantonese*, Unit 25), the important assertive particle **ge** 嘅 also has the variants **gé** 嘅 and **gá** 㗎. **gé** 嘅 has two main senses:

- Puzzlement about a situation:

  Dímgáai gāan fóng gam lyuhn gé?   How come the room is so messy?
  點解間房咁亂嘅？
  Kéuih dōu m̀h daap ngóh gé   He's not answering me (why not?)
  佢都唔答我嘅

- Reservation about a statement:

  Gám dōu hóu gé 咁都好嘅   That would be fine too, I suppose.
  Kéuih géi yáuh-yìhng gé 佢幾有型嘅   Well, I suppose he's quite stylish....

gá 㗎 suggests a stronger sense of reservation, especially in the sequence **sīn dāk gá** 先得㗎:

  Léih yīnggōi jī gá 你應該知㗎   You ought to know that.
  Léih jouh yéh mhóu gam maahn   Can't you try not to work so slowly?
  sīn dāk gá 你做嘢唔好咁慢先得㗎

Q: **Bātyùh léih heui paak hei lā**
不如你去拍戲啦

Why don't you make a film?

A: **Paak-jó chēut làih yáuh yàhn tái
sīn dāk gá** 拍咗出嚟有人睇先得㗎

Only if there are people to see it
when it's made

Combining particles

Combinations of particles, like contracted forms, combine the meanings and
functions of the individual particles involved. Common combinations include:
ge 嘅 + **la** 啦 (assertion + relevance):

Fūng seun yíhgīng gei-jó chēut heui ge la 封信已經寄咗出去嘅喇
The letter's already been sent out.
Ngóhdeih jauh dou ge la 我哋就到嘅喇
We're almost there.

ge 嘅 + **mē** 咩 (assertion + query):

Jānhaih m̀h béi dāk ngóh jī ge mē? 真係唔畀得我知嘅咩?
Am I really not allowed to know?
Ngóh m̀h yahp dāk làih ge mē? 我唔入得嚟嘅咩?
Can't I come in?
Léih chīsin ge mē? 你黐線嘅咩?
Are you crazy?

One characteristic of such combinations is that a particle preceding another
can be reduced from a full vowel to an unstressed vowel ([ə] or 'schwa'), which
we may write simply as **e**:
la 喇 + **mē** 咩 → **le mē** 呢咩

Léih yíhwàih gám jauh hóyíh ngāak dóu ngóh ge le mē?
你以為咁就可以呃到我嘅呢咩?
Did you actually think you could cheat me by doing this?

Interjections and exclamations

Common interjections include the following:

Hóu yéh! 好嘢!	Great!	**Wa (háai)!** 嘩(㗁)!	Wow!
Aiya! 哎呀!	Oh no!	**Óh** 哦!	Ah-ha!
Séi la/bai la! 死喇/弊喇!	Uh-oh!	**Chē!** 啤!	So what! (belittling)
Yí? 咦?	Hah?		

Hóu yéh, yáuh syut-gōu sihk!
好嘢, 有雪糕食!

Great, we have ice cream (to eat)!

Aiya, sèhng sān sāp saai!
哎呀, 成身濕晒!

Oh no, I'm wet all over!

wa 嘩 expresses surprise or shock:

Wa (háai)! Léih máaih gam dō láihmaht gé! 嘩(嗨)！你買咁多禮物嘅!
Wow, you bought so many gifts!
Wa! Kéuih ga-jó go yīkmaahn fu-hòuh a! 嘩！佢嫁咗個億萬富翁呀!
Wow! She married a billionaire!

yí? 咦? expresses surprise plus an element of puzzlement:

Yí, yùhnlòih dá cho houhmáh 咦, 原來打錯號碼
Huh, I dialled the wrong number.
Yí, māt léih dōu làih-jó àh? 咦, 乜你都嚟咗呀?
Hey, you've come too?

Note the use of **māt** 乜 'what' to indicate surprise or bewilderment.

óh 哦 'ah-ha' is usually lengthened to express realization and an element of surprise:

Óh, yùhnlòih lī go sīnji haih hūngsáu
哦, 原來呢個先至係兇手
Ah-hah, this one is the murderer. (finally realizing the real culprit at the end of the story)
Óh, ngóh jūngyū mìhngbaahk dímgáai léih yiu chìhjīk
哦, 我終於明白點解你要辭職
Oh, I finally understand why you had to resign.

chē 嘲! is disparaging or expresses contempt:

Chē! Léih hóu lēk mē? Haih yàhn dōu sīk lā
嘲！你好叻咩?係人都識啦
Huh! You think you're so clever? Anybody knows that.

chōi 啋 is typically used by women in response to someone's inauspicious remarks:

A: **Kéuih sèhngyaht sihk-yīn; hóu yùhngyih sāang ngàahm ga**
佢成日食煙; 好容易生癌㗎
He always smokes; he could easily get cancer.

B: **Chōi, m̀h hóu lyún āp yéh lā** 啋, 唔好亂噏嘢啦   Don't talk nonsense
or **Chōi gwo léih, daaih gāt leih sih** 啋過你, 大吉利是 (a set expression to neutralize the taboo topic, like 'Touch wood' or 'Let's keep our fingers crossed')

Exercise 23.1

Respond to the question given, using the particle **lō** 囉 or **āma** 吖嘛 for obviousness and **gwa** 啩 where uncertainty is indicated.

1 Q: **Heui Jīmsājéui daap géi dō houh bāsí a?**
   去尖沙咀搭幾多號巴士呀？
   A: **Ngh houh** 五號 _____
   Which bus goes to
   Tsimshatsui?
   The Number 5.

2 Q: **Kéuih dímgáai gam sēungsām a?**
   佢點解咁傷心呀？
   A: **Sāt-lyún** 失戀 _____
   Why is she so sad?

   Probably because she's
   fallen out of love.

3 Q: **Dímgáai kéuih móuh fāan-gūng a?**
   點解佢冇返工呀？
   A: **Heui-jó tái yīsāng** 去咗睇醫生 _____
   Why didn't she go to work?

   Because she went to see the
   doctor.

4 Q: **Léih tàuhfaat dímgáai bin-jó sīk gé?**
   你頭髮點解變咗色嘅？
   A: **Yíhm-jó** 染咗 _____
   How come your hair has
   changed colour?
   Because it's been dyed.

5 Q: **Heui Jīmsājéui daap géi dō houh bāsí a?**
   去尖沙咀搭幾多號巴士呀？
   A: **Yāt houh** 一號 _____
   Which bus goes to
   Tsimshatsui?
   The Number 1, I suppose.

6 Q: **Dímgáai kéuih móuh fāan-gūng a?**
   點解佢冇返工呀？
   A: **Heui-jó tái yīsāng** 去咗睇醫生_____
   Why didn't she go to work?

   I guess she went to see the
   doctor.

7 Q: **Dímgáai gam chìh ga?** 點解咁遲㗎？
   A: **Seuihdouh sāk-chē** 隧道塞車 _____
   Why are you so late?
   The tunnel was jammed, you
   know.

8 Q: **Géi dō houh gāau-jōu a?** 幾多號交租呀？
   A: **Yāt houh** 一號 _____
   On which day do we pay the
   rent?
   The first.

Exercise 23.2

Add the particles **há** 吓 or **hó** 呵 as appropriate:

1 **Léihdeih yiu tēng pòhpó wah, m̀h hóu láu-gái a ___**
   你哋要聽聽婆婆話，唔好扭計呀 ___
   You have to obey grandma. Stop playing up.

2 **Léih màaih-jó dāan ge le ___?**
   你買咗單嘅呢 ___?
   You have paid the bill, right?

3 **Léih juhng meih jáu jyuh a ___?**
   你仲未走住呀 ___?
   You're not leaving yet, right?

4 **Haih ngāam léih sīn hóu góng a ___**
係啱你先好講呀 ___
Say it only if it's right, OK.
5 **Léih dá-jó dihnwá heui ūkkéi la ___?**
你打咗電話去屋企喇 ___?
You called home, right?
6 **Léih mhóu jāuwàih heui, hái ūkkéi yāusīk dō dī lā ___?**
你唔好周圍去，喺屋企休息多啲啦 ___?
Don't go anywhere, just have plenty of rest at home, OK?
7 **Dī chēung sāan saai, douh mùhn só hóu la ___?**
啲窗閂晒，度門鎖好喇 ___?
The windows are all closed and the door locked, right?
8 **Tīngyaht gin lā ___?**
聽日見啦 ___?
See you tomorrow, OK?

Exercise 23.3

Add an appropriate interjection from the following:

wa(háai) 嘩(喺), **baih/séi la** 弊/死喇, **chē** 啤, **chōi** 啋, **óh** 哦, **yí** 咦

Example: ***Baih/Séi la.* mgin-jó tìuh sósìh** 弊/死喇。唔見咗條鎖匙
Oh dear, I've lost my key.

1 ________, **kéuih hóu leng mē?**
________ 佢好靚咩?
She's pretty? (showing contempt)
2 ________, **jauh gau jūng la, juhng meih jouh saai**
________ 就夠鐘喇，仲未做晒
Time's almost up, and I still haven't finished. (damned)
3 ________, **māt kéuih gihn sāam tùhng ngóh yāt yeuhng gé!**
________ 乜佢件衫同我一樣嘅!
How come her dress is the same as mine! (surprised and puzzled)
4 ________, **léih tou fānsā hóu leng a!**
________ 你套婚紗好靚呀!
Your wedding gown is beautiful! (impressed)
5 ________, **gám ge yéh dōu góng dāk chēut gé! Faai dī lēu háu-séui gong gwo a!**
________ 咁嘅嘢都講得出嘅！快啲┌口水再講過呀!
How could you speak of such things! Rinse out your mouth and say it again!
6 ________, **kéuihdeih haih hīngmúi lèihge, m̀h haih léuhng gūngpó**
________ 佢哋係兄妹嚟嘅，唔係兩公婆
I see, they are really brother and sister, not a couple.

UNIT 24
Colloquial syntax

Colloquial spoken Cantonese contains numerous features which would not be found in writing, and which rarely appear in textbooks either. Some of these patterns do not sit well with conventional ideas about Chinese grammar, with its fixed subject-verb-object word order. These deviations deserve mention because they are so commonly heard, at least in informal situations.

The pronoun kéuih 佢

In higher registers, the third person pronoun **kéuih** 佢 is used only to refer to people. In colloquial speech, its use is frequently extended:

- Referring to things rather than people, especially in imperatives:

  Léih sihk màaih kéuih lā! 你食埋佢啦! Eat it up!

- Referring to the object of **jēung** 將 (see Unit 10):

  Ngóhdeih bātyùh jēung dī gauh sāam dám-jó kéuih
  我哋不如將啲舊衫扰咗佢
  Let's get rid of these old clothes.
  (Note that **kéuih** 佢 here can even refer to a plural noun phrase.)

- Referring to nothing at all:

  Yám sing kéuih! 飲勝佢!   Bottoms up, cheers!
  Wah jī kéuih 話知佢   Couldn't care less.

- Reinforcing a noun phrase:

  A-Lìhng kéuih m̀h lōu la 阿玲佢唔撈喇   Ling is leaving. (her job)
  Ngóh tùhng a-Sām kéuih haih tō-yáu   Sam and I are dating.
  我同阿**Sam**佢係拖友

Afterthoughts and dislocations

Speakers have afterthoughts: adding some detail, modification or condition after completing a sentence. Some of these patterns have become so common that they no longer feel like afterthoughts but merely serve as alternative formulations for the same given content, much as in English: 'Pretty confident, she is'. This pattern is termed 'right dislocation' because the right-hand part, after the comma, appears to be out of place. Some of the elements most frequently 'dislocated' include:

- Subject pronouns and noun phrases:

    Séi-jó fó la, ga chē 死咗火喇, 架車   The car's stalled.
    Gām chi daaih-wohk la, léih   (You're) in trouble this time, you are.
    今次大鑊喇, 你

- Modal auxiliaries (see *Basic Cantonese*, Unit 20): these verbs have a particular tendency to appear as afterthoughts, serving to modify the preceding sentence:

    Léihdeih sái sáu a, yiu   You need to wash your hands.
    你哋洗手呀, 要
    Hóu faai fāan làih, yīnggōi   (He) should be back soon.
    好快返嚟, 應該
    Yāt jahn gāan tóuh-ngoh ga,   In a while, you'll be hungry.
    léih wúih 一陣間肚餓㗎, 你會   (mother to son)

    Note how both the subject and the auxiliary are dislocated together here.

- Adverbs, placed at the end of the sentence, serve to evaluate the whole proposition:

    Hóu hāt-yàhn-jāng, jānhaih   Really disgusting, it is.
    好乞人憎, 真係
    Géi yáuh-yisī, dōu 幾有意思, 都   It was quite interesting, actually.
    Ngóhdeih mhóu heui, bātyùh   Let's not go.
    我哋唔好去, 不如
    Yáuh-móuh m̀h mìhng a, juhng?   Is there anything you don't
    有冇唔明呀, 仲**?**   understand, anything else?

- Resultative constructions with **dou** 到 (Unit 14):

    Gáau dou ngóh hóu mángjáng   It made me frustrated.
    搞到我好瘱瘲
    → **hóu mángjáng, gáau dou ngóh**
    好瘱瘲, 搞到我
    or **ngóh hóu mángjáng, gáau dou**
    我好瘱瘲, 搞到

- Subordinate clauses and conditionals: although 'if' and 'because' clauses normally come first in the sentence (see Units 19, 20), it is also possible to add them after the main clause as afterthoughts:

Léih muhn jauh tái-háh boují lā 你悶就睇下報紙啦
If you're bored, read the newspaper for a while.
Léih tái-háh boují lā, muhn jauh 你睇下報紙啦, 悶就
Read the newspaper for a while, if you're bored, that is.

Classifiers

In some slang usages a classifier other than the usual **go** 個 is used for people:

gó tìuh yáu 嗰條友	that guy (colloquial)
léih tìuh jái/léui 你條仔/女	your boyfriend/girlfriend (vulgar)
wuhn gwo gihn 換過件	change one's boyfriend/girlfriend
giu (jek) gāi/aap 叫(隻)雞/鴨	call a prostitute (*lit.* chicken)/gigolo (*lit.* duck)

The effect is to treat human beings as physical entities or animals, with a demeaning effect:

Léih tìuh jái góng-yéh sèhng jek aap gám ga
你條仔講嘢成隻鴨咁㗎
(from a film)
The way your boyfriend talks is just like some gigolo.

This usage is sometimes 'corrected' as in the following example:

Léuihjái haih yāt go-go ge, mhaih yāt tìuh-tìuh ge
女仔係一個個嘅, 唔係一條條嘅
(from a comic film)
Girls are supposed to be referred to by **go** 個 not by **tìuh** 條.

The humour of this line lies in the contrast between the neutral register **go** 個 and the low register, vulgar use of **tìuh** 條 for women. Similarly, nouns formed with **gwái** 鬼 may take the classifier **jek** 隻 as used for animals:

Ngóh ūkkéi yáuh léuhng jek wā-gwái 我屋企有兩隻嘩鬼
There are two noisy devils in my house.

A number of measures are used colloquially for time, money etc.:

yāt pùhn séui 一盤水	ten thou'(sand dollars)
yāt gauh séui 一舊水	one hundred dollars
daaih-lāp-lóu 大粒佬	a 'big shot' (important person)
yāt lāp jūng 一粒鐘	an hour (normally **yāt go jūngtàuh** 一個鐘頭)

Léih jī-m̀h-jī ngóh dáng-jó léih sèhng lāp jūng a?
你知唔知我等咗你成粒鐘呀?
Do you realize I've been waiting for you for a whole flipping hour?
Gāmyaht dī daaih-lāp-lóu làih saai
今日啲大粒佬嚟晒
Today all the big shots were here.

There are also some colloquial verbal classifiers:

dá kéuih géi yéh 打佢幾嘢	hit him a few times (normally **dá kéuih géi háh** 打佢幾下)
dá (yāt) pōu gihng ge 打(一)舖勁嘅	have a good game (**dá-gēi** 打機, to play video games)

The magic of gwái 鬼

One of the most versatile elements in colloquial spoken Cantonese, **gwái** 鬼, gives a native flavour and colour to ordinary daily expressions in the language. From the Cantonese learner's point of view, to master the different properties of **gwái** 鬼 may be difficult without sufficient exposure to authentic input as spoken by ordinary people on the street. Examples are typically absent from textbooks, which follow the prescriptive tradition in providing formal, prestigious examples for learners. The literal meaning of **gwái** 鬼 is 'ghost', 'devil', but it has taken on other meanings which are extensions of the original ones, such as mischievousness, frivolousness, strangeness etc. Chinese people generally have a rich **gwái** 鬼 culture, and Cantonese is no exception: the ghost festival (**gwái-jit** 鬼節) falls on the fourteenth day of the seventh month of the Chinese calendar, which is the Chinese equivalent of Halloween in the West. **Gwái** 鬼 commonly appears:

* As the final element of a compound:

láahn-gwái 懶鬼	a lazy person
móuhdáam-gwái 冇膽鬼	a coward
sēui-gwái 衰鬼	rascal (may be affectionate, referring to someone intimate)

- As the initial element of a nominal compound:

gwáilóu 鬼佬	adult male foreigner	**gwáipòh** 鬼婆	adult female foreigner
gwáijái 鬼仔	child or young male foreigner	**gwáimūi** 鬼妹	child or young female foreigner

In these expressions, **gwái** 鬼 refers to foreigners who have Western features. A common practice is to refer to Westerners as **gwái** 鬼 as opposed to **yàhn** 人 'humans':

Kéuih haih yàhn dihnghaih gwái a?
佢係人定係鬼呀?
Is he Chinese or Western?
Ngóh dī jáiléui go yéung bun yàhn bun gwái
我啲仔女個樣半人半鬼
My children look half Chinese and half Western.
Hóu chói ngóh lóuhbáan gwái-gwái-déi ge
好彩我老闆鬼鬼哋嘅 (from an accountant)
Fortunately, my boss is pretty Westernized.

These terms have lost the 'devilish' connotations and are hardly insulting, though in polite company including foreigners they are avoided, **sāi-yàhn** 西人 (Westerner) and **ngoihgwok-yàhn** 外國人 (foreigner) being used instead.

- With adjective phrases: for emphasis and intensification, **gwái** 鬼 can occur after degree modifiers such as **hóu** 好 'very', **gam** 咁 'so' as an intensifier to modify an adjective:

Gām jīu gam gwái dung gé! 今朝咁鬼凍嘅!   It's so cold this morning!
Dímgáai léih gam gwái yīmjīm ga?   Why are you so choosy?
點解你咁鬼奄尖㗎?

gwái 鬼 can be inserted in the middle of a bisyllabic adjective:

màhfàahn 麻煩	troublesome	→	**màh-gwái-fàahn** 麻鬼煩	really troublesome
sih-daahn 是但	indifferent	→	**sih-gwái-daahn** 是鬼但	It doesn't matter a bit
dō-yùh 多餘	superfluous	→	**dō-gwái-yùh** 多鬼餘	totally unnecessary

- **gwái** 鬼 may come between the verb and aspect marker:

Ga gēi waaih-gwái-jó 架機壞鬼咗   The machine has gone and broken down.
Gūngsī kám-gwái-jyuh dī cháumàhn   The company is covering up
公司冚鬼住啲醜聞   the scandals.

These usages express frustration or annoyance. Although mildly expletive, **gwái** 鬼 is not particularly offensive to native speakers.

- In questions, where **gwái** 鬼 can also occur between **bīn** 邊 and **go** 個 as in **bīn-gwái-go** 邊鬼個 'who on earth' or between **bīn** 邊 and classifier:

Bīn gwái ga chē jong fá ngóh gó ga a? 邊鬼架車撞花我嗰架呀?	Which damned car scratched mine?
Bīn gwái jek sīn wúih sīng a? 邊鬼隻先會升呀?	Which damned (share) will rise?
mātyéh 乜嘢 what → **Māt-gwái-yéh?** 乜鬼嘢?	What on earth? What the hell?
jouh mātyéh 做乜嘢 what for → **Jouh māt-gwái-yéh?** 做乜鬼嘢?	What on earth for?
Léih gáau mát-gwái-yéh a? 你搞乜鬼嘢呀?	What on earth are you doing?
Kéuih jouh mát-gwái-yéh gam hōisām a? 佢做乜鬼嘢咁開心呀?	What on earth is he so happy about?

As the examples show, the effect is to challenge the point made or words used.

- In rhetorical questions (see Unit 17):

Gwái jī mē? 鬼知咩?	How on earth should I know?
Gwái bōng kéuih a 鬼幫佢呀	Only the devil will help him. (i.e. nobody will)

Exercise 24.1

Express the italicized part of the sentence as an 'afterthought'.

Example: *Ngóh wah* **móuh hēimohng la** 我話冇希望喇
→ **Móuh hēimohng la, ngóh wah** 冇希望喇, 我話

1 *Gāan ūk* **maaih-jó meih a?** 間屋賣咗未呀?
Have you sold the house yet?
2 *Bātyùh* **léihdeih yātchàih heui lā?** 不如你哋一齊去啦?
Why don't you go together?
3 **Ngóh chìh dou yānwaih** *Sījísāan Seuihdouh* **sāk-chē a**
我遲到因為獅子山隧道塞車呀
I'm late because the Lion Rock Tunnel was congested.

4 **Ngóh _jānhaih_ béi léih haak séi la**
我真係畀你嚇死喇
I was really scared by you.

5 **Ngóh _jī_ léih yātdihng wúih lám dóu baahnfaat ge**
我知你一定會諗到辦法嘅
I know that you definitely will think of a solution.

6 **Juhng yáuh sìhgaan, _hóyíh_ maahn-máan góng lohk-heui ā**
仲有時間, 可以慢慢講落去吖
There's still time; (you) can go on talking slowly.

7 **Léih _wúih_ tàih jóu teuiyāu mē?** 你會提早退休咩?
You will retire early?

8 **Léih _gei-jyuh_ síusām jā-chē a** 你記住小心揸車呀
Remember to drive carefully.

Exercise 24.2

Add the appropriate colloquial classifier.

Example: **Ngóh jouh-jó sèhng sāam _lāp_ jūng** 我做咗成三粒鐘
I've been working a whole three hours.

1 **Kéuih ___ jái géi chyun wo**
佢 ___ 仔幾寸喎
Her boyfriend is showing
quite an attitude.

2 **Ngóh je-jó géi ___ séui bèi go tùhngsih**
我寄咗幾 ___ 水畀個同事
I lent a few hundred dollars to
a colleague.

3 **Kéuih jeuk dou hóu chíh ___ gāi gám**
佢著到好似 ___ 雞咁
She dresses like a prostitute.

4 **Léih ___ léuih géi yìhng wo**
你 ___ 女幾型喎
Your girlfriend is pretty cool.

5 **Léih gam faai wuhn-jó ___ sān ge**
你咁快換咗 ___ 新嘅
You got yourself a new one
(boyfriend) so soon.

6 **Kéuih lāu dou dá-jó ngóh géi ___**
佢嬲到打咗我幾 ___
He's so angry that he hit me a
few times.

7 **Kéuih ūkkéi yáuh sāam ___ máhlāu-jái**
佢屋企有三 ___ 馬騮仔
She's got three little rascals at
home.

8 **Ngóh tùhng kéuih bōu-jūk bōu-jó géi ___ jūng**
我同佢煲粥幾 ___ 鐘
I've been talking on the phone
with him for a few hours.

Exercise 24.3

Add **gwái** 鬼 to indicate frustration in the following statements and questions.

Example: **Ngóh (gwái) jī mē?** 我(鬼)知咩?   How (on earth) should
I know?

1   **Tou hei hóu muhn** 套戲好悶   The film was pretty (damn) boring.
2   **Bīngo háidouh chóuh a?**   Who (on earth) is making such a
    邊個喺度嘈呀?   racket?
3   **Faisih heui la** 費事去喇   There's no (earthly) point in going.
4   **Ga chē maaih-jó la** 架車賣咗喇   The car's (damn well) been sold.
5   **Léih heui-jó bīndouh a?**   Where (the hell) have you been?
    你去咗邊度呀?
6   **Gam chèuhng-hei ga!** 咁長氣㗎!   He's so long-winded!
7   **Bīngo ga chē jó-jyuh saai a?**   Whose (damned) car is blocking the
    邊個架車阻住晒呀?   way?
8   **Ngóh m̀h lōu la** 我唔撈喇   I'm (damn well) quitting (my job).

UNIT 25
Code-mixing and loanwords

One of the most colourful features of Cantonese is the incorporation of foreign words – chiefly of English origin, but also from Japanese and other sources. Fluent bilinguals such as professional people and students can often be heard mixing Cantonese and English in the course of the same sentence. This typical bilingual behaviour is known as code-mixing. Because it is associated with high levels of education, residence abroad and a cosmopolitan outlook, it has a certain prestige in some circles. One Hong Kong radio station revels in its binguality:

First DJ: Next, we have bilingual news.
Second DJ: Haih a, hóu bilingual a 係呀, 好**bilingual**呀 (yes, very bilingual)

A morning radio show was entitled 'jo good morning sun' in which the English 'good morning' is playfully inserted into Cantonese **jóu sàhn** 早晨 'good morning'.

Readers should be warned that code-mixing as described in this unit is sometimes frowned upon and felt to be 'not Chinese' or somehow a corrupted form of language. One can hardly ignore the phenomenon, however, in describing Cantonese as it is spoken in Hong Kong. Code-mixing is also found wherever individuals or societies are bilingual and is a natural part of their use of language. Apart from its sociological interest, code-mixing is quite systematic; it has its own grammar.

The way code-mixing works is that English words are incorporated as far as possible into the sentence patterns of Cantonese. Consequently, Cantonese grammar is applied to English words, rather than vice versa:

- Aspect markers such as **jó** 咗, **jyuh** 住 and **gán** 緊 are added to English verbs:

Ngóh yíhgīng present-jó 我已經**present**咗	I've already presented.
Kéuih preg-jó géi loih a? 佢**preg**咗幾耐呀?	How long has she been pregnant?
Kéuihdeih yìhgá check-gán 佢哋而家**check**緊	They're just checking.
Dáng kéuih enjoy-háh 等佢**enjoy**下	Let him enjoy it.

169

Ngóh daai go léui heui in-háh
我帶個女去**in**下
I'm taking my daughter to have an interview.
Léih yiu lám baahnfaat keep-jyuh léih lóuhgūng
你要諗辦法**keep**住你老公
You have to think of a way to keep your husband.

- Similarly, English verbs may appear with verbal particles such as **fāan** 返, **yùhn** 完 and **saai** 晒:

  Ngóhdeih ngāam-ngāam shop yùhn fāan lèih 我哋啱啱**shop**完返嚟
  We're just back from shopping.
  Yāt yáuh sīusīk, jīkhāak call fāan ngóh 一有消息，即刻**call**返我
  Call me back as soon as there's any news.
  Kéuih yám-jó dī jáu, sèhng go high saai 佢飲咗啲酒，成個**high**晒
  She drank the wine and got all high.

- An English combination of verb and object can be separated in accordance with Cantonese grammar:

  Gauhlín budget cut-jó hóu dō   Last year's budget was cut a lot.
  舊年**budget cut**咗好多
  Mgōi léih hold jyuh tìuh line sīn   Would you please hold the line
  唔該你**hold**住條**line**先   for a minute?

- English nouns are given an appropriate classifier as in:

  tìuh 條 for 'line' (Cantonese **sin** 線)
  jek 隻 for 'model'
  fahn 份 for 'contract'

- Questions may be formed by reduplicating English verbs and adjectives:

  happy → **hēp-m̀h-hēp-pí? hēp**唔**hēp-pí?**   Are you happy?
  like → **lāi-m̀h-lāikí? lāi**唔**lāikí?**   Do you like (it)?
  delay → **de-m̀h-delay a? de**唔**delay**呀?   Will you delay (it)?
  Gūngsī de-m̀h-delay lī go project a?   Is the company delaying this
  公司**de**唔**delay**呢個**project**呀?   project?

Note that 'like' has been made into two syllables, **lāikí**, while in **hēppí**, the final syllable is in the high rising tone (see below on loanwords).

- The potential constructions with **m̀h** 唔 and particle surround an English verb:

  Ngóh yìhgā check m̀h dóu   I can't check now.
  我而家**check**唔到
  Léih predict m̀h dóu   You can't predict.
  你**predict**唔到

Tīngyaht sīn firm dóu go itin wo 聽日先**firm**到個**itin**喎 (from a travel agent)
I can't confirm the itinerary until tomorrow.

Even English prepositions may appear:
Go sáu-dói around yāt chīn mān dóu 個手袋**around**一千蚊到
The handbag is around a thousand dollars.
Lī go project haih under ngóh go department ge
呢個**project**係**under**我個**department**嘅 (from a civil servant)
This project is under my department.
Lī jek sàhnsīn gú within géi yaht jauh sīng-jó yāt púih
呢隻神仙股**within**幾日就升咗一倍 (from a stockbroker)
This miraculous stock has doubled its value within a few days.

Note that these fill a gap in the sense that the nearest Cantonese equivalents would come after the noun (for example, **géi yaht jíloih** 幾日之內 'within a few days').

Code-mixing as a relief strategy

Up to a point, code-mixing can be a useful strategy for learners who lack the vocabulary they need: just substitute an English word for the missing item, and the result is likely to be understood, at least by fluent bilingual speakers. This works especially well for technical terms; English computer and cyber-related words, for example, are regularly used by professionals and students in their conversation despite the availability of translation equivalents:

IT (Information Technology)	**jīseun fōgeih** 資訊科技
CD/CD-ROM	**(dihnlóuh) gwōngdíp** (電腦)光碟
cyber-classroom	**hēuiyíh gaausāt** 虛擬教室
upload	**seuhng chyùhn** 上存
download	**hah joi** 下載

One of the reasons Cantonese speakers mix is that the Cantonese terms are not well known or are even clumsy. CD-ROM seems simpler than **dihnlóuh gwōngdíp** 電腦光碟.

Loanwords

Although we have generally been writing them in standard English spelling, the English words often undergo some changes to make them sound closer to Cantonese words. The word 'class', for example, may be pronounced **klā-si** or even **kā-sí** in the sense of having class. By this process, the English words eventually become assimilated to Cantonese and become part of the everyday vocabulary, as in the case of words such as **bāsí** 巴士 (**bus**) and **dīksí** 的士 (taxi).

Known as loanwords, these are used by monolingual Cantonese speakers as well as by bilinguals.

Kéuih jeuigahn sīk-jó go lengléui, hóu hēppí 佢最近識咗個靚女, 好**happy**
He recently got to know a pretty girl and is very happy.
tái 睇 show → **tái sōu** 睇騷
show qualification → **sōu kōlí** 騷**kōlí**
Gàmlín hahtīn làuhhàhng lī go colour tùhng sexy look, dáng daaihgā hóyíh sōu-sōu kōlí 今年夏天流行呢個**colour**同**sexy look**, 等大家可以騷騷**kōlí**
This summer this colour and sexy look are in, letting people show off their figures (from a programme on fashion magazines).

If a word ends in a consonant, usually a new syllable with high rising tone is created:

gas → **gēsí**	**sāai gēsí** 嘥**gēsí**	waste one's breath
taste → **tēisí**	**móuh tēisí** 冇**tēisí**	without taste
bus → **bāsí**	**daap bāsí** 搭巴士	catch the bus
size → **sāaisí**	**Jeuk mātyéh sāaisí?** 著乜嘢**sāaisí**?	What size do you wear?
fuse → **fíusí**	**sīu fíusí** 燒**fíusí**	burn the fuse
face → **fēisí**	**móuh saai fēisí** 冇晒**fēisí**	completely lose face
tip(s) → **tīpsí**	**béi tīpsí** 畀貼士	give a tip
fans → **fēnsí**	**Ngóh haih léih ge chīukāp fēnsí** 我係你嘅超級**fēnsí**	I'm your super fan.
fail → **fèihlóu**	**Gām chi yauh fèihlóu àh?** 今次又肥佬呀?	Did you flunk again this time?
pass → **pāsìh**	A: **Léih háau sèhng dím a?** 你考成點呀?	How did the exam go?
	B: **Pāsìh lō** **Pāsìh**囉	Passed.
deuce → **dīusìh**	**Daih sei guhk dīusìh** 第四局**dīusìh**	The fourth game is deuce.

copy this file → **kāp lī go fāilóu kāp**呢個**fāilóu**
print out → **pīn chēut làih pīn**出嚟
short-circuited → **sōt-jó sōt**咗

Japanese words and phrases

As many aspects of Japanese culture have infiltrated Cantonese society, some of the related Japanese expressions have been adopted:

kālāai-ōukēi 卡拉**OK**　　karaoke
sauhsī 壽司　　sushi
wūdūng (mihn) 烏冬**(麵)**　　udon (noodles)

More commonly, Japanese phrases are translated literally using the Cantonese pronunciations for the Japanese Kanji characters:

sān-dāngchèuhng 新登場	new product (*lit.* new arrival)
bītsaat-geih 必殺技	secret lethal weapon (*lit.* sure winning technique)
chō-táiyihm 初體驗	first experience
daaih chēut hyut 大出血	big sale (*lit.* big out blood)
daaih got yáhn 大割印	big sale (*lit.* big cut . . .)
gāan-bā-dē 奸爸爹	cheer on
séjān-jaahp 寫真集	portfolio, series of pictures (sometimes nude)
yàhnhei (gāpsīng) 人氣(急升)	(sudden rise in) popularity

The pattern **yāt juhk** 一族 'one race' refers to a certain category of people:

séuhng-bāan yāt juhk 上班一族	(*lit.* go work one race) working people
keep-fit yāt juhk **keep-fit**一族	the keep-fit crowd
dāan-sān yāt juhk 單身一族	the single crowd
baahn-leng yāt juhk 扮靚一族	beauty queens

Exercise 25.1

Using the English verb as given in the translation, add the appropriate verb and aspect marker or verbal particle:

Example: **Ngóh yíhgīng *present-jó* la** 我已經*present*咗喇 I've already presented

1 **Léih _____ yīsāng meih a?** 你 _____ 醫生未呀?	Have you called the doctor yet?
2 **Faai dī _____ ngāam go mahtmáh lā** 快啲 _____ 啱個密碼啦	Set the code back to the correct one quickly.
3 **Kéuih haih-maih _____ a?** 佢係咪 _____ 呀?	Has he gone mad? (*lit.* Is he short-circuited?)
4 **Jingfú _____ lī go policy** 政府 _____ 呢個**policy**	The government is reviewing the policy.
5 **Ngóh tùhng kéuih _____** 我同佢 _____	I've swapped with him.

6 **Ngóh** _____ **kéuih géi chi**
我 _____ 佢幾次

I've dated him a few times.

7 **Léih jēung cheque yíhgīng** _____
你張**cheque**已經 _____

Your cheque has already
cleared.

8 **Kéuih ngāam-ngāam** _____ **fahn gūng**
我啱啱 _____ 份工

He has just quit his job.

9 **Bātyùh léih** _____ **làih béi ngóh lā?**
不如你 _____ 畀我啦?

Why don't you send it back
to me?

10 **Gūngsī yìhgā** _____ **lī géi jek sān product**
公司而家 _____ 呢隻新**product**

The company is promoting
these new products.

Exercise 25.2

Form questions based on the English verbs and adjectives provided:

    Example: Entertaining:
               Kéuih gokdāk hóu full 佢覺得好**full**   He feels full.
   →   **Kéuih gokdāk full-m̀h-full a?**   Does he feel full?
               佢覺得**full**唔**full**呀?

1 **Kéuih tùhng léih hóu friend (fēn)** 佢同你好**fēn**
   He and you are friendly.
2 **Léih predict dóu ngóh séung dím a?** 你**predict**到我想點呀?
   Can you predict how I want it?
3 **Kéuihdeih jeuigahn hóu busy** 佢哋最近好**busy**
   They've been busy lately.
4 **Lóuhbáan invite dī client heui dá golf** 老闆**invite**啲**client**去打**golf**
   The boss invites the clients to play golf.
5 **Ngóh hóu enjoy tái kéuih dī e-mail** 我好**enjoy**睇佢啲**e-mail**
   I enjoy reading his e-mail.
6 **Lóuhbáan tái yùhn go report, hóu impress** 老闆睇完個**report**, 好**impress**
   When the boss finished reading the report he was impressed.
7 **Go exam hóu easy a** 個**exam**好**easy**呀
   The exam was easy.
8 **Kéuih béi fān hóu fair ga** 佢畀分好**fair**㗎
   He's fair in marking.

Exercise 25.3

Identify the English loanwords in the following sentences (transcribed in Yale
romanization):

1 **Go fāailóu mgin-jó wo** 個**file**唔見咗喎
2 **Deui hàaih haih gafē-sīk ge** 對鞋係咖啡色嘅

3 **Léih séung-m̀h-séung sihk jēléi a?** 你想唔想食啫喱呀？
4 **Ngóhdeih daap wēnjái heui hóu m̀h hóu a?** 我哋搭van仔去好唔好呀？
5 **Dī sāammàhn-yú maaih saai la** 啲三文魚賣晒喇
6 **Léih ūkkéi géi houh lāmbá a?** 你屋企幾號冧把呀？
7 **Kéuih jíng dī sāléut hóu hóu-meih** 佢整啲沙律好好味
8 **Ngóu lóuhgūng hóu jūngyi sihk Faatgwok jīsí** 我老公好鍾意食法國芝士
9 **Léih máaih-jó yinsō meih a?** 你買咗燕梳未呀？
10 **Ngóh giu-jó jāudáyú-tōng** 我叫咗周打魚湯

KEY TO EXERCISES

Unit 1 Consonants and vowels

Exercise 1.4

1 **làahm-sih**;   2 **go-hói**;   3 **yùh-sāan**;   4 **m̀h gok wuih-yíh**;   5 **óh lāu go léih**;
6 **Gūn Tòhng**;   7 **Góngsāi**;   8 **M̀h Méih-laih**;   9 **Gok Fu-sìhng**;   10 **Làahm-gīng**

Unit 2 Tone contours

Exercise 2.1

1 low rising 23 vs. 33 mid level;   2 low rising 23 vs. 25 high rising;   3 low falling 21 vs. 55 high level;   4 low rising 23 vs. 22 low level;   5 high level 55 vs. 22 low level;   6 mid level 33 vs. 22 low level;   7 high level 55 vs. 25 high rising;   8 high rising 25 vs. 23 low rising

Unit 3 Changed tones

Exercise 3.1

1 **chau-cháu-déi** 臭臭哋 rather smelly;   2 **laahn-láan-déi** 爛爛哋 a bit broken;   3 **waaih-wáai-déi** 壞壞哋 not working very well;   4 **guih-gúi-déi** 劫劫哋 a bit tired;   5 **lyuhn-lyún-déi** 亂亂哋 rather messy;   6 **chèuhng-chéung-déi** 長長哋 rather long;   7 **lèuhng-léung-déi** 涼涼哋 rather cool;   8 **hàhn-hán-déi** 痕痕哋 rather itchy;   9 **làhm-lám-déi** 腍腍哋 rather tender, soft;   10 **lùhng-lúng-déi** 聾聾哋 a bit deaf;   11 **laaht-láat-déi** 辣辣哋 rather spicy hot;   12 **jī-jī-déi** 知知哋 know a little (about something)

Exercise 3.2

1 **gong-tíu**;   2 **hói-méi**;   3 **gauh-lín**;   4 **tói-mín**;   5 **ōnchyùhn-dáai**;   6 **tō-háai**;   7 **goklòk-táu**;   8 **máaih-láu**;   9 **taaiyèuhng ngáahn-géng**;   10 **Hēung-góng-déi**;   11 **sānmán**;   12 **góján**;   13 **gójahn-sí**;   14 **diht lohk déi**;   15 **yáuh**

yāt páai;   16 sān-léung;   17 sān-lóng;   18 sī-dái;   19 dá màhjéuk;   20 boují
tàuhtíu

Exercise 3.3

1 háp;   2 tìuh;   3 díp;   4 bóng;   5 pín;   6 dihp;   7 tíu;   8 hahp;   9 pùhn;   10 pún

Exercise 3.4

1 tīngmāan;   2 pòhpō;   3 séi-ngaahng-pāai;   4 goklōk;   5 lèuih-lēui;
6 móuh   géi   lōi/lói;   7 hēunghá-mūi;   8 mòuh-mōu   gūngjái;   9 ngáahn-
yāp-mōu;   10 sáujī-mēi

Unit 4 Reduplication

Exercise 4.1

1 **Gāan ūk kéih-kéih-léih-léih** 間屋企企理理.   2 **Go léui baahk-baahk-jehng-
jehng** 個女白白淨淨.   3 **Tou hei póu-póu-tūng-tūng** 套戲普普通通.   4 **Ngóhdeih ūkkéi yiht-yiht-laauh-laauh** 我哋屋企熱熱鬧鬧.   5 **Gó gāan hohkhaauh
séi-séi-báan-báan** 嗰間學校死死板板.   6 **Lóuhbáan gāmyaht máng-máng-
jáng-jáng** 老闆今日瘟瘟瘤瘤.   7 **Go dīksí sīgēi chōu-chōu-lóuh-lóuh** 個的士司
機粗粗魯魯.   8 **Kéuih go jái gōu-gōu-daaih-daaih** 佢個仔高高大大.   9 **Ngóh
fahn gūng ōn-ōn-dihng-dihng** 我份工安安定定.   10 **Gó go móhngkàuh mìhngsīng daaih-daaih-jek-jek** 嗰個網球明星大大隻隻.

Exercise 4.2

1 **Kéuih sailóu hàhm-hàhm-wùh-wùh daapying wàahn chín** 佢細佬含含糊糊答
應還錢.   2 **Kéuihdeih gáan-gáan-dāan-dāan bouji sān ūk** 佢哋簡簡單單佈置
新屋.   3 **Kéuih fuhmóuh sān-sān-fú-fú yéuhng daaih kéuih** 佢父母辛辛苦苦養
大佢.   4 **Lī gāan gūngsī jing-jing-sīk-sīk syūnbou pocháan** 呢間公司正正式式
宣布破產.   5 **Ngóh hēimohng léih kàhn-kàhn-lihk-lihk duhk-syū** 我希望你勤
勤力力讀書.   6 **Kéuih hīng-hīng-sūng-sūng gói saai dī gyún** 佢輕輕鬆鬆改晒
啲卷.   7 **Jūk léih seuhn-seuhn-leih-leih ló dóu hohk-wái** 祝你順順利利攞到學
位.   8 **Dáng ngóh chèuhng-chèuhng-sai-sai gáaisīk béi léih tēng** 等我詳詳細細
解釋畀你聽.

Exercise 4.3

1 f;   2 e;   3 g;   4 b;   5 d;   6 a;   7 h;   8 c;   9 j;   10 i

Exercise 4.4

1 **Kéuihdeih chān-chān-maht-maht, yīn-yīn-ngahn-ngahn** 佢哋親親密密，煙煙
韌韌.   2 **Gó go làahmyán sàhn-sàhn-bei-bei, gwái-gwái-syú-syú** 嗰個男人神神

177

秘秘, 鬼鬼鼠鼠. 3 **Ngóh lóuhgūng sìhng-sìhng-saht-saht, táan-táan-baahk-baahk** 我老公誠誠實實, 坦坦白白. 4 **Lī go jokgā sé ge yéh hūng-hūng-duhng-duhng, kèih-kèih-gwaai-gwaai** 呢個作家寫嘅嘢空空洞洞, 奇奇怪怪. 5 **Kéuih go yéung yìhm-yìhm-sūk-sūk, láahng-láahng-ngouh-ngouh** 佢個樣嚴嚴肅肅, 冷冷傲傲. 6 **Gāan ūk gōn-gōn-jehng-jehng, jíng-jíng-chàih-chàih** 間屋乾乾淨淨, 整整齊齊. 7 **Léih go léuih-pàhngyáuh sī-sī-màhn-màhn, daaih-daaih-fōng-fōng** 你個女朋友斯斯文文, 大大方方. 8 **Kéuih gāan seuihfóng syū-syū-fuhk-fuhk, hōi-hōi-yèuhng-yèuhng** 佢間睡房舒舒服服, 開開揚揚. 9 **Léih go beisyū mā-mā-fū-fū, fùh-fùh-lūk-lūk** 你個秘書馬馬虎虎, 符符碌碌. 10 **Ngóh sailóu gú-gú-waahk-waahk, gwái-gwái-máh-máh** 你細佬古古惑惑, 鬼鬼馬馬.

Exercise 4.5

1 i; 2 k; 3 a; 4 f; 5 h; 6 d; 7 m and b; 8 j and l; 9 g and c; 10 e and n

Unit 5 Word formation

Exercise 5.1

1 g; 2 h; 3 j/i; 4 b; 5 a; 6 i; 7 c; 8 d; 9 e; 10 f

Exercise 5.2

1 **yáuh-yiyih** 有意義; 2 **móuh-líu** 冇料; 3 **yáuh-mahntàih** 有問題; 4 **móuh-loih-sihng** 冇耐性; 5 **yáuh-bánmeih** 有品味; 6 **móuh-lèuhngsām** 冇良心; 7 **yáuh-leih** 有利; 8 **móuh-yùhnjāk** 冇原則; 9 **yáuh-haahn** 有限; 10 **móuh-jaakyahm-gám** 冇責任感

Exercise 5.3

1 **Jūng Ngàhn (or Ngán)** 中銀; 2 **Dahk Sáu** 特首; 3 **Máh Hòhng** 馬航; 4 **A Sih** 亞視; 5 **Sāi Seuih** 西隧; 6 **Bāk Daaih** 北大; 7 **Deih Tit** 地鐵; 8 **Góng Dāng** 港燈

Unit 6 Verb-object compounds

Exercise 6.1

1 **faahn/yéh** 飯/嘢; 2 **móuh** 舞; 3 **wá** 畫; 4 **seun** 信; 5 **chín** 錢; 6 **lèuhng** 涼; 7 **hohk** 學; 8 **gái** 偈; 9 **séui** 水; 10 **gō** 歌

Exercise 6.2

1 **jyú-gán-faahn** 煮緊飯; 2 **faat-gán pèihhei** 發緊脾氣; 3 **fong-jó-ga** 放咗假; 4 **duhk-gwo-syū** 讀過書; 5 **hàahng-yùhn-gūngsī** 行完公司; 6 **yám-gwo-jáu** 飲過酒; 7 **háau-gwo-síh** 考過試; 8 **dá-jó-dihnwá** 打咗電話

†Exercise 6.3

1 **Syū kéuih m̀h sīk gaau** 書佢唔識教. 2 **Syúga ngóhdeih ga dōu móuh dāk fong** 暑假我哋假都冇得放. 3 **Kéuih taai-táai jái yauh msái chau, gūng yauh msái fāan** 佢太太仔又唔使湊，工又唔使返. 4 **Jái chìh-jóu dōu yiu sāang** 仔遲早都要生. 5 **Fēigēi yauh m̀h daap, chē yauh m̀h jā** 飛機又唔搭，車又唔揸. 6 **Kéuih sāmchìhng m̀h hóu, faahn yauh m̀h sihk, gaau yauh m̀h fan** 佢心情唔好，飯又唔食，覺又唔瞓. 7 **Léih seun yauh m̀h sé, dihnwá yauh m̀h dá** 你信又唔寫，電話又唔打. 8 **Kéuih jōng yauh m̀h fa, tàuh yauh m̀h chēui** 佢妝又唔化，頭又唔吹.

Unit 7 Adjectives and stative verbs

Exercise 7.1

1 **kéuih go behng** 佢個病 (his illness); 2 **léih dī jáiléui** 你啲仔女 (your children); 3 **gahtját** 甲由 (of cockroaches); 4 **kéuih ge gihnhōng** 佢嘅健康 (her health); 5 **dī lēng-mūi-jái** 啲靚妹仔 (young girls); 6 **bīngo yīsāng** 邊個醫生 (which doctor); 7 **mātyéh** 乜嘢 (what); 8 **ngóh gòhgō** 我哥哥 (my elder brother)

Exercise 7.2

1 **fāan** 返; 2 **gwo** 過; 3 **jó** 咗; 4 **saai** 晒; 5 **màaih** 埋; 6 **jó** 咗; 7 **gwo** 過; 8 **fāan dī** 返啲; 9 **jó** 咗; 10 **fāan saai** 返晒

Exercise 7.3

1 **Ngóh hóu làahn tùhng kéuih hahpjok** 我好難同佢合作. 2 **Kéuih hóu yùhngyih lám dóu daapngon** 佢好容易諗到答案. 3 **Kéuihdeih hóu yùhngyih yèhng-jó lī chèuhng béichoi** 佢哋好容易贏咗呢場比賽. 4 **Lī go yúhn-gín sail-ouhjái hóu làahn yuhng dóu** 呢個軟件細路仔好難用到. 5 **Kéuihdeih hóu yùhngyi béi yàhn ngāak** 佢哋好容易畀人呃. 6 **Chín hóu làahn múhnjūk yāt go yàhn jānjing ge sēuiyiu** 錢好難滿足一個人真正嘅需要. 7 **Yīgā ge tīnhei, go-go dōu hóu yùhngyi sēungfūng** 而家嘅天氣，個個都好容易傷風. 8 **Dī yāmngohk hóu yùhngyi lihng ngóh lám fāan yíhchìhn ge sih** 啲音樂好容易令我諗返以前嘅事. 9 **Léih yíhwàih ngóh hóu yùhngyi yīngsìhng yàhn jouh-yéh àh?** 你以為我好容易應承人做嘢呀? 10 **Lī júng yàhn hóu làahn hái līdouh sāngchyùhn** 呢種人好難喺呢度生存.

Unit 8 Classifiers revisited

Exercise 8.1

1 **gāan séjihlàuh** 間寫字樓; 2 **jēun baahk-jáu** 樽白酒; 3 **tou sāi-jōng** 套西裝; 4 **daahp sān syū/dēui sān syū** 疊新書/堆新書; 5 **dī sósìh** 啲鎖匙/**chāu** 抽

(bunch) **sósìh** 鎖匙; 6 **jēung sānfánjing** 張身份證; 7 **fūng gaaisiuh seun** 份介
紹信; 8 **dī hohksāang/bāan hohksāang** 啲學生/班學生; 9 **ga páau-chē** 架跑
車; 10 **jek lùhnghā** 隻龍蝦

Exercise 8.2

1 **Go-go (hohksāang) dōu jáu-jó** 個個(學生)都走咗. 2 **Tou-tou (hei) dōu hóu
muhn** 套套(戲)都好悶. 3 **Tìuh-tìuh (tàihmuhk) dōu m̀h làahn** 條條(題目)都
唔難. 4 **Ga-ga (gēi) dōu baau saai** 架架(機)都爆晒. 5 **Kéuih bún-bún (syū)
dōu hóu hóu-maaih** 佢本本(書)都好好賣. 6 **Kéuih gihn-gihn (sāam) dōu hóu
gwai** 佢件件(衫)都好貴. 7 **Hahp-hahp (tóng) dōu bāau dāk hóu leng** 盒盒
(糖)都包得好靚. 8 **Ngóhdeih yeuhng-yeuhng (dím-sām) dōu giu-jó** 我哋樣樣
(點心)都叫咗.

Exercise 8.3

1 d; 2 f; 3 b; 4 c; 5 a; 6 e

Unit 9 Topic and focus

Exercise 9.1

A: 1 **Lī bún síusyut dī hohksāang meih tái-gwo** 呢本小說啲學生未睇過. 2 **Go
sai léui kéuih jeui sek** 個細女佢最錫. 3 **Gāan ūk kéuih hóu m̀h sé dāk maaih**
間屋佢好唔捨得賣. 4 **Gúdín yāmngohk ngóh m̀h sīk yānséung** 古典音樂我
唔識欣賞. 5 **Kéuih ūkkéi yàhn ngóh hóu suhk** 佢屋企人我好熟. B: 6 **Ngóh
gāmyaht ge sānmán m̀h dākhàahn tái** 我今日嘅新聞唔得閒睇. 7 **Ngóhdeih
Yahtmán sīk síu-síu** 我哋日文識少少. 8 **Kéuih gongkàhm hohk-jó sāam lìhn**
佢鋼琴學咗三年. 9 **Kéuih gam làahn ge yéh m̀h wúih jouh** 佢咁難嘅嘢唔會
做. 10 **Léih wahnduhng yīnggōi dō dī jouh** 你運動應該多啲做.

Exercise 9.2

1 **Ngóh lìhn jīpiu-bóu dou daai màaih làih** 我連支票簿都帶埋嚟. 2 **Kéuih lìhn
yú dōu m̀h sīk jīng** 佢連魚都唔識蒸. 3 **Kéuihdeih lìhn Chín Séui Wāan dōu
meih heui-gwo** 佢哋連淺水灣都未去過. 4 **Gíngchaat lìhn go yīsāng dōu m̀h
seun** 警察連個醫生都唔信. 5 **Kéuih lìhn ga chē dōu je béi ngóh** 佢連架車都
借畀我. 6 **Ngóh gēng dou lìhn láahnghohn dōu bīu màaih** 我驚到連冷汗都澼
埋. 7 **Kéuih lìhn go gúdúng fājēun dōu yiu maaih màaih** 佢連個古董花樽都
要賣埋. 8 **Ngóh lóuhgūng lìhn Chìuhjāu-wá dōu hohk màaih** 我老公連潮州
話都學埋. 9 **Kéuih ngoh dou lìhn gaakyeh sung dōu sihk màaih** 佢餓到連隔
夜餸都食埋. 10 **Lóuhbáan hāan dou lìhn láahnghei dōu m̀h hōi** 老闆慳到連
冷氣都唔開.

Exercise 9.3

1 **sīn** 先; 2 **sīn** 先; 3 **jauh** 就; 4 **sīn** 先; 5 **jauh** 就; 6 **sīn** 先; 7 **sīn** 先;
8 **jauh** 就

Unit 10 Using jēung 將

Exercise 10.1

1 **Ngóh jēung gūngfo gāau béi sīnsāang** 我將功課交畀先生. 2 **Kéuih jēung go mahtmáh wuhn-jó** 佢將個密碼換咗. 3 **Ngóh jēung go wuhháu chéuisīu-jó** 我將個戶口取消咗. 4 **Ngóh séung jēung fūk wá gwa héi** 我想將幅畫掛起. 5 **Tīn-waih jēung go yahtkèih gói-jó** 天慧將個日期改咗. 6 **Kéuih jūngyū jēung gāan fóng jāp hóu** 佢終於將間房執咗. 7 **Ngóh yiu jēung dī syū ló fāan heui hohkhaauh** 我要將啲書攞返去學校. 8 **Mùihmúi jēung dī fā chaap hái fājēun douh** 妹妹將啲花插喺花樽度. 9 **Kéuih jēung dī seun sāu-màaih saai** 佢將啲信收埋晒. 10 **Lóuhbáan jēung dī chín chyùhn-jó yahp ngàhnhòhng** 老闆將啲錢存咗入銀行.

Exercise 10.2

1 **hóu gōnjehng** 好乾淨; 2 **hóu dō chi** 好多次; 3 **léuhng chi** 兩次; 4 **hóu dyún** 好短; 5 **léuhng yaht** 兩日; 6 **sahp fānjūng** 十分鐘; 7 **yāt chi** 一次; 8 **géi chi** 幾次; 9 **sāam yaht** 三日; 10 **hóu leng** 好靚

Exercise 10.3

1 **(Léih) jēung gihn sāam ló lohk làih ā** (你)將件衫攞落嚟吖. 2 **Ngóhdeih jēung dī laahpsaap dám-jó kéuih lā** 我哋將啲垃圾抌咗佢啦. 3 **(Léih) faai dī jēung dī gyún gói saai kéuih** (你)快啲將啲卷改晒佢. 4 **Jīkhāk jēung go dihnchìh wuhn-jó kéuih** 即刻將啲電池換咗佢. 5 **Faai-faai-cheui-cheui jēung gāan fóng jāp hóu kéuih** 快快脆脆將間房執好佢. 6 **Chan yiht jēung dī Jūng yeuhk yám-jó kéuih** 趁熱將啲中藥飲咗佢. 7 **Jēung go syū bāau fong dāi hái deihhá** 將個書包放低喺地下. 8 **Jeui hóu jēung dī tàuhfaat dihn-jó kéuih** 最好將啲頭髮電咗佢. 9 **Jēung dī wūjōu sāam sái saai kéuih** 將啲污糟衫洗晒佢. 10 **Jēung gāan ūk jōngsāu hóu kéuih** 將間屋裝修好佢.

Unit 11 Serial verbs

Exercise 11.1

1 **bōng** 幫; 2 **yuhng** 用; 3 **bōng** 幫; 4 **wán/yuhng** 搵/用; 5 **yuhng** 用; 6 **doih** 代; 7 **yuhng** 用; 8 **doih** 代

Exercise 11.2

1 **Dáng ngóh bōng léih hōi mùhn lā** 等我幫你開門啦 Let me open the door for you. 2 **Kéuih heung ngóh kàuhfān** 佢向我求婚 He proposed to me. 3 **Dī chānchīk doih kéuih gāau-jōu** 啲親戚代佢交租 The relatives pay the rent on his behalf. 4 **Yīsāng bōng ngóh hōi-dōu sāang-jái** 醫生幫我開刀生仔 The surgeon performed a Caesarean for me. 5 **Gó go hohksāang gān ngóh hohk**

tiu-móuh 嗰個學生跟我學跳舞 That student learns dancing with me. 6 **Lī
jēung hóibou yuhng làih syūnchyùhn gāan sān gūngsī** 呢張海報用嚟宣傳間新
公司 This poster is to publicize the new company.   7 **Fuhmóuh waih-jó jáiléui
bok-mehng jaahn chín** 父母為咗仔女搏命賺錢 Parents strive to earn money
for their children's sake.   8 **Ngóh dī tùhngsih dahng ngóh hōisām** 我啲同事戥
我開心 My colleagues feel happy for me.   9 **Kéuih sèhngyaht deui-jyuh ngóh
góng hàahmsāp siuwá** 佢成日對住我講鹹濕笑話 He always tells dirty jokes to
my face.   10 **Kéuih pùih ngóh tái yaht-lohk** 佢陪我睇日落 He watches the sun-
set with me.

Exercise 11.3

1 **(làih) sóu paakjí** (嚟)數拍子 to count the beat;   2 **(làih) jouh sāléut** (嚟)
做沙律 to make a salad;   3 **(heui) tóuleuhn tìuh tàihmuhk** (去)討論題目 to
discuss the topic;   4 **baahn sáujuhk lèih-fān** 辦手續離婚 to sign the papers
for divorce; 5 **jouh fóngmahn** 做訪問 to do interviews; 6 **(heui) maat go
gongkàhm** (去)抹個鋼琴 to wipe the piano;   7 **jouh gímchàh**做檢查 to have
a check-up;   8 **taam ngóh a-màh** 探我阿嫲 to visit my grandmother;   9 **duhk
yúhyìhnhohk** 讀語言學 to study linguistics;   10 **wán ngóh** 搵我 to find me

Unit 12 Aspect markers

Exercise 12.1

1 **háh** 下; 2 **hōi** 開; 3 **háh** 下; 4 **hōi** 開; 5 **háh** 下; 6 **háh** 下; 7 **hōi**
開; 8 **háh** 下; 9 **hōi** 開; 10 **háh** 下

Exercise 12.2

1 **Léih yiu lihn-háh lī sáu gō** 你要練下呢首歌. 2 **Léih heui mahn-háh lā** 你去問
下啦.   3 **Léih si-háh gihn sāam sīn** 你試下件衫先.   4 **Ngóh yiu lám-háh sīn** 我
要諗下先. 5 **Mgōi léih dáng-háh sīn lā** 唔該你等下先啦. 6 **Ngóhdeih táu-háh
sīn** 我哋抖下先.   7 **Léih màhn-háh dī hēungséui ā** 你聞下啲香水吖. 8 **Faai dī
maat-háh faai mihn lā** 快啲抹下塊面啦.

Exercise 12.3

1 **léuhng yuhng** 兩用; 2 **léuhng gói** 兩改; 3 **góng-háh** 講下; 4 **sihk-háh** 食
下; 5 **léuhng-sé** 兩寫; 6 **léuhng-jeuk** 兩著; 7 **séuhng-háh** 上下; 8 **léuhng-
fan** 兩瞓; 9 **jyuh-háh** 住下; 10 **léuhng-lāai** 兩拉

Exercise 12.4

1 **Kéuih siu héi-séuhng-làih góján, go yéung hóu tìhm** 佢笑起上嚟嗰陣，個樣好
甜. 2 **Ngóh m̀h hóyíh joi ngàaih lohk-heui** 我唔可以再挨落去. 3 **Tīnhei jyun
héi-séuhng-làih, hóu yùhngyih behng** 天氣轉起上嚟，好容易病. 4 **Léihdeih**

joi chòuh lohk-heui, ngóh jauh giu gíngchaat làih 你哋再嘈落去，我就叫警
察嚟. 5 Seui-gúk chàh-héi-seui séuhng-làih, jauh màhfàahn 稅局查起稅上嚟，
就麻煩. 6 Gám yéung aau lohk-heui móuh yuhng 咁樣拗落去冇用. 7 Ngóhdeih kyutdihng m̀h dáng lohk-heui 我哋決定唔等落去. 8 Kéuih yāt chī-héi-
sin séuhng-làih, māt dōu jouh dāk chēut 佢一黐起線上嚟，乜都做得出.

Exercise 12.5

1 Kéuih yauh dit chān 佢又跌親. 2 Ngóh láu chān jek geuk 我扭親隻
腳. 3 Lohk-chān-yúh gāan ūk dōu wúih hóu sāp 落親雨間屋都會好
濕. 4 Ngóh béi yàhn cháai chān 我畀人踩親. 5 Go sailouhjái pūk chān
個細路仔仆親. 6 Kéuih yám-chān-jáu dōu jeui 佢飲親酒都醉. 7 Ngóhdeih béi taaiyèuhng saai chān 我哋畀太陽曬親. 8 Kéuih háau-chān-síh dōu
m̀h hahpgaak 佢考親試都唔合格. 9 M̀hóu ngoh-chān go bìhbī 唔好餓親個
BB. 10 Kéuih tái chān gó tou hei dōu haam 佢睇親套戲都喊.

Unit 13 Comparisons

Exercise 13.1

1 héi-kehk móuh bēi-kehk gam hóu-tái 喜劇冇悲劇咁好睇；2 hahtīn móuh
dūngtīn gam chèuhng 夏天冇冬天咁長；3 yīsāng móuh wuhsih gam mòhng 醫
生冇護士咁忙；4 Láuyeuk jitjau móuh Hēunggóng gam faai 紐約節奏冇香港
咁快；5 lihksí-haih móuh jithohk-haih gam yùhngyih yahp 歷史系冇哲學系
咁容易入；6 Wohnggok móuh Jīmsājéui gam bīk-yàhn 旺角冇尖沙咀咁迫人

Exercise 13.2

A: 1 Dīksí dihng fóchē faai dī a? 的士定火車快啲呀？ 2 Gātìhng dihng sihyihp
juhngyiu dī a? 家庭定事業重要啲呀？ 3 Jūng yeuhk dihng sāi yeuhk yáuh-
haauh dī a? 中藥定西藥有效啲呀？ 4 Daap-fēigēi dihng daap-syùhn syūfuhk
dī a? 搭飛機定搭船舒服啲呀？ 5 Duhk-syū dihng jouh-yéh sānfú dī a? 讀書定
做嘢辛苦啲呀？ B: 6 Go léui yáuh-móuh go jái gam pa-cháu a? 個女有冇個仔
咁怕醜呀？ 7 Tái dihnsih yáuh-móuh hàahng-gūngsī gam sāai-sìhgaan a? 睇電
視有冇行公司咁嘥時間呀？ 8 Seuhnghói yáuh-móuh Bākgīng gam yúhn a? 上
海有冇北京咁遠呀？ 9 Jūngdaaih yáuh-móuh Góngdaaih gam yáuh-méng a?
中大有冇港大咁有名呀？ 10 fōwaahn pín yáuh-móuh húngbou pín gam chigīk
a? 科幻片有冇恐怖片咁刺激呀？

Exercise 13.3

1 Dī gāsī taai pèhng/pèhng dāk jaih/pèhng gwotàuh 啲傢俬太平/平得滯/平
過頭. 2 Chau-jái taai-(gwo) sānfú/sānfú dāk jaih 湊仔太(過)辛苦/辛苦得
滯. 3 Kéuih jyú ge sung taai hàahm/hàahm gwotàuh/hàahm dāk jaih佢煮
嘅餸太鹹/鹹過頭/鹹得滯. 4 Yìuhgwán-ngohk taai chòuh/chòuh dāk jaih 搖
滾樂太嘈/嘈得滯. 5 Kéuih hàahng dou taai guih/guih dāk jaih佢行到太劫/

183

劲得滞. 6 **Hēunggóng bin dāk taai faai/faai dāk jaih** 香港變得太快/快得
滞. 7 **Jingfú taaidouh gihk douh/taai-gwo kèuhng-ngaahn** 政府態度極度/太過
強硬 8 **Kéuih làaih-láai taai làahn fuhksih**佢奶奶太難服侍. 9 **Ngóh ūkkéi ge
mahntàih taai fūkjaahp**我屋企嘅問題太複雜. 10 **Sīnsāang góng ge yéh gihk
douh sām-ou/taai-gwo sām-ou** 先生講嘅嘢極度深奧/太過深奧.

Unit 14 Resultative and causative sentences with dou 到

Exercise 14.1

A: 1 **hōisām dou fan m̀h jeuhk** 開心到瞓唔著 so happy that (she) can't
sleep; 2 **gēng dou m̀h gám fāan ūkkéi** 驚到唔敢返屋企 so scared that (he)
dared not go home; 3 **làu dou paak tòih paak dang** 嬲到拍枱拍凳 so angry
that (he) banged the table and chair; 4 **mángjáng dou lyún gam laauh yàhn** 瘟
瘤到亂咁鬧人 so frustrated that (he) scolded people indiscriminately; 5 **syūfuhk dou fan-jeuhk-jó** 舒服到瞓著咗 so comfortable that (she) fell asleep B: 1
Go hói-gíng leng dou wàhn 個海靚到暈 The sea view is breathtakingly beautiful. 2 **Gāan ūk gōnjehng dou fēihéi** 間屋乾淨到飛起 The house is so devastat-
ingly clean. 3 **Fūk wá daaih dou móuh yàhn seun** 幅畫大到冇人信 The picture
is incredibly big. 4 **Hēunggóng hahtīn yiht dou díng-m̀h-seuhn** 香港夏天熱到
頂唔順 A Hong Kong summer is unbearably hot. 5 **Kéuih dī chín dō dou sái
m̀h saai** 佢啲錢多到洗唔晒 He has more money than he can spend (Note: the
sentences can all end after **dou**, as in **Kéuih dī chín dō dou ā** 佢啲錢多到吖 ...
He has so much money.)

Exercise 14.2

1 **Lī jek yeuhk lihng dou léih yuht làih yuht leng** 呢隻新藥令到你愈嚟愈靚 This
medicine will make you look better and better. 2 **Ngóhdeih ge jéungbán dō
dou yàhn-yàhn yáuh fán** 我哋嘅獎品多到人人有份 Our prizes are so many that
there's something for everyone. 3 **Lī go jitmuhk jīngchói dou léih m̀h seun**
呢個節目精彩到你唔信 This programme is unbelievably brilliant. 4 **Ngóhdeih jáulàuh ge dím-sām sihk dou léih lém-lém-leih** 我哋酒樓嘅點心食到你
舐舐脷 Our restaurant's dim sum will make your mouth water (*lit.* lick your
tongue). 5 **Sung fūyàhn dī syū maaih dou tyúhn saai síh**宋夫人啲書賣到斷
晒市 Madam Sung's books sell so well that all the copies are gone from the
market.

Exercise 14.3

1 **gwai dou haak séi léih** 貴到嚇死你 so expensive that it'll shock you; 2 **chíh
dou mā-sāang yāt yeuhng** 似到孖生一樣 so much alike that they look like
twins; 3 **behng dou sihk m̀h lohk yéh** 病到食唔落嘢 so sick that it can't
eat; 4 **yī dou msái sihk yeuhk dōu hóyíh fan dóu** 醫到唔使食藥都可以瞓
到 cured to the extent that he can sleep without medication; 5 **johng dou**

chē-mùhn dōu laahn màaih 撞到車門都爛埋 so damaged that the car door was broken;   6 **hohk dou sīk góng siuwá** 學到識講笑話 I've learnt (Chinese) to the point where I can tell jokes;   7 **làu dou dá laahn saai dī yéh** 嬲到打爛晒啲嘢 so angry that she broke everything;   8 **mòhng dou hái sahtyihmsāt gwo yé** 忙到喺實驗室過夜 so busy that he spent the night in the laboratory

†Exercise 14.4

1 **Fūng seun tái dou ngóh hóu làu** 封信睇到我好嬲.   2 **Pīn mán sé dou ngóh ngāau saai tàuh** 篇文寫到我掅晒頭.   3 **Jēun jáu yám dou kéuih jeui-jó** 樽酒飲到佢醉咗.   4 **Go sahtyihm jouh dou ngóh jauhlèih chīsin** 個實驗做到我就嚟黐線.   5 **Jēung chòhng fan dou ngóh hóu msyūfuhk** 張床瞓到我好唔舒服.   6 **Go dihnsih tái dou ngóh ngáahn fā** 個電視睇到我眼花.   7 **Gó dī gwái-gú tēng dou kéuih fan m̀h dóu** 嗰啲鬼故聽到佢瞓唔到.   8 **Lī dī yeuhk sihk dou kéuih wàhn-tòh-tòh** 呢啲藥食到佢暈陀陀.

Unit 15 Quantification

Exercise 15.1

1 **Kéuih mātyéh beimaht dōu jī ge** 佢乜嘢秘密都知嘅.   2 **Gāan-gāan gūngsī dōu móuh sīusīk** 間間公司都冇消息.   3 **Ngóh go-go jih dōu m̀h sīk duhk** 我個個字都唔識讀.   4 **Ngóh fuhmóuh go-go jáiléui dōu gam sek** 我父母個個仔女都咁錫.   5 **Kéuih fún-fún sān chē dōu m̀h múhnyi** 佢款款新車都唔滿意.   6 **Lóuhbáan tìuh-tìuh sou dōu gai dāk hóu chīngchó** 老闆條條數都計得好清楚.   7 **Kéuih go-go yuht dōu jéunsìh gāau-jōu** 佢個個月都準時交租.   8 **Kéuih chi-chi dōu jāang-jyuh màaih-dāan** 佢次次都爭住埋單.

Exercise 15.2

1 **Go-go sīgēi dōu yáuh tūnghàhng-jing** 個個司機都有通行證.   2 **Jek-jek māau ngóh dōu jūngyi** 隻隻貓我都鍾意.   3 **Ngóhdeih gāan-gāan jáulàuh dōu heui-gwo/Gāan-gāan jáulàuh ngóhdeih dōu heui-gwo** 我哋間間酒樓都去過/間間酒樓我哋都去過.   4 **Kéuih tìuh-tìuh tàihmuhk dōu sīk daap/Tìuh-tìuh taihmuhk kéuih dōu sīk daap** 佢條條題目都識答/條條題目佢都識答.   5 **Ngóh jek-jek sáují dōu tung dou séi** 我隻隻手指都痛到死.   6 **Fūng-fūng seun dōu tái saai la** 封封信都睇晒喇.   7 **Fūk-fūk wá dōu hóu yáuh-yisī** 幅幅畫都好有意思.   8 **Sáu-sáu gō dōu hóu ngāam-tēng** 首首歌都好啱聽.   9 **Pō-pō syuh dōu yáuh jeukjái jyuh ge** 棵棵樹都有雀仔住嘅.   10 **Dihp-dihp choi dōu hóu hēung** 碟碟菜都好香.

Exercise 15.3

1 **Léih yiu dō dī tùhng jáiléui kīng-gái/Léih yiu tùhng jáiléui dō dī kīng-gái** 你要多啲同仔女傾偈/你要同仔女多啲傾偈.   2 **Ngóhdeih chéng dō-jó yāt wàih tói ge yàhn** 我哋請多咗一圍枱嘅人.   3 **Gāmyaht làih síu-jó go gúdūng** 今日嚟少咗個股東.   4 **Léih hó-m̀h-hóyíh góng síu dī, jouh dō dī a?** 你可唔可

以講少啲，做多啲呀? 5 **Léih jeui hóu síu dī dá màh-jéuk/Léih jeui hóu dá
síu dī màh-jéuk** 你最好少啲打麻雀/你最好打少啲麻雀. 6 **Chéng léih dō dī
gwāansām háh ūkkéi yàhn** 請你多啲關心下屋企人. 7 **Ngóh séung dō dī làuh
hái ūkkéi yāusīk háh** or **Ngóh séung làuh dō di hái ūkkéi yāusīk háh** 我想
多啲留喺屋企休息下/我想多啲喺屋企休息下. 8 **Jeuigahn sihk síu-jó Sāi-
gung dī hóisīn** 最近食少咗西貢啲海鮮. 9 **Gām-lín syúga dō-jó hóu dō yàuh-
haak** 今年暑假多咗好多遊客. 10 **Gāan ūk dō-jó (yāt) go fóng, síu-jó (yāt) go
gūngyàhn** 間屋多咗(一)個房，少咗(一)個工人.

Exercise 15.4

1 **saai** 晒; 2 **saai** 晒; 3 **màaih** 埋; 4 **màaih** 埋; 5 **màaih** 埋; 6 **saai** 晒;
7 **màaih** 埋; 8 **saai** 晒

Unit 16 Negative sentences

Exercise 16.1

1 **Kéuih m̀h/móuh joi tái gó go yīsāng** 佢唔/冇再睇嗰個醫生. 2 **Léih mhóu joi
ngāak jihgéi** 你唔好再呃自己. 3 **Lī gihn sih m̀h hóyíh joi tō lohk-heui** 呢件事
唔可以再拖落去. 4 **Mhóu joi gam yáih lā** 唔好再咁曳啦. 5 **Kéuih go sēungháu m̀h joi tung** 佢個傷口唔再痛. 6 **Kéuih gāmyaht móuh joi faat-pèihhei** 佢
今日冇再發脾氣. 7 **Léih msái joi gáaisīk** 你唔使再解釋. 8 **Ngóhdeih msái
joi jiugu kéuihdeih** 我哋唔使再照顧佢哋.

Exercise 16.2

1 **Máih/mhóu sāu-sin jyuh lā** 咪/唔好收線住啦. 2 **Ngóh m̀h/móuh dásyun būn
ūk jyuh** 我唔/冇打算搬屋住. 3 **Mhóu sāu-màaih fūng seun jyuh (lā)** 唔好收埋
封信住(啦). 4 **Ngóhdeih meih/m̀h heui dāk jyuh** 我哋未/唔去得住. 5 **Mhóu
faht go hohksāang jyuh (lā)** 唔好罰個學生住(啦). 6 **Mhóu dá hōi dī láihmaht
jyuh (lā)** 唔好打開啲禮物住(啦). 7 **Máih/mhóu séuhng chòhng fan-gaau
jyuh lā** 咪/唔好上床瞓覺住啦. 8 **Kéuih meih wán dóu gūng jyuh** 佢未搵到工
住. 9 **Léih m̀h yīnggōi fonghei jyuh** 你唔應該放棄住. 10 **Ngóh msái hohk
Póutūngwá jyuh** 我唔使學普通話住.

Exercise 16.3

1 **Ngóh móuh mātyéh/géi dō gāp sih** 我冇乜嘢/幾多急事. 2 **Léih gāmyaht
yáuh-móuh heui bīndouh máaih-sung a?** 你今日有冇去邊度買餸呀? 3 **Hói-
gwāan m̀h wúih dím (yéung) chàh léih ge** 海關唔會點(樣)查你嘅. 4 **Yùhgwó léih móuh mātyéh mahntàih, ngóhdeih yìhgā hóyíh chīm yeuk** 如果你
冇乜嘢問題，我哋而家可以簽約. 5 **Lóuhbáan m̀h wúih dím (yéung) laauh
léih ge** 老闆唔會點(樣)鬧你嘅. 6 **Yùhgwó yáuh mātyéh tàuhsou, hóyíh dá
lī go lāmbá** 如果有乜嘢投訴，可以打呢個冧把. 7 **Kéuih yáuh-móuh bīngo/
mātyéh chānchīk hóyíh jiugu kéuih ga?** 佢有冇邊個/乜嘢親戚可以照顧佢㗎?

8 **Yùhgwó léih heui bīndouh léuih-hàhng, geidāk daai màaih ngóh heui** 如果你去邊度旅行，記得帶埋我去. 9 **Ngóhdeih móuh géi dō/mātyéh chín sái** 我哋冇幾多/乜嘢錢洗. 10 **Móuh mātyéh/géi dō yàhn làih taam ngóh** 冇乜嘢/幾多人嚟探我.

Unit 17 Questions and answers

Exercise 17.1

A: 1 **Léih séung jouh yaht-gāang dihng yeh-gāang a?** 你想做日更定夜更呀? 2 **Léih séung gām-lín dihng chēut-lín fong-ga a?** 你想今年定出年放假呀? 3 **Léih séung tēng gúdín yāmngohk dihng làuhhàhng yāmngohk a?** 你想聽古典音樂定流行音樂呀? 4 **Léih séung tái Jūng-yī dihng sāi-yī a?** 你想睇中醫定西醫呀? 5 **Léih séung jyuh sīgā yīyún dihng gūnglahp yīyún a?** 你想住私家醫院定公立醫院呀? B: 6 **Léih yāthaih jīkhāak gāau-jōu yāthaih jīkhāak būn jáu** 你一係即刻交租一係即刻搬走 7 **Léih yāthaih duhk màhn-fō yāthaih duhk léih-fō** 你一係讀文科一係讀理科. 8 **Léih yāthaih tùhng ngóh yātchàih heui yāthaih jihgéi heui** 你一係同我一齊去一係自己去. 9 **Léih yāthaih chéng gūngyàhn chau-jái yāthaih jihgéi chau** 你一係請工人湊仔一係自己湊. 10 **Léih yāthaih tàih jóu teuiyāu yāthaih jyun part-time** 你一係提早退休一係轉 **part-time.**

Exercise 17.2

1 **Haih a (móuh wah wo)** 係呀(冇話喎)/**Mhaih ak (yáuh wah ngóh jī)** 唔係呃(有話我知). 2 **Haih a (msái)** 係呀(唔使)/**Mhaih ak (yáuh sìh dōu yiu ga)** 唔係呃(有時都要㗎). 3 **Haih a (móuh heui)** 係呀(冇去)/**Mhaih ak (ngóh yáuh heui)** 唔係呃(我有去). 4 **Haih a (móuh saai la)** 係呀(冇晒喇)/**Mhaih ak (juhng yáuh síu-síu)** 唔係呃(仲有少少). 5 **Haih a (móuh wo)** 係呀(冇喎)/**Mhaih ak (ngóh yáuh)** 唔係呃(我有). 6 **Haih a (msái)** 係呀(唔使)/**Mhaih ak (yiu)** 唔係呃(要). 7 **Haih a (juhng meih yáuh)** 係呀(仲未有)/**Mhaih ak (yáuh yāt go lèih-gán)** 唔係呃(有一個嚟緊). 8 **Haih a (m̀h háng a)** 係呀(唔肯呀)/**Mhaih ak, (kéuih háng)** 唔係呃, (佢肯).

Exercise 17.3

1 **Ngóh dím tēng dóu a? / Ngóh bīndouh tēng dóu a? / Ngóh tēng-gwái-dóu àh?** 我點聽到呀/我邊度聽到呀/我聽鬼到呀? 2 **Bīngo bōng kéuih jēk? / Gwái bōng kéuih mē?** 邊個幫佢唧/鬼幫佢咩? 3 **Ngóh géisìh yáuh ngāak-gwo léih a? / Ngóh bīn/gwai yáuh ngāak-gwo léih a?** 我幾時有呃過你呀/我邊/鬼有呃過你呀? 4 **Ngóhdeih gāmyaht dím jouh dāk saai a? / Ngóhdeih bīndouh jouh dāk saai a?** 我哋今日點做得晒呀/我哋邊度做得晒呀? 5 **Sái māt kéuih gaau ngóh a? / Bīn/gwai sái kéuih gaau ngóh a?** 使乜佢教我呀/邊/鬼使佢教我呀? 6 **Léih sái māt gam hóu sām a? / Gwái sái léih gam hóu sām àh?** 你使乜咁好心呀/鬼使你咁好心呀?

Unit 18 Relative clauses

Exercise 18.1

1 **Tàuhsīn dá-dihnwá làih gó go deihcháan gīnggéi** 頭先打電話嚟嗰個地產經紀 That estate agent who just called.   2 **Chìh-jó-jīk gó go wuihgaisī** 辭咗職嗰個會計師 The accountant who has resigned.   3 **Yíng-gán-séung gó dī geijé** 影緊相嗰啲記者 Those reporters who are taking pictures.   4 **Sātjūng-jó sāam yaht gó jek gáu** 失蹤咗三日嗰隻狗 The dog that went missing for three days.   5 **Jouh-gán sahtyihm gó dī hohksāang** 做緊實驗嗰啲學生 The students who are doing experiments.   6 **Chēut-jó yún gó go behngyàhn** 出咗院嗰個病人 The patient who has gotten out of the hospital.   7 **Yātchàih yìhn-gau lī go mahntàih gó dī jyūn-gā** 一齊研究呢個問題嗰啲專家 The specialists who are studying this problem together.   8 **Taam-gwo ngóh géi chi gó go pàhngyáuh** 探過我幾次嗰個朋友 The friend who has visited me a few times.   9 **Johng chān jek māau gó ga chē** 撞親隻貓嗰架車 The car which has bumped into a cat.   10 **Bōng kéuih hōi-dōu gó go yīsāng** 幫佢開刀嗰個醫生 The surgeon who did the operation for him.

Exercise 18.2

1 **Siht-jó hóu dō chín gó gāan gūngsī jāp-jó-lāp** 蝕咗好多錢嗰間公司執咗笠.   2 **Ngóh chàhmyaht johng dóu gó go làahmyán haih ngóh lóuhbáan** 我琴日撞到嗰個男人係我老闆.   3 **Kéuih sèhngyaht daai-jyuh gó jek bīu hóu leng** 佢成日戴住嗰隻錶好靚.   4 **Ngóhdeih taam-gwo yāt chi gó dī gaausauh haih Méi-hgwok-yàhn** 我哋探過一次嗰啲教授係美國人.   5 **Ngóh yuhng-gán gó go dihn-lóuh taai gauh** 我用緊嗰個電腦太舊.   6 **Ngóh sé-jó gó géi fūng seun mgin-jó** 我寫咗嗰幾封信唔見咗.   7 **Ngóhdeih máaih-jó gó dī Gwóngdūng-wá syū hóu gwai** 我哋買咗嗰啲廣東話書好貴.   8 **Léih jūngyi tái gó dī hei (dihnyíng) taai maahn la** 你鍾意睇嗰啲戲(電影)太慢喇.   9 **Kéuihdeih yám-jó gó dī jáu hóu hēung** 佢哋飲咗嗰啲酒好香.   10 **Kéuih sihk gó dī yeuhk hóu yáuh-haauh** 佢食嗰啲藥好有效.

Exercise 18.3

1 **Ngóh tái-hōi gó go yīsāng haih Gimkìuh bātyihp ge** 我睇開嗰個醫生係劍橋畢業嘅.   2 **Kéuih dī jáiléui duhk gó gāan hohkhaauh sāu hóu gwai hohk-fai** 佢啲仔女讀嗰間學校收好貴學費.   3 **Kéuih jyú gó dī sung móuh lohk yìhm** 佢煮嗰啲餸冇落鹽.   4 **Ngóh chéng gó dī yàhn-haak chyùhnbouh lèih chàih saai** 我請嗰啲人客全部嚟齊晒.   5 **Chìh dou gó dī hohksāang hóyíh chóh hái hauhbihn** 遲到嗰啲學生可以坐喺後便.   6 **Syūnbou yihpjīk hóu gó dī gūngsī jeuigahn kòhng sing** 宣布好業績嗰啲公司最近.   7 **Ngāam-ngāam máaih gó go gongkàhm yàuh Dākgwok wahn dou** 啱啱買嗰個鋼琴由德國運到.   8 **Go jái waahk gó dī wá hóyíh sung béi yàhn** 個仔畫嗰啲畫可以送畀人.   9 **Lóuhbáan chéng gó go beisyū meih chìh dou gwo** 老闆請嗰個秘書未遲到過.   10 **Ngóh jūngyi gó dī síusyut dōsou móuh bouhlihk ge** 我鍾意嗰啲小說多數冇暴力嘅.

Exercise 18.4

1 **Kéuih gei béi ngóh gó go bāau-gwó chúhng dou līng m̀h héi** 佢畀我嗰個包
裹重到拎唔起 The parcel he sent me is so heavy that I can't lift it.   2 **Léih
tēuijin gó go hohksāang háau-síh chēut-māau** 你推薦嗰個學生考試出貓
The student you recommended cheated in the exam.   3 **Léih gaaisiuh làih
gūngsī jouh-yé gó go tùhngsih haih ngóh gauh tùhnghohk** 你介紹嚟公司做嘢
嗰個同事係我舊同學 The colleague you introduced to work in our company
is an old classmate of mine.   4 **Chàhmyaht tái-jó gó tou hei ge jyúgok haih
ngóh ge muhng jūng chìhngyàhn** 琴日睇咗嗰套戲嘅主角係我嘅夢中情人 The
star of that film I saw yesterday is my dream lover.   5 **Go-go jaan (kéuih)
dākyi gó go sailouh haih wahnhyut-yìh** 個個讚(佢)得意嗰個細路係混血兒
The child that everyone praises for being pretty is mixed-race.   6 **Ngóhdeih syún-jó (kéuih) jouh yíhyùhn gó go leuhtsī m̀h jéun heui Bākgīng** 我
哋選咗(佢)做議員嗰個律師唔准去北京 The lawyer we elected as legislator
is not allowed to go to Beijing.   7 **Ngóh dehng-jó gó bún sān syū yuhng
làih jouh chāamháau** 我訂咗嗰本新書用嚟做參考 The new book I ordered
is used for reference.   8 **Kéuih wán dóu gó dī yeuhk yiu hūng-tóuh sihk ge**
佢搵到嗰啲藥要空肚食嘅 The medicine he found needs to be taken on an
empty stomach.   9 **Ngóh sung jek gaaijí béi kéuih gó go léuihjái haih ngóh
meih-fān-chāi** 我送隻戒指畀佢嗰個女仔係我未婚妻 The girl I gave a ring
to is my fiancée.   10 **Ngóh mùihmúi tùhng kéuih paak-tō gó go yīsāng làih
sihk-faahn** 我妹妹同佢拍拖嗰個醫生嚟食飯 The doctor my sister is dating is
coming to dinner.

Unit 19 Subordinate clauses

Exercise 19.1

1 **daahnhaih** 但係; 2 **dōu** 都; 3 **jīchìhn** 之前; 4 **jīhauh** 之後; 5 **jīchìhn**
之前; 6 **mòuhleuhn** 無論; 7 **jīhauh** 之後; 8 **mòuhleuhn** 無論; 9 **dōng**
當; 10 **yānwaih** 因為; 11 **gójahnsí** 嗰陣時; 12 **mòuhleuhn** 無論

Exercise 19.2

1 **jihchùhng...jīhauh** 自從...之後; 2 **dōng...ge sìh-hauh/gójahnsí** 當...嘅時
候/嗰陣時; 3 **yānwaih...sóyíh** 因為...所以; 4 **gójahnsí** 嗰陣時; 5 **chèuihjó
...jī-ngoih, juhng** 除咗...之外,仲; 6 **meih...jīchìhn** 未...之前; 7 **sēuiyìhn
...daahnhaih** 雖然...但係; 8 **mòuhleuhn...dōu** 無論...都; 9 **jihchùhng...
jīhauh** 自從...之後; 10 **sēuiyìhn...daahnhaih** 雖然...但係

Exercise 19.3

1 g; 2 a; 3 e; 4 b; 5 f; 6 c; 7 h; 8 d

Unit 20 Conditional sentences

Exercise 20.1

(Note that in most cases the conjunctions are optional.) 1 **(Yùhgwó) léih m̀h hahpgaak, ngóh jauh wúih hóu sātmohng** (如果)你唔合格，我就會好失望. 2 **(Yùhgwó) léih chóh háidouh, (léih jauh) wúih syūfuhk dī** (如果)你坐喺度，(你就)會舒服啲. 3 **(Yùhgwó) yáuh mātyéh sān líu, (jauh) gei-jyuh wán ngóh gòhgō** (如果)有乜嘢新料，(就)記住搵我哥哥. 4 **Kéuih (yùhgwó) haih jān pàhngyáuh, (kéuih) jauh wúih mòuh tìuhgín bōng léih** 佢(如果)係真朋友，(佢)就會無條件幫你. 5 **Léih (yùhgwó) juhng m̀h sāu-sin, ngóh (jauh) sāu-sin** 你(如果)仲唔收線，我(就)收線. 6 **(Yùhgwó) léih bou-gíng, ngóhdeih jauh séi ngaahng** (如果)你報警，我哋就死硬. 7 **Ngóh (yùhgwó) m̀h daai ngáahn-géng, yehmáahn (jauh) tái m̀h dóu louh páai** 我(如果)唔帶眼鏡，夜晚(就)睇唔到路牌. 8 **(Yùhgwó) léih kàhnlihk dī, (jauh) yātdihng hóyíh háauh dóu hóu hohkhaauh** (如果)你勤力啲，(就)一定可以考到好學校.

Exercise 20.2

1a **jauhsyun . . . dōu** 就算 . . . 都; b **chèuihfēi . . . yùhgwó mhaih** 除非 . . . 如果唔係; 2a **yùhgwó . . . jauh** 如果 . . . 就; b **yùhgwó . . . sīn** 如果 . . . 先; 3a **jauhsyun . . . dōu** 就算 . . . 都; b **chèuihfēi . . . yùhgwó mhaih** 除非 . . . 如果唔係; 4a **jíyiu . . . jauh** 只要 . . . 就; b **yùhgwó . . . jauh** 如果 . . . 就; 5a **chèuihfēi . . . yùhgwó mhaih** 除非 . . . 如果唔係; b **jauhsyun . . . dōu** 就算 . . . 都; 6a **jíyiu . . . jauh** 只要 . . . 就; b **yùhgwó . . . sīn** 如果 . . . 先; 7a **chèuihfēi . . . yùhgwó mhaih** 除非 . . . 如果唔係; b **jauhsyun . . . dōu** 就算 . . . 都; 8a **yùhgwó . . . sīn** 如果 . . . 先; b **jíyiu . . . jauh** 只要 . . . 就

Exercise 20.3

1a **Ngóh yuht làih yuht gēng** 我愈嚟愈驚. b **Ngóh yuht lám yuht gēng** 我愈諗愈驚. 2a **Ngóh yuht làih yuht gwa-jyuh kéuih** 我愈嚟愈掛住佢. b **Ngóh yuht gwa-jyuh kéuih, yuht séung gin kéuih** 我愈掛住佢，愈想見佢. 3a **Kéuih go léui yuht làih yuht leng wo** 佢個女愈嚟愈靚喎. b **Kéuih go léui yuht daaih yuht leng wo** 佢個女愈大愈靚喎. 4a **Ngóh yuht làih yuht jūngyi lī sáu gō** 我愈嚟愈鍾意呢首歌. b **Ngóh yuht tēng lī sáu gō yuht jūngyi/Lī sáu gō ngóh yuht tēng yuht jūngyi** 我愈聽呢首歌愈鍾意/呢首歌我愈聽愈鍾意. 5a **Gihn sih yuht làih yuht làahn gáaikyut** 件事愈嚟愈難解決. b **Gihn sih yuht tō yuht làahn gáaikyut** 件事愈拖愈難解決.

Unit 21 Reported speech

Exercise 21.1

1 **Mùihmúi wah (kéuih) móuh chín la (wóh)** 妹妹話(佢)冇錢喇(喎) Little sister says she's out of money. 2 **Sīnsāang wah ngóhdeih jáu dāk ga la (wóh)** 先生話我哋走得嘅喇(喎) The teacher said it's all right for us to leave. 3 **Gíngchaat**

wah (kéuihdeih) wán-gán jing-yàhn (wóh) 警察話(佢哋)搵緊證人(喎) The police said they're looking for witnesses. 4 **Leuhtsī wah ngóh yiu faai dī chīm-mēng (wóh)** 律師話我要快啲簽名(喎) The solicitor said I had to sign quickly. 5 **Yīsāng wah ngóh m̀h yīnggōi sihk tìhm yéh (wóh)** 醫生話我唔應該食甜嘢(喎) The doctor said I should not eat sweet things. 6 **Pòhpó wah kéuihdeih m̀h sīk louh fāan ūkkéi (wóh)** 婆婆話佢哋唔識路返屋企(喎) Grandma said they couldn't find their way home. 7 **A-Yī wah (kéuih) máaih-jó láihmaht béi ngóh dī jáiléui (wóh)** 阿姨話(佢)買咗禮物畀我啲仔女(喎) Aunty said she had bought some gifts for my children. 8 **Go léui wah (kéuih) yiu heui sāang-yaht-wúi (wóh)** 個女話(佢)要去生日會(喎) My daughter says she has to go to a birthday party. 9 **Bōsí wah gūngsī gām-lín m̀h gā yàhn-gūng (wóh)** 波士話公司今年唔加人工(喎) The boss said there'd be no pay raise this year. 10 **Ngóh taai-táai wah gām jīu yáuh geijé wán ngóh (wóh)** 我太太話今朝有記者搵我(喎) My wife said there were reporters looking for me this morning.

Exercise 21.2

1 **A-mā mahn kéuihdeih géisìh bātyihp wóh** 阿媽問佢哋幾時畢業喎. 2 **Mìhng-jái mahn ngóh jūng-m̀h-jūngyi tái hei wóh** 明仔問我鍾唔鍾意睇戲喎. 3 **Dī hohksāang mahn ngóh lóuhgūng haih-m̀h-haih Yīnggwok-yàhn wóh** 啲學生問我老公係唔係英國人喎. 4 **A-Sīn mahn ngóh séung-m̀h-séung làuh hái Hēunggóng wóh** 阿先問我想唔想留喺香港喎. 5 **A-Dāk mahn mātyéh haih ngóhdeih sìhnggūng ge beikyut wóh** 阿德問乜嘢係我哋成功嘅秘訣喎. 6 **Yīsāng mahn dímgáai ngóh gam gihnhōng wóh** 醫生問點解我咁健康喎. 7 **Go beisyū mahn ngóh jouh māt gam hīngfáhn wóh** 個秘書問我做乜咁興奮喎. 8 **Sī gaausauh mahn ngóh gokdāk bīngo jeui yáuh chìhmjāt wóh** 施教授問我覺得邊個最有潛質喎. 9 **Dī chānchīk mahn ngohdeih dī jáiléui góng Jūngmán dihng Yīngmán wóh** 啲親戚問我哋啲仔女講中文定英文喎. 10 **Go tùhngsih mahn dím sīn hóyíh máaih dóu lī go yúhn-gín wóh** 個同事問點先可以買到呢個軟件喎

Exercise 21.3

1 **Ngóh pàhngyáuh giu/hyun ngóh mhóu gam sēungsām** 我朋友叫/勸我唔好咁傷心 My friend asked/urged me not to be so sad. 2 **Sīnsāang giu ngóhdeih jīkhāak tìhng bāt** 先生叫我哋即刻停筆 The teacher told us to stop writing immediately. 3 **Go tùhngsih giu kéuih bōng-sáu** 個同事叫佢幫手 The colleague asked him to help. 4 **Gíngchaat mihnglihng ngóh jīkhāak fong dāi bá chēung** 警察命令我即刻放低把槍 The police ordered me to put down the gun immediately. 5 **Jyūn-gā gin-yíh ngóh maahn-máan dáng-háh sīn** 專家建議我慢慢等下先 Experts suggest that I should wait patiently. 6 **Yīsāng hyun ngóh faai dī gaai yīn** 醫生勸我快啲戒煙 The doctor urged me to give up smoking quickly. 7 **Lóuhpòh giu ngóh mhóu gam yeh fāan ūkkéi (wóh)** 老婆叫我唔好咁夜返屋企(喎) My wife asked me not to come home so late. 8 **Go tùhnghohk hyun ngóh yiu hóu hóu bóujuhng sāntái** 個同學勸我要好好保重身體 My classmate urged me to take care of my health. 9 **Go leuhtsī gin-yíh ngóh jīkhāak faat fūng leuhtsī seun béi go jōuhaak** 個律師建議我即刻發封律師信畀個租客

The lawyer suggested that I should serve notice on the tenant. 10 **Ngoh lóuh-gūng giu ngóh pùih kéuih chēut heui sihk-faahn** 我老公叫我陪佢出去食飯 My husband asked me to go out to dinner with him.

Unit 22 Cantonese speech conventions

Exercise 22.1

1 **lóuhbáan** 老闆; 2 **sīfú** 師傅; 3 **sīgēi** 司機; 4 **Wòhng Táai** 黃太; 5 **Faat-gō** 發哥; 6 **a-pòh** 阿婆

Exercise 22.2

1 **Māt gam āam a!** 乜咁啱呀! What a coincidence! 2 **Sānfān faailohk** 新婚快樂! Congratulations! (*lit.* newly wed happiness) 3 **Gūnghéi saai wo, go bìhbī gam dākyi.** 恭喜晒喎，個BB咁得意 Congratulations, the baby is so sweet. 4 **Sāang-yaht faailohk** 生日快樂 Happy birthday. 5 **Singdaan faailohk** 聖誕快樂 Merry Christmas. 6 **Jūk léih léuihtòuh yuhfaai** 祝你旅途愉快 (Wish you) have a pleasant journey. 7 **Jūk léih jóu yaht hōngfuhk** 祝你早日康復 (formal)/**Jūk léih faai dī hóu fāan** 祝你快啲好返 (informal) Get well soon. 8 **Yám sing (kéuih)** 飲勝(佢) Bottoms up. 9 **Gūnghéi faat chòih** 恭喜發財 Happy (Chinese) New Year. 10 **Jūk léih yāt louh seuhn fūng** 祝你一路順風 (Wish you) have a smooth journey.

Exercise 22.3

1 **Lī go/wái (haih) ngóh tùhngsih, (giu a-Cream)** 呢個/位(係)我同事，(叫阿Cream). 2 **lī wái haih Máh yīsāang** 呢位係馬醫生 3 **lī wái (haih) Yihp gaausauh (Prof. Yip)** 呢位(係)葉教授 4 **lī go (haih) ngóh tùhnghohk** 呢個(係)我同學 5 **lī wái (haih) ngóh taai-táai** 呢位(係)我太太 6 **lī go (haih) ngóh go chìhn-fū** 呢個(係)我個前夫 7 **lī go (haih) ngóh go daaih jái** 呢個(係)我個大仔 8 **lī go (haih) ngóh go chìhn-douh léuih-yáuh** 呢個(係)我個前度女友 9 **lī go (haih) ngóh yíhchìhn ge hohksāng** 呢個(係)我以前嘅學生 10 **lī go (haih) ngóh lóuhgūng/sīnsāang** 呢個(係)我老公/先生

Unit 23 Particles and interjections

Exercise 23.1

1 **lō/āma** 囉/吖嘛; 2 **gwa** 啩; 3 **lō/āma** 囉/吖嘛; 4 **lō/āma** 囉/吖嘛; 5 **gwa** 啩; 6 **gwa** 啩; 7 **lō/āma** 囉/吖嘛; 8 **lō/āma** 囉/吖嘛

Exercise 23.2

1 **há** 吓; 2 **hó** 呵; 3 **hó** 呵; 4 **há** 吓; 5 **hó** 呵; 6 **há** 吓; 7 **hó** 呵; 8 **há** 吓

Exercise 23.3

1 **chē** 唓; 2 **baih/séi la** 弊/死喇; 3 **yí** 咦; 4 **wa(háai)** 嘩(喺); 5 **chōi** 啋; 6 **óh** 哦

Unit 24 Colloquial syntax

Exercise 24.1

1 **Maaih-jó meih a,** *gāan ūk*? 賣咗未呀，間屋? 2 **Léihdeih yātchàih heui lā,** *bātyùh* 你哋一齊去啦，不如. 3 **Ngóh chìh dou yānwaih sāk-chē a,** *Sījísāan Seuihdouh* 我遲到因為塞車呀，獅子山隧道. 4 **Ngóh béi léih haak séi la,** *jānhaih* 我畀你嚇死喇，真係. 5 **Léih yātdihng wúih lám dóu baahnfaat ge,** *ngóh jī* 你一定會諗到辦法嘅，我知. 6 **Juhng yáuh sìhgaan, maahn-máan góng lohk-heui ā,** *hóyíh* 仲有時間，慢慢講落去吖，可以. 7 **Léih tàih jóu teu-iyāu mē,** *wúih*? 你提早退休咩，會? 8 **Léih síusām jā-chē a,** *gei-jyuh* 你小心揸車呀，記住.

Exercise 24.2

1 **tìuh** 條; 2 **gauh** 舊; 3 **jek** 隻; 4 **tìuh** 條; 5 **gihn** 件; 6 **yéh** 嘢; 7 **jek** 隻; 8 **lāp** 粒

Exercise 24.3

1 **Tou hei hóu gwái muhn** 套戲好鬼悶. 2 **Bīn-gwái-go háidouh chòuh a?** 邊鬼個喺度嘈呀? 3 **Fai-gwái-sih heui la** 費鬼事去喇. 4 **Ga chē maaih-gwái-jó la** 架車賣鬼咗喇. 5 **Léih heui-jó bīn-gwái-douh a?** 你去咗邊鬼度呀? 6 **Gam gwái chèuhng-hei ga!** 咁鬼長氣㗎! 7 **Bīngo ga chē jó-gwái-jyuh saai a?/Bīn-gwai-go ga chē jó-jyuh saai a?** 邊個架車阻鬼住晒呀/邊鬼個架車阻住晒呀? 8 **Ngóh m̀h gwái lōu la!** 我唔鬼撈喇!

Unit 25 Code-mixing and loanwords

Exercise 25.1

1 **call-jó** 咗; 2 **set fāan** 返; 3 **short-jó** 咗; 4 **review-gán** 緊; 5 **swap-jó** 咗; 6 **date-gwo** 過; 7 **clear-jó** 咗; 8 **quit-jó** 咗; 9 **send fāan** 返; 10 **promote-gán** 緊

Exercise 25.2

1 **Kéuih tùhng léih friend-m̀h-friend (fēn-m̀h-fēn) a?** 佢同你friend唔friend(fēn 唔fēn)呀? Are you and he friendly? 2 **Léih pre-m̀h-predict dóu ngóh séung dím a?** 你pre唔predict到我想點呀? Can you predict how I want it? 3 **Kéuihdeih jeuigahn bī-m̀h-bīsìh a?** 佢哋最近bī唔bīsìh呀? Have they been busy lately? 4

Lóuhbáan in-m̀h-invite dī client heui dá golf a? 老闆in唔invite啲client去打golf呀? Will the boss invite the clients to play golf? 5 **Léih en-m̀h-enjoy tái kéuih dī e-mail a?** 你en唔enjoy睇佢啲e-mail呀? Do you enjoy reading his e-mail? 6 **Lóuhbáan tái yùhn go report, im-m̀h-impress a?** 老闆睇完個report, im唔impress呀? When the boss finished reading the report, was he impressed? 7 **Go exam ea-m̀h-easy a?** 個exam ea唔easy呀? Was the exam easy? 8 **Kéuih béi fān fair-m̀h-fair a?** 佢畀分fair唔fair呀? Is he fair in marking?

Exercise 25.3

1 **fāailóu** = file; 2 **gafē-sīk** 咖啡色 = brown (*lit.* coffee colour); 3 **jēléi** 啫喱 = jelly; 4 **wēnjái van** 仔 = van; 5 **sāammàhn-yú** 三文魚 = salmon (fish); 6 **lāmbá** 冧把 = number; 7 **sāléut** 沙律 = salad; 8 **jīsí** 芝士 = cheese; 9 **yinsō** 燕梳 = insurance; 10 **jāudá-yú-tōng** 周打魚湯 = chowder (fish soup)

GLOSSARY OF GRAMMATICAL TERMS

aspect   A distinction between ways of describing an action or situation, such as the habitual aspect in **sihk-hōi sāi-chāan** 食開西餐 'to eat Western food regularly' and the delimitative aspect in **sihk-háh sāi-chāan** 食下西餐 'to eat Western food once in a while'.

attributive   An adjective used to indicate an attribute, as in **cho ge táifaat** 錯 嘅睇法 'wrong views'.

causative   A sentence type expressing how an event is caused to happen, as in 'He made me cry'.

changed tone   A tone which differs from the citation tone, usually becoming the high rising tone as in the second syllable of **léuih-yán** 女人 'woman'.

citation tone   The tone used when a word is cited in isolation, e.g. when it is read from a written character.

concessive   A type of sentence used to concede a point, as in 'although I am poor . . . ' which concedes being poor.

contraction   A case when two or more words are reduced, as when English 'it is' becomes 'it's', Cantonese **si yāt si** 試一試 'have a try' becomes **sí-si** 試試 (with change of tone).

coverb   A verb which characteristically occurs together with another verb, like **tùhng** 同 'with' or 'accompany(ing)'.

diphthong   A sound combining two or more vowel sounds, e.g. **dōu** 都 'all', 'also' which begins with the sound of **o** and ends with *u*.

focus   An element of the sentence which is stressed and represents new or important information, as in 'He asked ME (of all people)'.

indirect command   A type of sentence which reports a command, e.g. 'He asked me to pay the bill'.

intransitive verb   A verb used without an object, like the verb 'cry' in 'She's crying'.

minimal pair   A pair of words, sentences etc. differing in only one respect, e.g. **gāi** 雞 'chicken' vs. **gāai** 'street' which differ only in the length of the diphthong.

palatalization   A change in the sound of a consonant caused by contact between the tongue and the palate (the roof of the mouth).

predicative   An adjective used to state a property of something, as in **Lī go táifaat cho ge** 呢個睇法錯嘅 'this view is wrong'.

quantification The area of meaning concerning expressions such as 'all', 'some' etc., which refer to relative quantities of things rather than to individual things.

reduplication Grammatical pattern in which a word or syllable is repeated.

register A form of speech associated with a certain degree of formality, e.g. colloquial register.

reported speech Those types of sentences which report what someone else has said, e.g. 'She says there's no time for that'.

serial verbs Two or more verbs used in a series within the same clause as in 'Let's go and eat'.

subordinate A subordinate clause is not complete by itself but accompanies a main clause to which it is subordinate. For example, a clause beginning with 'although', as in 'Although we know little about this topic' is a subordinate clause, which must be followed by a main clause.

topicalization Taking an element of a sentence and putting it in the first (or occasionally second) position, making it the 'topic' of the sentence, as in 'Oysters I can't eat'.

transitive verb A verb used with an object following it, like the verb 'push' in 'She's pushing the trolley'.

INDEX

Printed and bound by CPI Group (UK) Ltd, Croydon, CR0 4YY